NEXT

GORDON PINSENT

NEXT

———◆———

WITH GEORGE ANTHONY

McClelland & Stewart

Library and Archives Canada Cataloguing in Publication

Pinsent, Gordon, 1930-
Next / Gordon Pinsent.

ISBN 978-0-7710-7137-9

1. Pinsent, Gordon, 1930-. 2. Actors – Canada – Biography.
I. Title.

PN2308.P49A3 2012   792.02'8092   C2012-900972-5

We acknowledge the financial support of the Government of Canada through the Canada Book Fund and that of the Government of Ontario through the Ontario Media Development Corporation's Ontario Book Initiative. We further acknowledge the support of the Canada Council for the Arts and the Ontario Arts Council for our publishing program.

Typeset in Jenson by M&S, Toronto
Printed and bound in the United States of America

This book was produced using recycled materials.

McClelland & Stewart,
a division of Random House of Canada Limited
One Toronto Street
Toronto, Ontario
M5C 2V6
www.mcclelland.com

1 2 3 4 5   16 15 14 13 12

Charm, this is for you,
as is everything I do.

foreword

Who is Gordon Pinsent?

He's an actor, a movie star, a painter, a writer, a poet, a lyricist. And, first and foremost, an artist.

We sit at the kitchen table in his downtown penthouse apartment, looking out at the west side of Toronto. My assignment, my task, is to elicit memories. We talk about the Winnipeg years, the Hollywood years, and his boyhood in Newfoundland, and suddenly he starts singing a verse of "Farewell, Amanda," the Cole Porter song that David Wayne crooned to Katharine Hepburn in *Adam's Rib*.

"Of all things to remember!" he says, chiding himself. Yes, of all things to remember – a song from an MGM movie that came out in 1949, more than six decades ago, when he was an admittedly callow youth of nineteen.

Gordon the Actor has an actor's memory. Gordon the Poet rhymes words I've never heard rhymed before and makes verbs out of nouns.

Old ladies, plain old ladies,
lackadaisin' under a tree that's shady . . .

Gadflies and gals, Pepsodent pals in the sun
wonderin' how it will be when the war is won . . .

Old gentry, hoi polloi gentry
gentlemen distinctive and parliamentary . . .*

Has anyone ever before or since made a rhyming lyric of "parliamentary"?

No wonder we get along so well.

In many ways we had grown up in show business together. In one earlier professional incarnation, I interviewed actors and movie stars for a living. And because I was raised in screening rooms and spent so much time in Hollywood, I knew almost all those films he saw as a child, who was in them, and why he was so taken by them. So it was, for me, pure pleasure to coax and cajole those stories from him, so he could revisit all those moments and share them with all of us in this autobiography.

It was also fascinating, and more than a bit heartwarming, for me to hear him talk about his life with Charmion King. As you will learn, Gordon and Charmion met when she was starring on stage and he was cast as her love interest. ("And was apparently of some interest to her," he notes, "on the luckiest day of my life.")

I was already familiar with Charmion King's work on the big screen and the small screen; she made her moments count. I remembered her work with Don McKellar, playing the Meals on Wheels lady in his quirky television series *Twitch City*, and the cameo she did for him in the first feature film he directed,

* From *Sweet Orchids*, by Gordon Pinsent.

Last Night. But my memories of her work on stage are far more vivid. I'll never forget her portrayal of Ethel Barrymore in *Royal Family* at the Shaw Festival, or the huge laughs she sparked when she rocked the house as Jessica in *Jitters*.

I also have this fond, funny memory of going through U.S. customs with her one day at the Toronto airport. I was on my way to L.A. to interview some movie star, and Charm was on her way to Houston to do a play. She had bought a box of very good Cuban cigars as a gift for the director, a man whom she knew was exceedingly fond of cigars, at a time when you couldn't get good Cubans in America. Much to her clearly apparent chagrin, two male U.S. customs officials refused to let her take the Cuban cigars to Texas. When she asked what the hell she was supposed to do with them, she was told to "just leave them with us." At which point she smiled sweetly at the customs officer and replied, "No. No, I don't think I'll be doing that." She then opened the box of Cuban cigars, walked over to a large trash can and destroyed each cigar – breaking them one by one, rendering them unsalvageable – and dropped each one, now torn asunder, into the trash, while the U.S. customs officials watched in horror.

Witnessing her performance that day was the highlight of my trip.

I still regret that I never saw her that very last time, doing *Our Town* with Soulpepper in Toronto in 2006. It was such a big hit that they had already announced they were bringing it back again; I thought there was plenty of time. But, there wasn't. My wife and I ended up, along with most of Canadian show business, at Albert Schultz's memorial tribute to her, held at the Young Centre on the same stage she had shared with him in *Our Town*. Richard Ouzounian wrote in the *Toronto Star*, "She was the class act of Canadian show business." *Next* is, in so many ways, a love letter to Charmion King.

The author of the love letter remains open yet enigmatic, practical yet romantic. Gordon Pinsent's lifelong friend Perry Rosemond sees him as a true Renaissance man: "He acts, he writes, he directs, he paints – he even builds furniture!"

Another long-time friend, Larry Dane, sees Gordon as a man whose greatest work of art is himself – a man who knows his own brand.

"Gordon has a reputation of being an actor," he says, "of being someone who can really act. And yes, there are a lot of actors out there, but most of them are not considered that way. The way you are perceived will lay the groundwork for your entire career. And that perception has to come from you. You pass it on to your agents, and you pass it on to the world of show business. *I will do this, but I will not do that.* It's up to you to set the tone.

"From the very beginning, Gordon was considered and regarded as an Actor. He isn't playing the same part in the same series for years and years, so audiences don't get tired of him. And Gordon is happy when he's working, as long as you treat him with respect. He does have a line that he will draw; there are certain things he will not do. When he says 'I won't do this, and I won't do that,' producers may get pissed off for a few minutes, but ultimately they like it. Because they know where they stand with him, and they respect him for it. And that creates longevity."

And how. Pinsent has been onstage and onscreen for more than half a century. He is a member of a select group of actors – Christopher Plummer, William Shatner, and Donald Sutherland among them – who have never stopped working. Only HRM Queen Elizabeth II has held her job longer than they have – and she never had to audition. Paul Gross, a relatively new Old Friend in Pinsent chronology, has described him as "preternaturally young, bottomlessly creative; his contribution to our country is immeasurable and his passion for our country is inexhaustible." And the fact that Pinsent decided to live and work in Canada was not lost on Gross, who, in his own words, did "a similar sort of thing." He says, "I went down to L.A. and came back home to do *Due South*. And I thought, *well, he's done it. Maybe I don't have to go back to L.A. Maybe I can do it here.* And that's an important legacy."

That Pinsent continues to win the affection, admiration, and respect of new generations may be in part a reflection of his own affection, admiration, and respect for his fans.

"He hates it when I do this," Larry Dane confides, "but there's a quote about Steven Spielberg that I think also applies to Gordon: *Much nicer than he has to be.* And he is. He doesn't want to let people down. If you go out for lunch or dinner with him, be prepared to wait an extra twenty or thirty minutes while you're leaving the restaurant, because people will want to talk to him, and he will stop and talk to every single one. Sometimes I'll just yell, 'Okay, Gordon, talk to you tomorrow!' and go home. But it's still a quality of his that I very much admire."

Me too.

Gordon, we're all yours.

George Anthony

NEXT

born to make believe

———◆———

I AM IN BED WITH JULIE CHRISTIE.

Me, who used to practice kissing on trees.

I'm in bed with Julie Christie.

We lie naked under the blanket together.

Well . . . half-naked.

She strokes my arm lovingly. I look deep into her eyes and I see her past lives. The luminous Lara of *Doctor Zhivago*. The sexy seductress of *Shampoo*. The passionate wife who romanced tragedy in *Don't Look Now*.

A voice interrupts my reverie. "And . . . *cut!*"

Julie Christie gives me a hug.

"Well done, Gordon, well done!" she purrs, in her plummy English.

That's going in the resumé.

I act. Always have.

Sir Ralph Richardson said of us, "We are printers." I suppose by that he meant that we copy life, and the living. We ride invisible horses, wear fall-away costumes, until they fall apart and we exchange them for others. One job does us for a while until that ends and we see or hear something else that takes us over.

It took a while to figure out how to "hit notes" – to colour them properly, to play the right chords. And I guess I hit them pretty well. So now I know what to do with them. I can bring them down, down, down. And I can still be true to the rendition when I do it. All I need is the job.

I see an excellent Glenn Gould documentary by filmmaker Peter Raymont and I get sucked into a silence where I am all alone, as Gould was at times, vulnerable, and wanting to be; where I would try to understand him, to the point that I, like Gould, would not enjoy a hearty hello or a meaningful handshake. I would dress in a scarf, and gloves, and cap, perhaps … No. Okay. Just the flaccid handshake would do to assume his sense of isolation and quietude, with just the tiniest bit of hope that someone had noticed how much more peculiar and enigmatic I was next to anyone else.

Being someone that no one really knows … this is not pretense, entirely. It's needed, but scary during weekends when the phones don't ring, and all you have to do is to have enough breathing left to make it to Monday when you fire up your synapses again, quickly rattling in Italian, aloud, script-wise, while choosing bananas at the market next door, being not at all embarrassed by your own mumbling at the checkout counter. All this before that night's performance, when you are able to remind the three-hundred-seat house that you are there for them, and haven't actually starved yourself into complete and utter self-neglect.

I once played to two old ladies and a pigeon. But I'm getting ahead of myself.

Porky Pinsent, at your beck and call.

To be more formally precise: Gordon Edward Pinsent. Born July 12, 1930. Yes, 1930. No, that's not a typographical error. But thanks just the same.

Son of Stephen Arthur Pinsent and Flossie Cooper, of Grand Falls, Newfoundland. My father was a highly industrious fellow; when illness forced him to leave the paper mill, he taught himself to become an expert cobbler. My mother was a servant girl, born into a time when a woman got up in the morning and made breakfast for her children and made a place for her husband to come home to. My mother did all of that, and more.

I was not an only child. Nita Hilda was the eldest, followed by Raymond and Morley, both of whom died in their infancy, followed by Hazel Winnifred, followed by Harry Thomas, then Lilith Leah, then Haig Alonzo, and then, finally, me. The runt of the litter.

Before you picture me as a chubby baby who became a chubby little boy who eventually grew up and finally conquered his chubbiness, let me confess that hardly anyone, including me, remembers how or why I ended up with the nickname Porky. Early photos show me as an average kid with an average build and an average weight. But one short-pants summer I did go through a more robustly corpulent phase, thus winning me that nickname.

Because I had rickets I didn't walk until I was five. In our family pictures, I was always sitting, or sprawled out on the floor, or lying around in the grass. When my sisters thought it was time we had a picture of me upright, they hoisted me up against a tree in our backyard, then pulled me up to a stand-ing position and stuck some of the lower tree branches under the back of my sweater, so that I appeared to be standing on my own. But of course it was a rather precarious position to be in, and I started to lean towards the camera, that little Brownie box camera we all had back then, and the only thing that was keeping me from falling forward were the tree branches that were slowly pulling away from my shirt. But my sisters got their picture. "Gord, stand up, for God's sake!" And there I was, standing upright, proud as hell; it didn't take much to make me happy. And then there I was, falling over, slowly, but still waving to someone who was passing by, as if it was the most natural thing in the world for Porky Pinsent to be standing.

You'd think I'd remember the first time I stood up on my own, without the aid of my sisters or an innocent, unsuspect-ing tree. But I don't. It just happened one day. I wasn't waiting for it to happen. I couldn't walk, but then I had never walked, so I just didn't know any different.

Because I had rickets I also started school a year after every-body else. Being a year late, I think I was probably playing catch-up, because everybody else had gone on without me, and I was left behind. That was the start of the anxiety and the insecurity that would plague me for the rest of my days. But I made sure at the same time to fake it, to act as though I had been there forever, just like in that photo; that I was an old hand at this. Didn't know I was already acting. Just staying alive. Maybe I was old at heart, but I was able to fit in fairly well. Even though I could see around me others' ideas of who I was, I could skirt around those and believe only in myself. I was born to make believe.

I was not an over-privileged child – well, none of us were. Maybe Charles Dickens had *Great Expectations*, but ours were not so grand. Passed-down gifts were lost, then mysteriously resurfaced when there was little to give at some Christmas or other. My mother and father needn't have tried so hard. I had never expected anything. Never the long face from me when there wasn't enough under the tree. Even at my youngest, life just was. Whatever it would bring, or not, would do. And because of this, things did stumble my way, as though they were in search of he who had not gone searching.

My favourite hideaway was the small confines of the family woodshed. Here I would spend countless hours, on countless occasions. My father had transformed the woodshed into a cobbler's den, where he would drive his fiddly tacks and slice his soles and heels. I was as happy crawling under it as playing inside it. And occasionally, when school or other compulsory distractions intervened, being the magnanimous kid I was, I'd let my dad have the whole shed to himself.

My mother didn't have an awful lot to say in our life, but there isn't a hair on her head I can't remember. Poor Mom. Mom would be ironing, and I'd say, "Well, Mom, I'm engaged." I'd be ten, maybe twelve. And she would just keep ironing. And I'd say "Well, Mom, I just robbed a bank, I guess I'm in real trouble now." Her expression would never change. She would just keep ironing.

Legitimate. Wanted to think of myself as that. I knew I was in the most obvious way legitimate – Mom's face, Pop's chin. I made so much noise that I can hear it still. I needed proof of being counted. For something. It looked doubtful during those early years with the world rehearsing for the Second World War. No matter – the noise I made, the laughter alone, would help me be recognized surely. They'd hear me coming, a harbinger of mostly unwanted attention piping up for no reason except to be heard. John Philip Sousa could've used me. But it couldn't be helped. I would dissuade timidity at the cost of childish arrogance.

But why this great need to be legitimate? Where did that fear come from, that I was not? I would ponder this seemingly bottomless concept forever, if necessary; not being needed for anything special from breakfast to breakfast, porridge to porridge, of any given day awarded me as a boy.

When the biggest book of all of this planet's living, breathing human particles was written, would I, could I, be found among them, for the sake of the final census, shall we say? One would hope so.

I didn't know how I was being summed up – the ego and all – by others great and small around me. I was barely noticed, or so my ego told me.

Certainly I wanted to be included. I wouldn't have liked to find food and sustenance for myself. Shag that! Still, there was this need to give "normalcy" a chance, even though I wasn't sure what that was. Doing things for others would help to a degree. Maybe that was a start, but it wasn't my fault that others – maybe all others – would be far better suited to that than I, than me. How the hell would I ever have time to look outward? When would I have time and the interest to look inward, where the "I" was, that no one understood? Or had an interest in deciphering? But somehow I steadfastly gave the impression that I was only fascinated in me.

Mind you, I had had feelings at times that I might have been no more important than a nickname.

Fine. Inside me, I knew the roads, and the rocks, and the hideouts, caves, yes, and stalactites, to throw off those who could, impossibly, have reason to call me to supper. Where I couldn't be as foolish as I wanted.

I wish I could tell you more about my father. I can't, but I wish I could, because then I would know so much more about him than I actually do. I could have asked him, of course; should have asked him, no question about that now. But what was the rush? Fathers live forever, and he was only in his fifties. No need to store up memories of him; he was here just a minute ago. And then he was gone. I was nine years old, and when my father's Oddfellow cronies brought food baskets to us, as brand-new survivors of one of their members, I thought we'd won the lottery. Harry, who was ten years older but still only nineteen, was horrified by this gesture of charity, as any grown man would be when reminded that he couldn't take care of his own family.

I couldn't wait to be ten. I wore bobskates all year long, hoping to get there faster. I was racing ahead now, and by the time I was twelve I was such a fan of Harry James that I joined the Church Lads Brigade and discovered, to my utter delight, that I could play the bugle better lying down. Which didn't help a lot in parades.

That's okay, I had other talents. I was already cute as hell. With dimples, for God's sake! I couldn't think of anyone, not a single kid uptown or downtown, far and wide, who possessed dimples. Not this side of Hollywood, anyway.

There'd be no stopping me later on, when I'd hit thirteen, say.

Dimples. They should've counted for something, dammit! Not that they would have the girls from Grade Eight onward tripping over their laces at the sight of me – I'd have to create a newer persona to fit the moment. And that moment was coming up fast. I'd soon be turning that last corner, where I would be overawed by "the big white house" named – suitably – *high* school!

Jesus, what a smack across the face and a kick in the arse that was, at first sight; curdling what had previously been ingested so that I had to nip the cheeks together for longer than I should have.

The high school spoke to me. Right away. It said:

Run, you little bastard! You dumpy, pee-smelling, heart-thumping little downtown shagger! Run from what you don't understand! My name is the Grand Falls Academy! And you don't come anywhere near me in the way of importance! Dimples, what dimples? I don't see dimples! Oh yes. Them. Don't mean a thing. A boot in the bum. Worth nothing more. Now, if you manage to get the heavy front doors open on your own, you might be able to stand at the back of the assembly hall where no one will be tempted to see your irrationally pathetic self.

"Hello," I'd say to myself a few times, before fulfilling my secret mission in case there were spies from the upper grades about. "Hello, back," I'd say, in a voice that someday I'd be paid for.

That's better. Tight little fists. Determined strides of a much older me, soon brushing against higher high schoolers, with the courage of Ernest Hemingway, whom I'd never heard of yet. I was fine now. With a desk of my own, almost. Ink in the inkwell. No one staring at me. Couldn't see me maybe. That's fine. Getting older by the minute. And bigger too. And smarter. Smart enough to have an opinion. Just not pushy enough to feel like outsmarting any of them.

Main thing was: I felt stronger, with me to lean me on. It seemed natural. And I'd always be closer than the closest friend, maybe, which was way better than feeling useless next to these others, engaged in a huge brain-exchange. Aryan-like mama's boys and girls, who were already "on their way" out the main door, diplomas held high, beribboned no less. Another secret I would only dream of. All of them legitimate!

I recall, at the same school, having the most gripping crush on the most comely girl in evidence there. There wasn't, of course, a chance for me. Could not have been. Not with the far more uptowned, moneyed, fashionably attired and handsome swain around. So, with not a favourite marble to lose, I picked my nose, wiped it down my faded, rustic pants, and shouted "FUCK" all the way home; which, as it turned out, was the first time anyone had used the phrase, right out that way, since it had been swept in on the wings of the first American contingent, now set up at the fringe of town. I recall one of our more outgoing local girls, known for the growing habit of being on occasion "seen" with those crisp, razor-sharped gabardine Yanks, saying to me: "I hates that word. I hates them when they says it. I don't mind the other word, which means the same thing; but I hates the sound of that one starting with a capital F!"

Some kids my age were getting religion. Me? If I'd known the Catholics had a drama club at their school, I'd have converted. The Anglicans had one, but they would take long, long breaks, and that simply wouldn't do. So I continued to rehearse my greatest roles in the family woodshed.

I rehearsed for all my girlfriends too, the ones I was too shy to talk to at school, by coming home and kissing the side of the house. And waited for that first kiss. And waited. And waited. It finally happened on a Saturday night in the summer of '42 and a bit.

My plan was to reach greatness. Any kind of greatness. That was the plan, at least, and, dreaming my way through the tail end of the Depression, I turned that corner into my teens, and dressed myself for the world at large. I knew that only then would I be brave enough to walk by a stranger's dog. Yes, I was afraid of dogs as well, though you would never know it, not when a decent-sized audience was around.

I was sketching now. The step after sketching is water-colours, but it depends on what your parents can afford, which may not be very much. So you really had to depend on the schools, and what they could provide, and their will to provide it. I just kept illustrating. I did a lot of illustrating before I left home. It sounds fancy, but it wasn't fancy at all. No one in the world of illustration was saying, *Well, we really need someone like him.* I thought my illustrations were pretty good, but they meant nothing on the mainland, nothing in Toronto or

Montreal or anywhere else. I was aware, to some degree, that it was a talent of sorts. But the concern, the priority, was about developing a talent that would put food on the table. So yes, Porky could sketch, Porky could draw, but that was hardly paramount to our existence. We just didn't think about it all that much.

What was this time all about? What really, if I was of no use to anyone at this age and time? Barely fixed in the family album by corner stickers, like everyone else. Old aunts would finger their way through, proudly sharpening their memories: "Now, who's that? Oh yes, Flossie, née Cooper, Stephen Arthur, the sisters, Nita Hilda, Hazel Winnifred, Lilith Leah, and the brothers Harry Thomas, and Haig Alonzo, and who's that?" – pointing to some small blur, who'd moved and spoiled the picture – "Oh yes, must be Gordon Edward, already on his way off the margin to God-knows-where!"

The blur had places to go and things to do that would not identify themselves until he came to a full stop.

I began to say "Yes, I can" alongside just about anyone. But the truth was that, with a sliver of the earlier insecurity still lodged in the root cellar of my character, I'd never considered myself high on life's roster for consideration for anything. Besides, the family woodshed was one theatre that I didn't have to pay to get into, because there was no one taking tickets.

Because, you see, by now – had you guessed? – I had discovered the movies. And the movies had found their greatest fan: Me.

lost in celluloid

—◆—

ONE OF THE MOST POPULAR EXPRESSIONS I RECALL
from my earliest days – or teens, from peers, I guess – happened
to be:

Who do you think you are?

Now, it must be said that this was not aimed at me exclu-
sively. Everyone got it at one time or another. But it was perfect
for me – that, and *Get out of my sight!* That was big. My brother's
nickname for me was *Go 'way boy!* And let's not forget *Go to the
woodshed 'til supper's ready!* That was big too. But the question
Who do you think you are? just always hung there, meaning more
than any of these other tossed-off lines, because that was one
I sure couldn't answer.

The whole school – my whole world – seemed to be obli-
gated to choose what they were going to do in the way of a life's
work. This frightened me. I would be the only one to not be
ready. Indeed, I'd be thrown out of house, island, country,
world, for having gone against the grain.

*I know, I said. I'll be an actor. I'll be so completely lost in the realm
of imagined characters that they'll never find me. I'll drive the census
people nuts.*

In Grand Falls Mom never knew who was coming through the door, because I had seen a movie with someone else in it and I was already impersonating my way around town.

To me actors were faraway Dream People. When movies played at the Nickel in Grand Falls – a.k.a. Paddy Edwards' Palace of Dreams – they played only two nights, so everyone went one night or the other. As kids we went to the matinees, of course, because we weren't old enough to go at night. But whenever we could we would sneak into the evening shows to see Bogart and Cagney.

The Nickel was short for the Nickelodeon, and kids could get in for a nickel. If you were accompanied by your parents, you could get in free. Most of the time I was a nickel short but a dollar smart. I would walk into those late afternoon shows with a new set of parents each time – even though their fresh-eyed "offspring" bore a striking resemblance to the kid who was at the matinee three hours earlier. I was lucky, because the ticket taker at the Nickel was tragically nearsighted.

The movies were a magical elixir for me. Every time I left the cinema I felt stronger, physically, mentally, creatively – stronger in every way. I would walk the streets of our small town, singing up a storm after an Al Jolson or Fred Astaire movie, and the good people of Grand Falls still made room for me. Just smiled and waved and treated me like I was next to normal.

All those amazing people on the screen. And I started to resemble them. I took steps to prove it. One week I looked like Walter Hampton. The next I looked like Turhan Bey. My first moustache? Rakish, no two ways about it. And then Alan Ladd came on the screen. We learned from American movie magazines that Alan Ladd had married Sue Carroll, who had been an actress in the twenties, and she managed his career. In some photographs he looked quite slight, and I was quite slight, and yet he looked big and strong and sturdy onscreen.

As far as I was concerned, these movies were being made just for me. I wanted to believe that these lives were being lived, that these dramas were being played out in real life. And I fitted myself in there – I cast myself in every story I could. Watching the flickering light on the screen, I'd come close to hearing my name mentioned during scenes by the actors.

Casablanca:
YOU AND PORKY ARE GETTING ON THAT PLANE!

The Grapes of Wrath:
WHEREVER THERE'S A FIGHT SO HUNGRY PEOPLE CAN EAT,
PORKY WILL BE THERE!
WHENEVER THERE'S A COP BEATIN' UP A GUY,
PORKY WILL BE THERE!

Sometimes I'd get so involved, I'd cry, until the people next to me – who would know me as the kid who had delivered their Christmas turkey – would think I needed help. But I wasn't there. I was either in a Flying Tiger with John Wayne, or lighting a cigarette for Bette Davis, or delivering mail for the Pony Express, happy to be answering for lives I would never have.

When I was in this peculiar space, I always thought I was on a train I didn't have a ticket for, but doing a remarkable service for the entertainment industry, with fans in all the great capitals of the world. I kind of thought of myself as belonging to this tremendous club, hanging out with the best of them. An important part of it all; being a limb on this enormous tree called MGM, or at the very least, Republic. On a first-name basis with some of the cowboy heroes of the time: Tom Mix, Buck Jones, and Don "Red" Barry.

I saw nothing wrong with showing a human frailty or two. I probably would have played a great quisling in war films, if I couldn't be the hero or, at the very least, the hero's side-kick. I went so far into celluloid that no one knew me. And if it wasn't for Mom and the smell of her freshly baked raisin bread, I would've been married to Lana Turner or splitting the loot with James Cagney.

I knew that I wanted a certain kind of life, but I did not know how to acquire it, so I certainly did not expect it. And I could not put a scholastic wrap around it. So I went for the fanciful, the imaginary. I had been everywhere in the movies – Sherwood Forest, China, Treasure Island, to India with Sabu, in Alcatraz with Humphrey Bogart. I was in Africa last Saturday with Stanley and Livingstone by way of Spencer Tracy and Cedric Hardwicke. Next Saturday I might meet up with Clark Gable, Regis Toomey, Gale Sondergaard, Leo Gorcey, Maria Ouspenskaya, Loretta Young, or Brian Donlevy.

Eventually it dawned on me that there could be some money in this. There could be a future in this. Other people were becoming doctors and lawyers. But I was so immersed as a child in the world of movies that of course it affected my thinking. Answering for fictional lives that would last only the length of a matinee, and sensing one's own fallibility when hitting the street outside. It made me not appreciate a moment exactly when experiencing it; not being on time with my own being, discounting the reality of the home town and the car wheels not owned by John Garfield or Bogart. Meanwhile, somewhere between my burnt toast and Jell-O, World War II had begun. My brother Harry had already enlisted. Our phone number in Grand Falls was 301-R, and I would sit under the wall phone, waiting for the call that would tell us that the trains were coming in and Harry was coming home. We wouldn't get that call for quite a while. Still, was there any place more strategically important to the war effort than Grand Falls? Not if my imagination had anything to do with it!

By now Gander's airport was the largest on the planet, essential to the war effort in getting aircraft from North America to Britain. First place a plane could land was Gander on this side of the ocean, and Shannon, Ireland, on the other side. The inhabitants of the town of Gander, the homes and shops in the surrounding area, were the families of all the people who worked at the airport, and their grocers and butchers and so on. There was no other significant industry to speak of.

By now American movie stars were flying overseas on USO tours to entertain the troops. To get there they had to stop in Gander to refuel. We were all suitably impressed, but I was downright dazzled. The Dream People, the heroes and heroines of our weekend fantasies, were coming to Newfoundland.

At fifteen I made my first major journey. I boarded The Bullet in Grand Falls and, about an hour later, got off in Gander to stay with my sister Hazel. Hazel had married Cecil

Bishop, an able-bodied seaman who worked in communications. She was the sweetest, fairest woman I ever knew – and she was my champion. "It wasn't Gord's fault!" she'd insist, even when it was. But Hazel wasn't the reason I went to Gander. I went to Gander because I had applied for, and won, the highly coveted (by me) job of busboy at the then-legendary Airlines Hotel.

One night the word was out that, because of the weather, none of the planes could take off. So the actors and all the others were all around us, sitting in the bars, and I thought, *My God, I've died and gone to heaven.* I paid twenty-five cents to another busboy to borrow his white jacket and I walked around emptying ashtrays. I think Barry Fitzgerald was there, and Edgar Bergen with Charlie McCarthy, and I was walking around them, in this other world of fancy china and crystal, thinking I was King Tut, happy to be emptying ashtrays as long as I could see actors go by. I wasn't entirely sure they were real, and once I convinced myself that they were, I did a little better with it, but I still didn't sleep for nights. Ginny Simms. Mel Tormé, Deanna Durbin, all coming or going. And Jean-Pierre Aumont. And Maria Montez – I was only a busboy, but I got to dance a few steps with her!

Churchill would come to Botwood, which was a seaplane port in the Bay of Exploits, between Gander and Grand Falls, on his way to make speeches in New York. And I got to see where he stayed, and where he slept. At least, the room where they said he might have slept. Next to a wireless room. Incredible.

They were camouflagin' stardust
only half the world was free
and while Gander was havin' its way with you
you were havin' your way with me
Did ever we have madness then
did ever we have trouble
and when our champagne heads had cleared
*did ever we have rubble**

If movie stars were coming by sea they'd also come to Botwood, and then sometimes to our town, Grand Falls. That's how one of Hollywood's most illustrious citizens, Bob Hope, ended up making a visit to our local bakery with Frances Langford, Jerry Colonna, and Les Brown. As you might imagine, the four of them were barely in the door when word-of-mouth started travelling faster than a Justin Bieber video on YouTube. *"Bob Hope's at the bake shop!"* And so he was.

I had it in my head that this was it. *It's all gonna happen to me today. It's Bob and me, me and Bob. He's going to throw me into his car, give me a contract, and I'll be in Hollywood in a week.* And when I saw him at the bake shop I was sure I heard him say, "Go home and wash your face, kid." Although fourteen other young lads will tell you that that's what he said to them. But I insist it was me he said it to. Blessing me, in a sense. "Go on, kid, go on. Come on down to Hollywood and join us as soon as you can." And that's all I needed to hear. Because there was always that

* From *Gander! Gander!* by Gordon Pinsent.

feeling of something else. I always felt I was supposed to be part of something larger. I just didn't know what it was.

So now I knew for certain that I could ride this acting animal – promised to me by some early unknown force – to some sort of recognition in a world larger than Grand Falls. A way out, or in, where I might find others like myself. It was very personal. And I was so sure I owed something to this promise that I would stay with it 'til it was accomplished, however unstable and far-reaching it proved to be.

Inside, I might have been a nobody. Outside, I was everybody! If ever the two came together, I'd be a somebody!

leaving home

How does it feel when the rock was here?
How is it that we can't get there now?
What did you do to it, or they?
What happened to it, yesterday?

How did you know how to last till then
and not know how to last till now?*

DID I MENTION THAT I CAME TO NORTH AMERICA from a foreign land?

Newfoundland, the exotic country I grew up in, was once a sovereign state – an independent dominion of hearty, colourful, and decidedly independent souls adrift in the Atlantic.

What can I tell you of my lovely, lonely island that hasn't already been sung? Most of our history, dating back to the Viking settlements of AD 1000, has been set to music by one troubadour or another. And we've produced some great

* From "How Was It When the Rock Was Born," by Gordon Pinsent.

ones – Ron Hynes, Alan Doyle and Great Big Sea, Figgy Duff, Neil Bishop and The Gig – and continue to do so.

We were a British colony at one time, before we gained our independence; but the Depression took such a toll on us that we voted to become a British colony again. And then, in 1940, with World War II raging around us, Winston Churchill and Franklin Delano Roosevelt, as partners in defence, decided that Newfoundland would be the key British naval base in the Atlantic. The Yanks poured in, and we were reasonably prosperous again. After the war we thought we'd have to decide who to go with – the U.S. or Britain – until Canada made us an offer we (and by "we" I mean some of us) couldn't refuse.*

The Rock was beautiful to us long before Newfoundland & Labrador Tourism discovered it. Nobody ever truly wanted to leave. Well, nobody our family knew. But one day, after a whole lot of dreaming, and after receiving a decent-sized cigarette butt from a mill worker, I knew it was time to go. My feet knew it. My mind knew it. I had an energy that didn't seem to fit with the idea of staying. That energy had to get out, somehow, somewhere. It had to be unleashed. How far it would take me I didn't know, but somehow I had to find a way, and I walked through the town to the end of my indecision.

Next, I needed a single paycheque, a prerequisite for emigrating to Canada. Oh yes, and X-rays. This was the latter part of 1948, after all, and not 'til the following April would we be

---

* An older generation who considered isolation a winning way of life still regard Confederation as the day Canada joined Newfoundland.

able to call ourselves Canadian. By the time I left home, Harry was back from the war and had already taken over the family reins. And all three sisters had been married in the last two years of the war. As I mentioned before, Hazel had married Cecil Bishop, and they were living in Gander. My sister Nita had married a taxi driver, Les Knight. Lilith's husband, Ron Smith, worked at the paper mill and was also involved in the union. And my brother Haig had worked in the paper mill until he was old enough to leave home, and then ended up in the Air Force.

In August 1948, after all the fond farewells, I took The Bullet across the island to Port aux Basques to board the passenger ship for my first visit to Canada. Yes, The Bullet. In those days we still had our own railway. We called it The Bullet. People on bikes used to pass it. You could walk across the island faster. And if you took it from one side of the island to the other, you were bound to have a couple of birthdays along the way. So it was not the fastest way to get somewhere. But it was our way.

On the crossing to Canada on the wave-churned Cabot Strait I decided to hang out with a small group of seasoned party animals who were far more fluent in screech than I was. By the time the ship docked in North Sydney, Nova Scotia, I wasn't young anymore. And Canada, much to my chagrin, appeared to be little more than a customs shed.

"Wanna see me X-rays?" I asked the surly customs official who collared me.

"No, I want to see $250, which is what you're supposed to have if you intend to stay here."

I didn't have $250 on me that very second.

My pocket jangled with the princely sum of thirteen cents.

So, I performed.

And, I performed well. I performed a stage-worthy soliloquy of youthful helplessness, immigrant ignorance, and abject sadness, with a proper pinch of vulnerability. I insisted that my lack of funds could hardly constitute a relevant issue as I was bound to be hired by eager employers as soon as I set foot on the main street. And I am proud to report that I pleaded my fragile case so successfully that my once-grumpy interrogator summoned the nurse to look me over. (Politicians would kill for that sincerity.)

The Canadian customs official told me to put away my thirteen cents and my spare set of shoelaces. They would let me into the country provided I stay in Sydney until they could verify, in three days' time, that I indeed had a job, and that I would not be a drain on Canada's financial resources.

Three customs officials – *three!* – showed up to check on me three days later. I was mixing and pouring cement into newly constructed frames inside a corner store, and when I saw them coming, I smeared my face with cement, just to add a touch of drama. The closer they got, the harder I appeared to be working. Shovelling, mixing, scooping, shovelling, mixing, scooping. They were suitably impressed, and expressed the hope that I would continue to labour in this noble profession.

"Oh yes, I loves it!" I assured them. "I'm nutting without a pick and shovel! Can't see meself ever doing anyting else!"

They left.

I quit the job I never had.

I snagged a few short-term jobs, a string of them, and inched my way to Toronto, province by province. A tough potato-picking engagement in Prince Edward Island was followed by equally unfortunate employment gigs in New Brunswick. I broke my hand hauling ice blocks, broke my back picking spuds, and broke my toe in bridge construction.

Was I worried? Of course not. I was eighteen.

Besides, Herbert Marshall had lost a leg in World War I and had walked through one hundred movies without anyone catching on. So broken toe be damned. I just kept plugging away until I got the price of a one-way CNR second-class ticket to Toronto. And got robbed of that by a bum who said, "You're a bum like me, except you're a young bum!" I never forgot that.

By the time I finally arrived at Union Station in Toronto I had only three cents in my pocket. And eyes the size of saucers when I came out of the station and saw, right in front of me, the second-tallest building in the British Commonwealth, the Royal York Hotel. (It didn't take all that much to amaze us back then.)

Biggest news of the day was the escape of the Boyd Gang – their second successful unauthorized exit from Toronto's sinister-looking Don Jail. Lorne Greene was doing live updates on the Canadian Broadcasting Corporation's brand-new Canadian television network. Mesmerizing.

Over the next two months – September and October – I had at least six jobs, all of them short-lived. I suppose the mistake my employers made was to give anyone as sensitive as an aspiring thespian a job. And I say that with no regrets.

Although I still had a personal wish list, I confess that a desire to excel at making Dixie cups, distributing free soap samples, wrapping crystal at Sears, painting signs, and insulating houses was not on it.

What I lacked in skill I made up for in confidence – totally unjustified, of course. But I had cleats on my boots, and in those days if you could walk around and be heard . . . well, I thought I was the smartest thing ever, and brought those boots into every office I went to. Including the employment agencies.

"All right," said one interviewer, "what do you want to do?"

"I'm an actor," I said. (Bald-faced lie. But, still . . .)

"An actor," he said. "Well, what did you do before that?"

"I was a shepherd," I said.

"Well," he said, "there are not too many sheep in Toronto."

"Well then," I said, "you're going to have to get me work as an actor!"

I was at that time happy to call myself an Actor. Not that anyone else did. But if you'd had time to study me for a moment longer than "hello" I might have reminded you of someone from the big screen. Almost anyone from the big screen; if I saw that I didn't strike you engagingly in the first moment, I'd get you at next glance. Tragedy. Comedy. The whole map of human behaviour was right there, and would fit whatever moment in your good or bad hair day you'd require.

Plus – did I mention that I was just eighteen? – I was enchanted by Toronto's glamorous nightlife. First night in the big city. The Silver Rail, the Brown Derby, Club Kingsway; mickies under the table, with still enough shine in an old jacket for copying Frankie Laine, hard at "Jezebel" on Toronto's ticket.

Afterwards, for one who hadn't come with one, or left with one, you found yourself in the shadow life of the different Toronto the Good. And if you weren't interested in maturing right away, you could make a lot of those nights in Toronto shadows, which may or may not have had moving people in 'em, Shapes only, when the world turned seamless amber, and you were at a place where no one knew you and you didn't get sent home. No questions asked. You were inside now, on a doubtful set of stairs, not having left a clue behind you; and something would be waiting for you that you hadn't met before, and you wouldn't have to take it with you. It would stay. Then, cracked lips from nowhere brushed yours with the music of the moment. No flattery here. You didn't ask to be remembered, and you had just enough youth on your face to undo the eyes of a forgotten fiancée, taking her sadness out on a tired and uninterested candle. And at the Casino, Lili St. Cyr, she of the bathtub, and Sally Rand, she of the giant balloons. Be still, my boyish heart! (Not to mention my nether regions.) I was informed later that Sally had been older than the theatre on the day I saw her. Regardless, a lot of young Canadians grew up watching Sally, and a lot of old men didn't get home in time. And who could forget Chuck Gregory & His Dancing Girls, whose pulchritudinous ranks included the lovely and talented Kitty Kat McDonald, wife of U.S. mobster Mickey McDonald, who was right up there on the public enemies list. And Chuck always introduced his Dancing Girls with a hit tune of the day:

Little girl . . .
This big ol' world will be divine
When you're mine, little girl, all mine

The Casino on Queen Street West showcased such formidable talents as Bill Daniels, Rosemary Clooney, Sammy Davis Jr., the Four Lads, Patti Page and Josh White, and would be torn down to make way for the Sheraton Centre opposite Toronto's "new" City Hall. The Victory Burlesque Theatre dominated Spadina Road for three decades.*

On nights like these I gained an invaluable insight about who I was becoming: I loved being in the audience. I loved being in the moment. At times I wondered which side of the stage I should be on. And even then the answer seemed inevitable. Both sides, Porky. Both sides.

* Years later I would attend a dinner at the Canadian Consulate in Beijing. Sitting across from me was Sir Run Run Shaw, the Hong Kong movie mogul who ran a huge movie empire but was arguably more famous for letting Bruce Lee and Jackie Chan slip through his fingers. And he said, "You are from Toronto? Really? . . . how is The Victory doing?" Apparently he owned it.

jump

———◆———

BY LATE AUTUMN, TWO MONTHS AFTER MY UNHERALDED
arrival in Toronto, I had yet to be hired as an actor.

Incredible! you say. I agree. Incredible. And yet, strange as it
may sound, the people in Toronto who were in the business of
hiring actors seemed to want actors with at least some credentials, credits, or experience – none of which, due to various
twists of fate, I had gotten around to acquiring.

So I joined the Army instead.

Okay, that's not entirely true. I joined the Army for a number
of reasons, mostly because I was homesick. Frankly, I was caught
off guard and confused by this thing called freedom. It felt odd,
even uncomfortable, to be able to do whatever I pleased without anyone's permission.

Harry Thomas, my oldest brother, had gone off to war and
come home a hero. Everyone thought the world of Harry, and
I wanted everyone to think the world of me too. So I joined
the Canadian infantry on November 12, 1948 – peacetime
army, of course; no sense getting shot up, I might lose something I was going to need later on – and for the next three
years would seldom, if ever, get to do what I pleased without

first getting permission from the Royal Canadian Regiment.

This was me. Played convincingly by me. Late teens, I was a patch job where character was concerned. Living on half an alphabet. Fragmented to where it wasn't altogether too rewarding to share my company for longer than a hyphen. You'd feel the need to excuse yourself and hurry back to your common sense. That is, if you were serious about anything.

At the completion of our basic training in Ontario at Camp Borden in the late forties, we had been given the option of being assigned to our choice of regiment. At that time there were three. It was only for me to make the choice: the Princess Patricia's Canadian Light Infantry (PPCLI); the Royal Canadian Regiment; or the Royal 22nd Regiment (the Van Doos of French Canada). I chose to go to the Van Doos. Did I speak French? No. Did I ever have a real sit-down with a person of French descent? No. It must have been because I liked their hat badge. Oh yes. Hat badge. You'd be amazed at how much attention that could bring you, when walking the streets of a given army town on a weekend pass, say. The Van Doo badge in particular stood out in bas-relief, and looked great buffed to all heaven, beaver and all. And of course their tricoloured shoulder flashes. Now, with the shoulder flashes sewn on and the hat badge attached, I fairly tickled myself into waiting for the first Van Doo to come and address me in French. Not as a gag; I seriously wanted to be addressed in French. This didn't happen that I recall. Don't know why. They could easily have taken me for French, with the name Pinsent. As in *Pan-son*. But *non*. What would I have done? It seems I knew I was stupid but didn't take the results as seriously as the beauty of the initial experience. Plus, you may wonder, didn't I realize that by volunteering to join the Van Doos, I'd have to go to one of their bases: St. Jean, or Valcartier? Of course I didn't! So then I was allowed to swing over to the Royal Canadian Regiment while they would still have me.

I was stationed at Camp Borden for a while, and then Petawawa, and hitchhiked to Toronto on precious weekend furloughs. That is, if and when some kindly motorist would pick me up. After the war it seemed as if the colour khaki no longer registered, and I soon concluded that no one in the history of the armed forces was as unimportant in the eyes of civilians as the peacetime soldier.

Back at the camp I wondered if the First Battalion might be sent to Korea. But we were an airborne regiment, so the popular assumption going around was that the government had invested too much in our paratroop training to use us as infantry.

Being a member of an airborne regiment presented its own special challenges. I was not, to put it mildly, a natural jumper. On my first flight I was the last one out of the plane. At least, I was the last in line to jump. Everyone else had gone. So I left my foot inside the door, just in case. And I changed the direction of my hand. I had at first positioned my hand outside the door, to help push me forward. But I decided instead to bring my hand back inside the door, where I could stay and be warm. So the plane carried on, and other people were landing on the ground now, and I was still up at the door of the plane, spread out against the fuselage like an insignia. And I started to talk to myself again, as I always did. And I thought, *Could I land like*

[30]

this? I wonder if I could land like this. Just slide off the plane, literally, after it landed.

Despite that nagging question I would soon experience the knee-cracking mock tower, the gut-knotting high tower, the smack of the raw propeller blast upon exiting the plane, the piss-making jump, and the bone-jarring coming to earth. These were not experiences I willingly embraced. I really didn't so much jump as get too close to the exit not to go. And I did this on as few occasions as I could get away with, doggedly unwilling to risk life and limb for such a small audience.

Posing a far greater risk to my personal life and limbs was the fact that my comrades in arms were by and large seasoned barroom brawlers – and I was not. Oh, I could hold my own for a while in mano-a-mano scuffles with fellow privates, but never long enough to finish. So I had to find a way to make myself indispensable to the guys in my regiment, and concluded that they would regard me as invaluable if I shared my special talent with them.

No, not acting. Opening beers with my teeth.

Did I mention that I was eighteen?

Opening bottle caps with my teeth was my version of having muscles. *Don't mess with me, buddy, I crack beers with my bicuspids.* Blessed with one particularly strong lower bicuspid, I cracked those beers with style and panache, to the delight of my potential head-bashers. Unfortunately the tooth gave out before the Molsons did, so I had to fall back on my next talent – sketching. Get out the old pad and pencil and whip up some flattering sketches of the guys who looked Most Likely to Punch You Out. When that gambit grew old hat, I switched to letter writing.

Clearly a Cyrano ahead of my time, I'd compose love letters for the boys to send off to their girls, and in no time they were lining up around the dorm.

When that party trick ran its course, I sent away for an easy book on easy guitar playing for dumber-than-toilet-bowl soldiers with no talent for fighting, picked up a third-hand guitar, learned four chords, and amused them with my impersonations of Bing Crosby, Vaughn Monroe, the Mills Brothers, and the Ink Spots – singing all the parts wasn't easy – and my pièce de résistance, Hank Snow. This was my greatest crowd-pleaser until Hank Snow himself showed up at a concert at the camp, and my fellow grunts quickly discerned that Hank Snow sounded more like Hank Snow than I did, so I had to drop him from my repertoire!

Of course the very idea that I wore a uniform was ridiculous. I had lived in my own world of play-making for so long, at the movies or in the family woodshed, that when times came up when I was going to be truly embarrassed, or badly hurt, I would immediately feel that I was the only person on earth to feel this way, and for the least reason I would go over the hill if I felt like it, rather than face the captain.

I was an artist, for God's sake! So they put me in a little shack at one point, doing artwork for signs. The fellow who was with me was a wonderful illustrator who liked to do illustrations of ideal girls and boys in compromising positions. And we were both caught. I was caught looking at them, and they thought that I had done them. And I said *No, no, I can do much better than this!* But we were both called up on the carpet for it. And suddenly I was a schoolboy again, afraid to raise my hand. Because the loneliness of that moment was overwhelming.

I was tempted to go over the hill that day. Because we were sent to the brig for punishment, which was unfair, because we deserved to be in that shack. We had the talent. I just wanted to do my little signs. All the others could do was put bullets in guns and hit targets. *Hit the target? Are you joking?* I was playing at being. Yes, playing at being, the acting thing. It never stopped. Let's see – was there anything else before moving on? Oh yes. My circumcision, by an army doctor type. Why did I have this done? Because someone else had, and it was cheap – nothing, in fact – except for a fair amount of embarrassment, and pain, of course. Pain out of character for circumcision, I thought. The initial unwrapping of it was . . . unwinding . . . and then that last tug, which might have brought people out of comas. Other reasons: The circumcision took place in Windsor, and I'd never been to Windsor. Plus, it got me out of a Colonel's inspection. Still, I carried myself like a soldier who had been in the army for forty years, and had always wanted to be, because I was determined to look experienced. Looking experienced was an acting technique that would serve me very well down the road, when I started actually getting paid for it.

I had done the same thing in childhood, starting school after everybody else but acting like I knew all there was to know about it, or at least all there was that was worth knowing. Starting a year back, I was always playing catch-up, always wanting to be able to compare notes with the kids who were in the grade ahead of me.

Which has more than a little to do with that great speech from *Troilus and Cressida*:

> For emulation hath a thousand sons
> That one by one pursue: if you give way,
> Or hedge aside from the direct forthright,
> Like to an enter'd tide, they all rush by
> And leave you hindmost;
> Or like a gallant horse fall'n in first rank,
> Lie there for pavement to the abject rear,
> O'er-run and trampled on . . .
>
> (Act III, Scene 3)

Oh yes, they'll go right by you on horseback if you let 'em. And they won't get hurt, either! They may fall off, but they won't get hurt.

So my life in the military continued to play out like one of those black-and-white comedies Donald O'Connor made for Universal-International.

And then one day everything changed.

The lists were up on the board for people to go to Korea. The Second Battalion had been formed. I was in the First Battalion of the Royal Canadian Regiment. The training was at Petawawa, the Regiment's headquarters – training the new ones and re-training the fellows who had served in World War II, so they could go as well.

We went out on the training field, where everything was set up – ten separate mortar stations all in a row, about six or eight feet apart. I was number five.

We all got down behind our guns, stretched out on the ground, and the trainers, those of us who were doing the training, were kneeling very close behind our men, leaning over their shoulders.

I was a trainer, not because I was so good at it but because I had done it before. (I mean, I didn't want to excel at it – I might get a stripe out of it, and then actually have to be responsible for something.)

All our trainees were holding the barrels with their left hands, leaning in so they could reach to the right where they had a row of maybe six bombs. And they would take the bomb and slide it down the chute, and away they'd go.

This particular time, down went the bomb, and everything turned black. The bomb exploded inside the barrel, and went in every direction. I was number five, and the man in front of me was killed.

From number five to number one – there were between eight and ten people killed in all – the blast went just one way. A piece must've gone by my shoulder, past me, into him, because of the way we were positioned. And of course you can't really see how much damage has been done until it's all over. There was this terrific blast, and everything turned black, and I fell backwards. And they immediately started to count off the people on the line, asking us to call out our names, and I was still flat on my back, and I heard someone say, "Pinsent's got it!" The force of the blast had showered me with a whole lot of dirt. And when I rallied I couldn't hear anything, not a thing, and I saw that the fellow in front of me was dead, and other fellows had started to apply first-aid and bandages. The fellow next to me, Puddicombe, was supposed to be getting married the next weekend. His clothes were blown off from halfway down, and his arse was bare, and I remember seeing this big hole in him, with blood settling in it. And I was thinking *My God, it's like drawings, it's like artwork.* It was the strangest sensation, this disaster. I remember looking at Puddicombe and practically crying. I was shaking, trying to help as best I could with the bandaging, and the padre arrived almost immediately and started administering last rites on the field. The sirens were still going, but he conducted a service right on the spot.

Our ears were still ringing, but they ordered us to get down behind the guns again, so it wouldn't be a problem for us later on. So we had to shoot off some bombs ourselves. After that, we sang a hymn, I think, and then back we went, piling into our trucks to return to the barracks. I remember telling some fellows in the barracks what had happened, because they hadn't heard even a whisper about it. And then, a bit later, we heard that the cause was faulty ammunition.

To me it was a shattering experience, an epiphany. At eighteen, faced with shocking, sudden death, you are strengthened because it wasn't you. The first thing I thought of, or close to it, was that yes, it was real, all this blood and pain, and guys blown apart, and you still had that shiver, that shock in your head. That would be there for a while. But at the same time, what was being done was done. And you were not part of it. So it couldn't have been you. And you might still live to be a million years old. So that represented victory. *Because I can live to tell the tale.* And there's the guilt, of course, feeling guilty because you thought, I'm glad it's not me. *Home of the Brave.*

But what a fresh start. What a fresh outlook.

One of the things I remember most, getting off the truck and walking into the barracks, was the sweetness of the fresh air. Fresh air! It was as if some page of my life had been finished, completed. It was a very particular thing. And, coming quite unexpectedly, a feeling also of pride. Later I could never understand when people accepting awards would say, "I'm proud of my work in this most of all." I could never say that. ("Proud" was a word that your grandfather hit you over the head for.) But in a peculiar way I was proud of being part of that experience. I was no longer a novice, no longer a rookie.

I volunteered to go to Korea, but they wouldn't send me. The popular assumption that had been going around was correct. They wouldn't send me because I was First Battalion, training for parachute jumps, and they had already spent a considerable amount of money on us. So they sent straight infantry instead.

I said, *Well, send me somewhere, for Christ's sake!* So they sent me to Fort Churchill, Manitoba, to another group of earthbound fighting men. And happily for me the guys at Fort Churchill hadn't seen Hank Snow in concert. So back into my musical kit bag he went.

shall we dance?

<hr/>

PRIVATE G. E. PINSENT WAS DISCHARGED IN NOVEMBER, 1951 – in Winnipeg, which seemed somewhat counter-productive to my grand scheme to take Broadway by storm.

As we celebrated our found-again freedom one of my fellow dischargees, a soldier named Billy Reid, invited me home for dinner. Billy was a buddy, a great guy, and while we were enlisted he had persuaded me (with very little coaxing) to become pen pals with his sister Irene.

After months of flirting via Canada Post, Irene and I had finally met, under somewhat unusual circumstances. Since our unit was training at the Rivers, Manitoba, base, we were called in to help with sandbags and evacuations resulting from the Winnipeg flood in 1950. There was a bridge spanning the Red River near the suburb where Irene lived with her parents and, as it so happens, her dog. It was Irene's dog who insisted on jumping into the river, and in a foolish romantic moment I boldly followed suit. I was sure I looked every inch Beau Geste as I made my way out to retrieve her barking pet. I couldn't swim but her bloody dog could, so it was the dog who brought me ashore. And yes, it would be cruel of you to ask me if I still would have waded in for the mutt had she not been standing there. But she was, and I did, and in no time at all we had fallen in love, and in no time at all we were married.

Getting married seemed to be a step other people were taking. *Oh, I'll follow that.* I followed trends, everywhere in life. I had always copied what other people were doing. So, okay, *I guess that's what I'm supposed to do next.*

Irene's family were good, solid working-class people. They worked. And of course there was I, thinking that I would be going in a different direction. I would try to be the proper husband, and good house builder. But at twenty-one I still couldn't get my mind off the arts, and a whole other lifestyle.

Soon we had two children, Barry and Beverly, and I was a working man, going from one lacklustre gig to another: Manitoba Telephone System, meter reader, streetcar ticketer, sign painter, commercial artist. Got the last two jobs when I went looking for work as an illustrator. Never had any training, of course. Didn't know there was such a thing. I thought if you had it, you had it. Which is not entirely true. I ended up painting signs and doing artwork in a place called Display Industries in St. Boniface. And later, much later, when I was acting on stage, I would do the posters. If I had any cocksuredness it was because I knew I could do these certain things to a certain point, whether it was acting or drawing or this or that. With that in mind I used to get up in the morning feeling pretty good about myself. But I was nowhere near as ready as I thought I was.

Most fun, for me, was becoming a bona fide ballroom dance instructor at the Arthur Murray Dance Studios, which were thoughtfully located one flight up from a personal loan company – just in case you needed to borrow some cash to continue your lessons. Especially after basically untrained teachers like me had assured you of your above-average potential.

I found the whole group of people at the Arthur Murray studio in Winnipeg to be very … well … *odd*. And oddly enough, I found that very appealing. They seemed to me to be very New York-y, or at least what I imagined New York people might be like: Not at all like the rest of Winnipeg.

Dance studios were common in the fifties, but the two most popular were those franchised by Fred Astaire and my boss once-removed, Arthur Murray. Murray was a brainy U.S. entrepreneur who made a hobby (and ultimately a fortune) out of social dancing, at a time when dancing was still regarded as romantic. For guys it was a chance to hold a girl in your arms. For girls it was a chance to dance with tall, dark, and handsome strangers, just like the ones who swept fair maidens off their feet in the love stories published in magazines like *Redbook* and *McCall's*.

Murray was a brilliant promoter. He sold dance lessons by mail, spent a lot of money on advertising, and sold his first franchise to a businessman in Minneapolis in 1938. A few years later Betty Hutton and Jimmy Dorsey made a big noise on the hit parade – remember the hit parade? – with a tune called *Arthur Murray Taught Me Dancing in a Hurry*, and by 1946 there were more than seventy Arthur Murray Dance Studios in the United States By the time I arrived in Winnipeg, Arthur Murray was a household name, thanks to his television series. Murray had bought airtime on a major American television network in 1950 to launch an elegant and entertaining weekly infomercial before that word had even been coined. As host he installed his wife Kathryn, his effervescent dance and business partner, who actually wrote the manuals given to me and every Arthur Murray dance instructor to study. *Arthur Murray Dance Party* was a runaway hit, reaching millions of potential customers every week. Including ours.

In retrospect I suppose the Fred Astaire and Arthur Murray dance studios were the lonelyhearts clubs of their era. Single women, unmarried or widowed, paid their instructor/escort to wheel them around a dance floor, bolstering their shaky confidence and low self-esteem. Suddenly they could take pride in their own achievement, and that exceptional sense of satisfaction, so rare in their everyday lives, might carry them all week – or at least until their next lesson. Every few weeks all of the instructors would gather in one room to watch a film of Arthur and Kathryn demonstrating a new dance step. And off we would go.

At times we also had to be fast on our feet off the dance floor. One of our clients, a wonderful woman, a widow, had lost her first dance instructor – apparently he had moved on to a real job – and I was informed that I was her new teacher. I was not a great dancer, but I had rhythm. And I had grown the appropriate moustache for my new role as an Arthur Murray designate. And she had already paid a lot of money, $10,000, I believe, and was registered in a lifetime course. So I took her out on the floor, and we did the foxtrot. (That one even Porky knew, from all those Knights of Columbus dances on Friday night in Grand Falls.)

She said, "I don't want to do the foxtrot. I want to do the *paso doble!*"

"The *paso doble!*" I exclaimed. "Oh my dear, you need to do a little more work on your balance before we try the *paso doble!*"

I took her to a private room and gave her two exercises to do, to work on her balance. And then I excused myself for a moment, ran all the way back to the teachers' green room and cried, "How the fuck do you do the *paso doble?*" I learned two quick steps and went back to the room where she was practicing her balance.

"Very good!" I said. "And now we will do the *paso doble!*"

And *paso doble* we did.

Dancing was easy. Marriage was hard. I had a head full of dreams, and the dreams just could not fit inside the marriage. I was not the man Irene needed me to be. What I was learning, sadly, was that I didn't want to be that man. So it seemed like the only way to resolve it was to separate the two lifestyles, hers and mine. I had to choose between my family and my dream, in one of those awful moments when things aren't what they should be and life isn't on an even keel anymore. Suddenly you're in a time of crisis and reaching that point where you realize it's never going to be the same again.

Barry was five and Beverly was three. I remember leaning over their bunk bed to kiss them goodbye, and I remember wondering if I would ever see them again. I was in a terrible state at the time, and I remember feeling glad that they couldn't tell how upset I was. I remember wondering if, when they grew up, they would ever understand what had happened, and why I had left. Finishing, kissing, not allowing myself to stop, boom boom boom and out the front door, standing alone on the street.

I remember feeling as if I had been given money to go to the store, and that I had lost it, or spent it on something else. I felt dreadful, and useless, concentrating on a life that might not pay me a living – certainly not enough to raise a family. And yet this hunger, this thing that I had not done before, would now force me to go out and see if it could happen.

Standing before a judge and agreeing not to see my children, so their mother could make a fresh start, was the lowest point of my immature young life. For the next two decades my children would see me only on television. Years later, thanks to their love and persistence, we would find each other again, and some thorny issues and unanswered questions would finally be resolved.

In an interview with Newfoundland filmmaker Barbara Doran my daughter Beverly described my departure from their daily lives with a perspective and a generosity I lacked at the time.

"My dad had to go," she told her. "Issues in the marriage aside, the heart wants what the heart wants. You have to go. He couldn't have been Gordon Pinsent without that. You can't hold that kind of hunger down. It would be letting the hungry dogs out of the basement. When you do they would wreak havoc. So best let them out when they're just a little bit hungry."

"go get him, ernie!"

———◆———

"All the world's a stage," quoth the Bard, "and all the men and women merely players. They have their exits and their entrances, and one man in his time plays many parts."

Easy for you to say, Mr. Shakespeare. Especially in Winnipeg.

Here's what I want to know: If all the world's a stage, when do I go on?

In 1954 I met my first director. A wonderful woman named Lena E. Lovegrove. Dowager type. Pince-nez and the lot. She had formed a small theatre group who played only three nights at a time on a little stage they rented at the YMHA. We did Ruth Gordon's play *Years Ago*. In 1953 MGM had made it into a movie with Spencer Tracy and Jean Simmons called *The Actress*, and I played the part Tracy had played. And there we were, doing it in Winnipeg.

I'd never acted before, never been on stage, but Ms. Lovegrove had asked me beforehand if I had been on stage, and I said I had, of course – hell yes! But, I added, I don't know how to do small parts. For some reason they were simply beyond me; I just couldn't imagine how other people managed to do them. Far too difficult for me, I said; I only do leads. Besides, where I was living was beyond the city limits, and commuting every day, going back and forth every day for a small part, just wouldn't be worth my while. So she gave me the lead in *Years Ago* and I had to watch other actors putting on makeup, because I didn't even know how to do that.

While we were in rehearsals I discovered that there was another stage company in town, another little theatre group up on Main Street. And someone from our cast was talking to someone from their cast, and someone from their cast had dropped out of the role of Sebastian in the show they were doing. I ran up the street and got the part of Sebastian in the show they were doing – *Twelfth Night*.

With no experience yet, no instance where I had actually walked across a stage, I now had two parts, in two different plays – one of them by William Shakespeare.

I haven't had such guts since.

My first review came from *Winnipeg Press* theatre critic Frank Morriss, who would soon trade his Manitoba theatre beat for the more prestigious role of film critic for the *Globe and Mail* in Toronto. Of my debut in the Ruth Gordon play he wrote something like: "Despite his obvious youth, and ill-advised make-up, Pinset [sic] played his part with vigour." Or relish. Whatever. Who cares? Name in the paper and all. And not for any indictable offence!

My Shakespearean debut was somewhat less auspicious. I developed a nervous giggle that became a bloody nuisance to everyone else in the cast, a tick that still comes back to haunt me from time to time. Somehow I got away with the language, even when I exchanged *calm* for my more Newfoundlandese *cam.* Before I could get too embarrassed about it, the purists in the crowd decided that *cam* was probably truer to the Renaissance English spoken by Shakespeare and his company, and by the time we opened the entire cast had adopted my bastardized pronunciation as their own.

(God only knows what the audience thought. We couldn't round up enough of them to find out.)

So I played those two roles, and hoped something else would come along. And it did – a shipboard romantic comedy called *Just Married* which, despite all manufactured legends to the contrary, was the first play ever performed on the Rainbow Stage, an enduring and endearing outdoor theatre which was still struggling to establish itself as a showcase for musical comedies. Meanwhile, Lena Lovegrove was mounting a new production of *Gaslight. Gaslight* had starred Charles Boyer and Ingrid Bergman onscreen after premiering on Broadway as *Angel Street* with Vincent Price and Judith Evelyn. I played the sinister husband, and I also did the artwork for the poster, and it all went very well. According to the review by Frank Morriss, who this time round graciously included all the consonants in my last name, I too did very well. And of course I believed that, and took it with me wherever I would go. You couldn't bring me down again with claws. As far as I was concerned, I was on my way.

I started to get some radio work at CBC. I loved doing it – still do – but back then it was also a wonderful way to work on my dialect problem. I still had a Newfoundland accent as thick as Gander fog. It wasn't that I didn't want to sound like I came from Newfoundland; I didn't want to sound like I came from anywhere. That way I might get across the message that I was very worldly, that I was very much at home on international stages, and that they would be very lucky to get me.

I was hoping the girls I met would feel the same way. As new as I was to theatre, I recall practicing the pretense of being experienced in the world of romance on a young actress. I remember trying to come off as a boy-man of the world in all things at this shaky time of personal development, which my mirror had been witness to, before my hitting the streets; not unlike De Niro had done in *Taxi Driver*.

Having exhausted the mirror, but convincingly identifying myself in that same mirror as a passable bargain to the as yet faceless paramour born to mate me, I was not at all prepared for the assessment I would receive from the one I had planted my roving feet for.

Having used up a good-sized part of the evening at the theatre, at what would turn out to be a silent farce for the Blind institute – oh yes, sight gags for the unsighted – I took the young date to a late supper – a snail and snapper seafood reminder never to eat snail or snapper as long as I ate.

Not to worry. Could I erase the whole of this black Friday's night with a pleasurable walk from the bus to her place, perhaps? She answered "yes." And I almost had enough of things of interest to fill the final half-kilometre or so, which I had already shared with the mirror. Though wit is not as appreciated when reheated – have you noticed that?

It was obvious by the post-snail dinner travesty that this evening might wind up on lips that were not mine. As I closed in on her mouth, she came up perhaps with the only remark that stood a chance to shrink every part of me but my shoes, and the certainty of a decent curtain.

I had complimented her effusively, I thought, expecting one in return, and didn't it come?

"I don't mean this the way it will sound," said she. "And you're very nice," she added. "Almost unexpectedly so, but . . ."

Well! Was I going to get a kick in my nuts in payment for a night of poor theatre and an unsuccessful snail-and-snapper yak-tasty supper and my frayed collar and cuffs?

"No," she said. "But I can't see us as a serious item, physically."

I shouldn't have pressed. She next suggested that I had "a man's face on a boy's body."

What? screamed my pride, silently. *Are you the same thing I put in a half a day of my life with?*

"What the fuck does that mean? A boy's body? Feel that!" I screamed, loud enough to unhinge rutting neighbourhood dogs.

She cast her eyes elsewhere, as if to say: *I happen to think that type is very important, and I haven't found mine yet.*

"Well, good luck, baby," said I, on a romantic note. "Even the heart is a muscle, and mine would stand up to the best of them!"

With that, I made it to my rented room, and another trip to the fucking mirror!

"Lying bastard!" said I.

"Prove her wrong," said It.

"Make up your shagging mind!" I topped.

It took me barely short of eighteen months to buff the boy's body to at least that of a suitable car jockey at an annual

Brazilian ball. Trouble was, I now had a boy's head on a man's body. And I could hear my mirror laugh me into manhood.

Being on stage at night meant rearranging my calendar. I could teach ballroom dancing only in the afternoons, because mornings were occupied with my third career as a sign painter. Still, could Broadway be much closer?

Winnipeg had a vibrant history of legitimate theatre and vaudeville. The two major houses were the Dominion, which had opened in 1904, and the Pantages, which had opened as a vaudeville theatre in 1914. The Pantages had originally presented three performances each day, and showcased such comedians as Stan Laurel and Buster Keaton and novelty acts like U.S. heavyweight champion Jack Dempsey, who challenged members of the audience to go a few rounds with him on stage. The Dominion alternated between "high-class" vaudeville and touring companies, hosting its own musical stock company as well as sponsoring many amateur performances.

As a city Winnipeg might as well have been surrounded by water. Our audiences didn't depend on anyone else. They served themselves. The lifestyle was warm and welcoming, primarily because of the European influences on the community, which happily included a love of theatre. Immediately ahead of me, looming large on my narrow horizon, were the two men who would create the most thrilling time I've spent in theatre before or since. John Hirsch, who became one of the most brilliant directors this country has ever produced, had joined forces with the writer and actor Tom Hendry, who became one of the most brilliant producers this country has ever produced, and the two opened their own theatre company at the old Dominion. They called it Theatre 77, because it was exactly seventy-seven steps from the intersection at the heart of the city, Portage and Main.

The first production was *The Italian Straw Hat*, and I was cast as the butler. (No, not the lead; Hirsch and Hendry were not so easy to fool.) I then proceeded to contract the scurrilous Asian flu, and ten minutes before show time I was still burning up, flat on my back in the wings, encased in a blanket, shaking uncontrollably, with no possible way of going on. But when I heard the strains of *God Save the Queen* I got to my feet, threw off the blanket, did the play, and subsequently partied all night with the cast. It was my first experience, but not my last, with the power of theatre as an antidote for flu, fever, and just about anything.

The artistry that John Hirsch brought to Arthur Miller's classic *Death of a Salesman* single-handedly resurrected Winnipeg theatre in 1958. That stellar production also introduced me to an ambitious young actor who would become my lifelong friend. John Hirsch and Tom Hendry were looking to build a nucleus of actors, and Perry Rosemond was one of their recruits. I played Happy – Willy Loman's amoral youngest son, Hap – and Perry played Bernard, the next-door neighbour's son, a childhood friend of Hap's older brother Biff and now a successful lawyer. My role was bigger than his, and Perry made sure I knew he coveted it. Every night, as we waited in the wings to go on, Perry would start to sing, in a small voice barely above a whisper:

I want to be / Happy
If you can be / Happy
*Why can't I be / Happy too?**

Perry often said, "Nobody has ever played Bernard like me!" And that's true. Because he always connected humour to everything he did. He also adored show business humour – especially the stories you couldn't make up. In one scene in *Salesman* my character, Hap, sits in a bar with his older brother Biff – Donnelly Rhodes played the waiter – and a couple of curvaceous young hookers walk in. One girl is particularly well endowed, prompting my character Hap to remark, "Hey, get a load of them binoculars!"

We got through the read-throughs and the rehearsals, and finally the dress rehearsal, but I could see that the actress playing the hooker with the big bosom was unhappy about something, because she kept sulking.

"What's wrong?" I asked her.

"Everybody's got their props but me!" she complained. "When do I get my binoculars?"

You can imagine Perry's reaction.

Perry's mother and father were wonderful. They were naturally funny people, so he came by it honestly. We'd be watching a ball game on television and his mother would pass by on her way to the kitchen. "That Yogi!" she would say, glancing at the screen, "he got fat!" When Perry was living in Toronto and,

* "I Want to Be Happy," Vincent Youmans and Irving Caesar, from *No, No, Nanette* (1925).

[51]

later, Los Angeles, I would still stay with them when I went back to Winnipeg for jobs, and at one point my picture was on their living room mantel, next to his.

One time I came back to Winnipeg to do *Two for the Seesaw* with Lillian Lewis, a talented local actress. The play was a very demanding two-hander, with Lillian and I attempting to top the original performances of Anne Bancroft and Henry Fonda on Broadway in 1958 and Shirley MacLaine and Robert Mitchum onscreen in 1962. Perry had also returned to Winnipeg and applied for a job at the CBC, and while he was waiting for his phone to ring he took a small part in the Manitoba Theatre Centre production of *Mister Roberts*, playing Mannion, the lead supporting sailor in the play. John Hirsch was directing this new production, and Perry and I were bunking together at his parents' place while I was in rehearsal for *Seesaw*. One evening Perry fell on stage and hurt his leg, and by morning the leg had swelled up beyond belief. And he had a performance that night. And he said, "Gordon, I don't think I'm going to make it. Would you go on for me?"

"But Perry,'" I said, "I'm in rehearsals for *Two for the Seesaw!*"

Perry had this whine he would use, and he'd say, *Oh. Come. On. Gordon* in this pleading voice until it was pointless to refuse.

"All right, all right!" I said, "I'll do it."

We start rehearsing some of the lines. This is around four o'clock in the afternoon, and curtain is at 8 p.m. And Perry keeps pumping the lines at me, and I keep trying to learn them. At about 6:30 p.m. we take a cab to the theatre, and of course John Hirsch has no idea what we're planning, but he happens to be at the performance that night. And Len Cariou is getting into makeup – he's playing Ensign Pulver, the role David Wayne played on Broadway and Jack Lemmon played in the movie. And Donnelly Rhodes is already there, he's in it too, and he's getting into his sailor suit. I approach Nadine Kelly, the wardrobe lady, to see if she has an extra sailor suit, which she does. So I put it on. And suddenly Perry limps in, and he's wearing a sailor suit. And I say, "What are you doing?" And he says, "Well, I thought you could do the fight and I could do the lines."

"Fight?" I say. "What fight?'" Because this is the first I've heard about it.

"You have a fight on stage with Donnelly," he says. "So you can do the fight, and I can do the lines."

So now suddenly *Mister Roberts* has an extra sailor going on stage. Instead of Mannion coming out alone, two guys, me and Perry, walk out on stage together. And it's coming to Mannion's first line, we both know the cue, and we both know whoever says it will be stuck with the part for the night. And Perry looks at me, and I look at him, and he says Mannion's first line. We play out the rest of the scene, and Perry and Donnelly start to get into it – "Oh yeah?" "Yeah!" "Oh yeah?" "Yeah!" – and Perry calls Donnelly a dirty sonovabitch, and Donnelly tells Perry he can go to hell.

Perry says, "You can't talk to me that way!" and is about to plunge in for the fight. Or would be, except for his bad leg and his new sidekick. So instead he turns to me and says, "Go get him, Ernie!"

Suddenly my character – who doesn't exist – has a name: Ernie. So I go in and do the fight. And John Hirsch is just sitting there, shaking his head, wondering what we're going to do next. And the producer of *Two for the Seesaw* is also in the audience that night, and almost goes into cardiac arrest when he sees me on stage, because if I injure myself they will be doing *One for the Seesaw*. And the next day Perry is in the hospital, having his knee attended to, and somebody else – not me! – is playing Mannion.

Perry and I laugh about it every time we hear the name Ernie. "And I think, my God, did that really happen?" says Perry. Yes, it really did.

The name of the company, Theatre 77, had been changed almost immediately to the Manitoba Theatre Centre, and I was gob-smacked happy to be working on its stage. I played Mortimer Brewster in *Arsenic and Old Lace*, Johnny Pope in *A Hatful of Rain*, George in *Of Mice and Men*, Tom in *The Glass Menagerie*. I had said goodbye to daylight, but the MTC was an extraordinary classroom for me. Tom Hendry thrived in the shadows, in his usual mode of controlled concern for the over-all, and John Hirsch was the most truthful director I would ever work with. The work he did at the Rainbow Stage could match work done anywhere. He could shift effortlessly from musical comedy to the classics; it didn't appear to faze him one bit. Years later I was lucky enough to enjoy his influence again, when he revolutionized the drama department at CBC Television. And when I left Winnipeg, which had become and still remains one of my favourite cities, he knew he could call me at any time, for anything – providing it was the lead – and I would come running.

A dozen or so years later I was living in Hollywood, and in

my free time, which I had entirely too much of, I used to go hiking in the Hollywood Hills with Marlon Brando. John Hirsch called and asked me if I wanted to do *Guys and Dolls* with Denise Fergusson, Dean Regan, and Judy Armstrong at the Manitoba Theatre Centre. I would be playing Sky Masterson, the role that Brando had played in the 1955 MGM film version.

I jumped at it, of course. But Brando was shocked.

"Wait a minute, wait a minute," said Marlon with a disdainful squint. "You're going to *Winnipeg?* To do a twenty-year-old musical?"

"No," I said, "I'm going to Winnipeg to do a show for John Hirsch."

let's kiss and make up

I was lying on the straw floor of a scummy South American jail, writhing in pain.

I caught a glimpse of my reflection in a jagged piece of glass. There was no getting around it. I looked terrible. But then, that was the whole idea.

My first network drama – thank you, CBC Winnipeg! – and I could just imagine the scene in Grand Falls, with the whole family hunkered around the black-and-white TV set, watching my auspicious screen debut in 1955.

This new medium of television, I'd decided, could learn a lot from us theatre folk. For one thing, what was the big deal about going "live"? We came from the *Theatre*. We went "live" every night. And for another, the CBC makeup department didn't seem to have a knack for realism. I was playing a rebel hero who had just received a beating from two prison guards, but the makeup they had put on me was, in my opinion, far too subtle.

I had heard that such famous fellow thespians as Bette Davis had experienced the same kind of creative incompetence. In one of her movies the character she was playing was supposed to be in hospital after a car crash, and Ms. Davis felt the Warner Bros. makeup artists were more concerned about making her look pretty than injured. So when the crew broke for lunch she went to a doctor friend and said, "I've been in a terrible car crash. I'm lucky to be alive. What would I look like?" An hour later she returned to the studio with her left leg in a cast, her right arm in a sling, and her head bandaged in such a way that you could hardly see her left eye.

As the story goes, her big boss Jack Warner took one look at her and almost had a heart attack.

"My God, Bette, what happened?" he cried.

"I've been in a terrible car crash, Jack," said Bette – "and *this* is what it looks like."

Fortunately I was by now an old hand at applying makeup, so I decided to enhance the CBC work with some special touches of my own. Soon I had deeper "bruises" and fresher "cuts," and in another innovative stroke I jammed a mile or so of bloodied gauze inside my mouth on one side, to create the effect the script required, i.e., to look swollen and beaten as if my face had been "smashed with a rifle butt."

Lights. Camera. Action.

The two guards who have just beaten me – two actor friends of mine – have barely dumped me in the cell when I hear the soft voice of the female prisoner in the next cell. Slowly I drag myself to the bars between our cells, one of which is a microphone disguised as a prison bar. Having made enough mic noise to rival a thunderstorm, I'm now in a very tight close-up with my beautiful leading lady, Louise Walters, and begin to deliver a full page of dialogue. Which I suddenly go up on.

Dry up completely.

Totally blank.

My beautiful leading lady's expression moves from astonishment to fear to abject terror. The silence is deafening. As the seconds tick by I come up with a solution. I reach through the bars, grab her by the back of her head, and kiss her, sure that my lines will come back to me.

Which they do.

Until I see that the CBC paint on the fake prison bars is not quite dry, and that two distinct bar impressions now decorate the margins of her gorgeous face. Along with a few smudges of my bloody makeup.

Which causes me to forget my lines. Again.

So I reach through the bars, again, and pull her face to mine, again, and kiss her, again, this time even more longingly. And all my words come back to me like a song, and as I release her, to begin my dialogue, we both become aware that the tail end of the mile of bloody gauze stowed inside my mouth is now attached to her mouth, a thin ridge of gauze hanging from her lips, swinging like a tiny rope bridge, beautifully lit by the CBC.

Bette Davis notwithstanding, maybe there was more to learn about this "live" television thing than I'd thought. And suddenly my urge to get to New York wasn't nearly as strong. I would try to tame this TV animal first, and I would do it in the jungle where it lived and flourished: Toronto.

I was in Winnipeg when I saw my first live black-and-white television show from Toronto. Toronto was where most of Canadian television was happening, the electronic nut to crack if you wanted to work as an actor. MGM's tagline was "More stars than there are in heaven." Well, CBC had the people. CBC had the performers. CBC had performers of every stripe and colour, and some of the top singers, too. I was living in Manitoba but I knew every face on CBC. Because they were our stars at that time.

Perry Rosemond got to Toronto first, about six months ahead of me. He had originally planned to stay at his old University of Toronto frat house, but changed his plan as soon as he saw it. "What a dump!" he reported gloomily. At that time he had a couple of friends who were studying to be dentists, and they suggested that he move in with them. So he coughed up the enormous fee of $52 a month – for room and board – and stayed at the School of Dentistry frat house at 42 Bedford Road in Toronto's downtown Annex neighbourhood. He shared a room with Allan Blye, a singer who would later become a very successful Hollywood producer, and a guy from Australia named Jimmy Hannan, who was also a singer. I was still in Winnipeg, staying with Perry's parents. At that point, as testament to my great good luck, one Jimmy Hannan moved out of the frat house and one Gordon Pinsent moved in to take his place. Allan was the only one working – he was doing one of Billy O'Connor's music shows – and Perry still suspects that Allan declared both me and Perry as dependents on his 1959 tax return.

Perry had already ingratiated himself with the casting office at CBC Television, and he had been cast in "The Death Around Us," an episode of a weekly dramatic series sponsored by General Motors. Artistically speaking it was not the most challenging role; he was supposed to play a dead body on a hospital gurney.

When I walked into 42 Bedford for the first time, having just arrived back in Toronto, Perry was on the pay phone in the lobby, talking to Liz Butterfield, who was responsible for casting *GM Presents*. He was pretty excited, too, because he had just received word that he had been upgraded to a two-line bit. Alfie Scopp, the actor who had originally owned the two-line bit, had apparently moved on to bigger and better things. So Perry now had every actor's dream – a speaking part.

I walked in while he was still on the phone, and after gratefully accepting his new speaking part, Perry said, "Have you re-cast the dead body yet?"

Liz said no, they hadn't.

"Well, in that case," said Perry, "have I got a corpse for you!"

So I got Perry's part. With no lines to learn.

At the read-through the casting director said he needed someone to be seen sweeping the floors of the hospital hallway when the principal actors walked by. "I can do that!" I said. And I got it. At rehearsal they decided they needed an extra to play a young intern walking down the hall. "I can do that!" I said. And I got that one too.

At the end of the day I made more money than Perry did, because I racked up three roles. Every time they turned on the camera, there I was. And Perry told that story to everyone.

When we weren't waiting for the phone to ring (and when weren't we?) we came up with temp jobs to pay the rent. I was a painter, so I painted graduate students, oil portraits for their family, that sort of thing, for $30 a head. I had it worked out that if I got one small one-line speaking part on television and one small non-speaking part on television, I could get through the month. I would do six grad students at a time, line them up in six chairs, while Perry would provide a running commentary: "He's just finishing the chin on number four, no, wait, he's moving to the nose on number two, okay, okay, he's fixing the eye line on number six . . ." And when he wasn't giving the play-by-play on my artistic endeavours, Perry kept himself reasonably solvent by selling shoes downtown at the Betty Jane Shoe Store.

The benefits of staying in the Jewish dental fraternity were not insignificant. Because we were in residence at the Alpha Omega frat, we also got free dental work at the dental college: 100 chairs, no waiting. After my bottle-cap-biting days, I was an ideal candidate. Oh sure, open a bottle cap with bravado, then cry like a baby at a root canal!

There was only one television set, in the basement. The frat housekeeper and the handyman were a married couple, Burt and Lisa Bergman. English was their second language, and Burt and Lisa could understand only one show, *The Red Skelton Show*, because Skelton did a lot of mime when he performed. So they loved to sit down Sunday night at eight o'clock and watch Red Skelton. Perry and I, of course, wanted to watch *GM Presents* on Sunday night at eight o'clock, to see, in Perry's words, who would be playing the roles that we were born to play. But we always had to acquiesce to Burt and Lisa. In the months to come we had a whole coterie of people – Al Waxman and Martin Lavut and Larry Zolf and that whole Yorkville gang – who would gather in the basement of the dental fraternity to watch black-and-white TV dramas on CBC.

I remember playing an extra in "Dr. Ocularis" with Douglas Rain and Lois Nettleton. Dougie and Lois had lines, of course, but I had the best coat. Humphrey Bogart, right out of *Casablanca*. I walked out on the deck of the ship, paused for a moment with the sound of the sea behind me, and then walked out of frame again.

Perry, of course, couldn't resist such a tantalizing cue. "For a moment there," he said, eyes twinkling, "I thought you were going to speak!"

Another time we were watching *The Grapes of Wrath* with Henry Fonda and Jane Darwell and I saw a familiar shadow on the wall. "Here comes O. Z. Whitehead," I said. Sure enough, Whitehead, a supporting actor who received seventh-place billing in the movie, suddenly sauntered onscreen.

"How do you do that!" Perry cried, as if I had just done my best party trick ever. "What's your secret?"

"Growing up in Grand Falls," I said.

One night it was a television production of *Death of a Salesman*, and Perry had auditioned for the part of Bernard, the part that he had played in Winnipeg for John Hirsch. He thought getting it would be a cinch, too, since he had just come off a magnificent stage engagement of the very same play. But the part went to Sean Sullivan instead, so we were desperate to see the show. Perry and I decided that we would have to get Burt and Lisa to abstain from watching Red Skelton, if only on this one occasion. I went downstairs, and I pretended that I had a cousin in the production, and Burt and Lisa were quite intrigued, and stayed to watch it with us.

To this day Perry still claims that it was me who got him out of acting. As we watched *Salesman* Sean Sullivan came on, in the part Perry insisted he was born to play, and Perry evaluated his performance. And after the telecast he turned to me and said, "You know, Gordon, he's better than I would have been."

I nodded in agreement. "Perry," I said, "get out of the business *now!*"

At least, that's what I said according to Perry. If I'd known how successful he would become as a producer and director, not to mention his phenomenal success in bringing Air Farce, Canada's most beloved comedy troupe, to television, I would have told him sooner. For even then he was enchanted with the whole behind-the-scenes thing, hanging out in control rooms and taking television courses at Ryerson, a technological institute that would decades later become Ryerson University.

Besides, he didn't have the ego to be an actor. Perry would come home from an audition, or even just from wandering the halls of the CBC, and he would take all his clothes off and go to bed. It didn't matter what time of day it was. As far as he was concerned, his day's work was done.

More to the point, Perry had read a book on producing and thought he should explore his options backstage rather than in front of the camera. "I only get cast as Jews or Indians," he noted wryly, "and I don't see a big future in that."

saying yes

———◆———

MY VERY FIRST TV ROLE IN TORONTO, AND HERE I AM, lying on the ground under a tarp, desperately hoping no one will discover me. Which feels extremely counterproductive, considering I came back to Toronto with the sole purpose of being discovered. But since I'm playing a stowaway on a ship, discretion is not only called for, it is demanded.

"Do the stars have to sit on me?" I whine to the first assistant director.

"The stars aren't supposed to know you're there," the A.D. replies. "That's the whole point. We don't want them to know you're there, not until the end of the show. So please stop wiggling under the tarp!"

Afterwards I rush home to the frat house, where Perry and the others have just watched the live telecast in the freezing basement.

"How was I?" I ask.

"Really good!" says Perry, without a moment's hesitation.

"I was only on for a second."

"I know," he says. "But that second was like a minute. You were that convincing."

"I shoulda had the lead," I sigh.

Oh well.

I was playing many small TV parts – and yes, there *are* small parts, Virginia, not just small actors – and getting to do more radio, sometimes for the legendary Andrew Allen. Andrew always referred to his actors as Mister and Miss, something that added a special note of dignity to your craft. The minute you stepped inside Studio G at the CBC building on Jarvis Street to make your contribution to the revered medium of radio drama, you felt you had somehow reached a special level in your normally unstable status as a performing artist.

Lots of TV series were shooting in town. John Hart was the star of *Last of the Mohicans*. Lon Chaney Jr. played Chingachcook and he got through it with the worst wig you ever saw in your life, with braids on it that had things crawling in 'em, and a bottle of Black Velvet a day. But I was still awestruck, because his was one of the names I had learned in my boyhood, when I was always the last one to leave the matinee. Barry Nelson was doing a series called *Hudson's Bay*. Perry acted in one episode and still has a snapshot of himself with Barry. That's what we wanted in those days – photographs! Photos to show that we were part of their story, and they were part of ours. And then there was *Tugboat Annie*, and *Cannonball*, and you were watching the medium grow up around you, taking baby steps.

I was still saying Yes to everything. Can you ride a horse?" "Yes!" "Can you drive a car?" "Yes!"

In 1960 I got back in uniform again to play one of the grunts in a CBC war drama called *Rehearsal for Invasion*. Director Ron Weyman had cast an Ottawa actor named Lawrence Z. Dane in the lead, and we were all suitably impressed. No less a celestial personage than Paul Almond himself had brought Dane in from Ottawa to do his TV drama *Shadow of a Pale Horse*. In one scene in our TV drama Larry had to use a rope to scale a wall. So they threw a rope over the wall and he started to climb – and then the magic of television took over. Ron Weyman cut to the top of the wall, at which point they put up a ladder which you couldn't see on camera, and Larry promptly scrambled up the ladder to go over the top of the wall. For some reason I found this hysterically funny, and for some reason Lawrence Z. Dane was amused by my inappropriate and unprofessional reaction, and a great friendship was born.

Although we weren't aware of it at the time, Larry and I had a lot in common. We had different yet similar upbringings. He was one of six children in a Lebanese family up in Ottawa, always conscious of perception, always concerned about what other people might think. We could both remember getting kicked under the table when someone offered us a second piece of pie, in case we'd forgotten that we were supposed to say No Thank You. Growing up in close-knit communities, both of us were always conscious of perception. What else was there?

Larry had caught the showbiz bug even earlier than I had. He was on stage when he was just a kid, competing in a variety show at the Elmdale Theatre in Ottawa, doing his stellar impression of Al Jolson. (He lost to a French-Canadian kid who did *his* stellar impression of Al Jolson with a French accent. Go figure.)

Before we met, Larry had worked on the *R.C.M.P.* series shooting in Ottawa. The three leads were Gilles Pelletier,

Don Francks, and an American actor named John Perkins. Larry was hired to be John Perkins' stand-in double and consequently got to spend a lot of time on set, with all sorts of guest stars like Jack Creley, John Drainie, Frances Hyland, and Toby Robins, and got to work with Paul Almond, who was hired by the producer, Budge Crawley, to direct some of the thirty-nine episodes. And it was Paul Almond, of course, who had brought Larry to Toronto, so he could roam the halls of CBC like the rest of us, trolling for the next job.

I was dating a bit and flirting a lot. So was the Very Tall, Dark, and Ruggedly Handsome Lawrence Z. Dane. Larry and I both liked women, but Larry liked beauty. He was immediately drawn to the most beautiful girl in the room. And it didn't matter if she didn't have very much to say. He wasn't in it for the conversation.

I decided to go the other route. I was sure no one was going to see me as a matinee idol, so I would pick out the lonely girls and talk to them. Chatting with lovely ladies of all kinds was wonderful, and exciting, and at times romantic. And crucial to my growing up. In those days people were not as open to friendships between men and women, but friendship was very important to me. And I was as good at chatting as I was at catting.

Meanwhile, I was working not only on sound stages but on real stages, too, at the New Play Society, shepherded by Dora Mavor Moore. The first Canadian actor to perform at the Old Vic in London, the indomitable Dora had launched her ambitious theatre troupe right after the war, in 1946. Dora's modest but boldly creative company would end up supplying more than half the onstage talent when her friend Tyrone Guthrie helped Tom Patterson found the Stratford Festival in 1953. I loved working with her, and her company of players.

On one occasion the esteemed *Globe and Mail* theatre critic Herbert Whittaker, a stage veteran himself, was directing a new production of André Obrey's *Noah*, inspired by a great British production he'd seen in his youth, with John Gielgud playing Noah and Alec Guinness playing the Wolf. In our production Hugh Webster was playing Noah, and as you can imagine a lot of the actors in the production were wearing animal costumes. At one rehearsal Hugh suggested that he should make his entrance holding the hand of one of the monkeys.

"No, Hugh, you won't be doing that," said Herbie.

"But Herbie," Hugh began, "I think it would be charming – "

"This is *Noah*, Hugh," said Herbie flatly. "This is not a Tarzan movie!"

As any Bible student worth his salt can tell you, Noah had three sons – Shem, Ham, and Japheth. I was cast as the middle son, but the part was not nearly flamboyant enough for my taste.

"When I make my entrance," I proposed, "how about I come out and take my shirt off?"

"No, Gordon," said Herbie.

Consequently I had to come up with other ways to detour the spotlight from my stage brothers Shem and Japheth onto me, and I did manage to upstage them both on more than one occasion.

My dedication to scene-stealing was not lost on Herbie.

"Gordon," he said, "your performance continues to prove to me that I was right to give you the part of *Ham*."

Okay, maybe I overdid it a little. But it must have worked, because soon Dora Mavor Moore herself tapped me to play Orpheus in her remount of Jean Anouilh's *Eurydice*. I couldn't have been more pleased. Especially after Dora took me aside and whispered, "Gordon, *please* don't tell anyone, but I'm giving you a dollar more than anyone else." Heady days indeed.

I was also finding stage work at the Crest Theatre. Canadian theatre pioneers Donald and Murray Davis had created the Crest as a showcase for the country's top theatrical talent, including their gifted sister Barbara Chilcott and a mesmerizing, smoky-voiced leading lady named Charmion King. They had all performed together at Hart House, the esteemed theatre space of the University of Toronto, and they were the same fearless foursome who had formed the Straw Hat Players in Muskoka, the Ontario lake district which was well on its way to becoming the summer playground of the rich. The riveting Miss King (and make no mistake, it was *Miss* King, not *Ms.*) and her cohorts were fearless in their theatrical choices, from such classics as *Three Sisters* to *Long Day's Journey Into Night* to such established crowd-pleasers as *Hay Fever* and *The Man Who Came to Dinner* – not to mention their now-legendary annual musical revue *Spring Thaw*. Consequently I was lucky enough to be cast as the love interest – the male ingénue, if you will – opposite Miss King when she starred in the title role of Jean Giraudoux's *Madwoman of Chaillot* at the Crest in November 1961, eight years before Katharine Hepburn tackled the screen version. Giraudoux's play has an unusually large cast of characters, and

I was the new boy in a glittering company that included Barbara Chilcott, Bruno Gerussi, and Julie Rekai, as well as Miss King's two former New York roommates, her two best friends Kate Reid and Barbara Hamilton.

In one scene Miss King was supposed to whistle through her teeth and, much to the general amazement of the cast, it was one skill she had not mastered.

"I can do that!" I said, quick to volunteer. So I would stand just offstage, and she would come close as close as she could without actually coming offstage, and she would stick two fingers in her mouth and I would whistle. And we would have nightly conferences on how that was working out. And because she had a car, a Vauxhall, she would give me a lift home every now and then, and then more often, and then every night.

I pinched myself. She had a car. She had the star dressing room.

I had a girlfriend with *her own car.*

It boggled my imagination.

Every other night, during the run of *Madwoman*, Miss King received a rose from an anonymous admirer. She never knew from whom, and over time came to suspect that I had sent them. When she questioned me, I would never admit it, but I would never deny it, either. Truth is, they were not from me. For one thing, I would have sent her a rose every night, not every other night, but even if I had wanted to send her a rose every other night, I hardly had the money to do so. Still, I was more than happy to take credit for it!

By now I had discovered that Charm and her soulmates Kate and Barbara were all cut from the same cloth. They were theatre people who worked in film and television to pay the rent, and were grateful for the opportunity to do so. But it was not the camera that seduced them, it was the footlights. Always, the footlights. Whether she was playing New Haven or Toronto, Stratford or Shaw, Charm was happiest when she was about to go onstage. While I was competing for parts in Winnipeg she was on Broadway, being directed by Tyrone Guthrie in *Love and Libel*.

Kate Reid, too, was more at home on stage than anywhere else. She was about to make her Broadway debut, playing Uta Hagen's role twice a week in matinee performances of *Who's Afraid of Virginia Woolf?* It was a wonderful time for Kate, because she had trained with Uta Hagen and Herbert Berghof in New York. The only drawback was her acute fear of flying. "I do *not* have a fear of flying!" Kate would insist. "I have a fear of *crashing*." Consequently she despaired of her twice-weekly white-knuckle trips to Manhattan from Toronto, especially since she couldn't allow herself to have a calming Scotch or six on the flight. She would go from the airport to the theatre to her dressing room to the stage, take her bows and taxi back to the airport as her mentor and benefactor Uta Hagen was preparing for the evening performance. But somehow it all worked out, and by the end of the decade Kate would be regarded primarily as a New York actress, winning Tony nominations for her work with Alec Guinness in *Dylan* and Margaret Leighton in Tennessee Williams' *Slapstick Tragedy*, and would make another Broadway splash starring in Arthur Miller's newest play *The Price*, with Pat Hingle and Arthur Kennedy. (Kate, *New York Times* critic Clive Barnes would note in his review, "gets the very most out of the play's best conceived role.")

Barbara Hamilton could set new box office records when she performed in original musical revues created to showcase her considerable comedic gifts. A seasoned actress with almost magical timing, she had joined the cast of the satirical revue *Spring Thaw* in 1958, and by the time I met her she had already established herself as the funniest woman in Canada. Future newspaper columnist Sylvia Train was her agent at that time, and would later insist that she had personally produced one of Barbara's biggest hits, an original revue called *That Hamilton Woman*, at the Crest, "so I wouldn't have to listen to her whine about not working!" By the end of the decade our beloved Barbara would originate the role of Marilla in the world premiere of the musical *Anne of Green Gables* at the Charlottetown Summer Festival, later picking up a London Drama Critics award for Best Actress when she reprised her role in the West End.

So my introduction to Toronto theatre was also my introduction to three powerhouse ladies. No, not ladies. Women. Very ladylike, in their way – unless you happened to get in their way. Which was, candidly, not a good idea. At any time. Ever.

Coming into that scene at the Crest, I suppose I could've been overwhelmed. But I wasn't, not really, because I felt I knew these women. I had heard them on radio and seen them on television. That was the beauty of only having one or two channels. In Winnipeg I saw people on TV and knew their faces when I arrived. Jack Creley was in everything that Larry Mann wasn't in. And Lloyd Bochner. And, and, and.

Amusingly – especially when I look back on it now – Charm had to answer to both Kate and Barbara, and Barbara Chilcott too, when she started driving me home every night. "You're driving him home *again?*" But Barbara Hamilton secretly had a rooting interest.

"I told you about him, Charm," she would whisper to Miss King. "I told you I saw him on television. He's *The One.*"

It was Barbara, in fact – Barbara Ham, as she was affectionately known by all those who loved her (and probably by a few who didn't) – who took one long hard look at Charm and me, on stage and off, and proclaimed, as only she could: "You two look like you belong together."

I couldn't have agreed more. But I didn't want to mislead anyone – especially Charm.

"Did I mention that I was married?" I said one day, trying to sound as casual as I could. "To a wonderful girl named Irene. We had two wonderful children. But, with my life and hers, she wasn't in the theatre and . . ." I shrugged. "It didn't work out."

Charm clucked her tongue sympathetically. "Too bad."

"Yes, it was."

Suddenly her eyes lit up. "Did I ever mention that *I* was married?"

I gulped. "No, I don't think so!"

"Well I was!" she said. "For a minute or two." She paused thoughtfully. "Now what the fuck was his name . . ."*

The Davis brothers, Murray and Donald, and their sister Barbara Chilcott, were very protective of Charm and not at

* Radio producer Alan Savage.

all sure they approved of me. They seemed to me at the time to be a tight little club, the four of them, and I was the interloper, disturbing what I'm sure Murray and Donald saw as the natural order of their creative existence. I thought I could sense Barbara ever so slightly warming to me; she had a glorious laugh, second only to Charm's. I believed they might have judged me by my rye-and-ginger – my drink choice at the time – and as such, thought I might have to endear myself to them in ways less grounded, so to speak. Might even have to learn bridge. But no, not necessary, as it turned out. Being invisible worked just as well. And I liked them for loving Charm. Because by now I was hopelessly smitten with the offstage Miss King. She was five years older than I was, and at least ten years more mature, but I was determined to enter her life by whatever road possible. In a stroke of unexpectedly and uncommonly good fortune, she seemed to be warming to me. Years later she told an interviewer, "Once I realized that the idea of having a relationship with him was even a remote possibility – that he was in fact free and, you know, out of puberty – I thought, well, this is amazing, this is great. And the more I got to know him, the more I liked him. I mean, I liked the *person*. I liked the man inside the pretty face."

After *Madwoman* closed at the Crest Theatre I was doing my best to steal the show in a production of Edward Albee's *Roots* – another ambitious undertaking – by seducing the audience whenever I could. Making the audience like you is the best way to make producers like you. And when you're living from role to role, you keep hoping that your current job will lead to your next job, and that your next job will lead to your future job.

Audiences at the Crest seemed to like me, so I wasn't completely taken aback when Stratford chief Michael Langham came backstage to see me one night after a performance. Would I be interested in joining his esteemed Shakespearean company's 1962 season "as cast"? I wasn't sure what "as cast" meant, but since he had made a point of asking me in front of the rest of the *Roots* cast – asking only me, you understand – was I about to quibble about what roles they wanted me to play? No. Well, maybe. I'd heard that it was going to be a big season for directors – Peter Coe, George McCowan, and Langham among them – and that Christopher Plummer was going to star in a new production of *Cyrano*. Maybe I could play Christian?

Michael Langham smiled. "But seriously, Gordon."

Yes. Seriously.

"I'm afraid that's gone."

When I suggested I could be an ideal Macduff in the Scottish play, he smiled again, and told me he thought he might be able to guarantee me a couple of good understudy spots.

"*Understudy?*" I said, indignantly curling my tongue around the word.

"Yes," he said. And then: "Will I see you there?"

Yes.

I said Yes.

I always said Yes.

By such twists of fate are entire careers made and lost.

As it turned out, Michael Langham had no interest whatsoever in me. Charm's friend Kate Reid was one of the leading lights of Stratford, and one of those rare creatures: An actor who was also a box office draw. I think she was set to do *Taming of the Shrew* with John Colicos, and I think John Vernon was on deck at Stratford that summer too, so there was no discernible shortage of talented leading men. But Kate had asked Michael Langham for a favour and, wise man that he was, Michael Langham did not want to disappoint Kate Reid.

Consequently, I was invited to join his esteemed Shakespearean company, mostly as a supernumerary, which is theatre jargon for extra. Also called "background player," mostly in Britain, or "spear-carrier" in opera-talk. So I got to stand around doing precious little in quite a few shows, frequently with Larry, who was in the same Shakespearean spear-carrying coterie as I was. But we were in exceptionally good company, with Dinah Christie, Tom Kneebone, and Louis Negin among our ranks, before all three went on to become major cabaret stars.

And talk about timing! On my very first day at Stratford I walked over to the rehearsal hall and there he was – Christopher Plummer in person, in the veritable flesh – stretched out on the grass, holding the script for *Macbeth* in his hands, learning his lines.

"How ya doing?" sez I.

Nothing.

"Whatzzit? Macbeth?"

Nothing.

"Want me to hold the book for ya?"

At which point he looked straight at me, and opened his mouth, and said something. A greeting of sorts. The twittering of the birds in the open Stratford sky drowned out the first word, but I could hear the second word quite distinctly: "... *off!*"

As I walked to the stage door to go into rehearsals, I thought to myself, *Well, Porky, pretty good! You've only been here one day, and already you've had a conversation with Christopher Plummer!*

Chris was brilliantly touching as Cyrano and brilliantly tortured as Macbeth that summer. Me? I played a tree in *The Tempest.* But at least I got to understudy Bruno Gerussi, who was playing Ariel, in director George McCowan's production.

George McCowan would later play a significant role in my screen career; this was our decidedly inauspicious introduction to each other. Did Bruno ever get sick and have to miss a performance so I could get my crack at playing Ariel? Did Bruno ever get so much as a common cold? Of course not! He was as strong as a horse, and already a shining pillar of the Stratford Festival. So I continued to play a tree, attempting to grow roots at the same time. I also played so many soldiers in the Scottish play that I ended up simultaneously attacking and defending Dunsinane. When at the next-to-last minute director Peter Coe decided he wanted a song to welcome the Scottish King, my hand shot up like a rocket. I got that job, too, and was doing it fairly well, I thought, until Louis Negin made me crack up onstage. "That's not the King!" he hissed, stage-whispering in my ear. "I've got the King's picture!" And my opening night jitters became opening night titters.

As predicted, I didn't get to play Christian in *Cyrano,* or even understudy him. Instead I was assigned to understudy John Horton, who was playing the Vicomte de Valvert. Meanwhile, Chris was receiving a number of visitors that summer, including Paul Newman, and Geraldine Page and Rip Torn, who were still a couple then, and some VIPs from Hallmark who decided they wanted to capture Chris' *Cyrano* on one of their classy Hallmark Hall of Fame television specials. The folks at Hallmark wanted to bring the original Stratford production to NBC, and for reasons I can't recall, John Horton was unable to reprise his role as the Vicomte de Valvert. So his reluctant understudy – yes, that would be me – ended up in New York with Don Harron, Bill Hutt, John Colicos, and Eric Christmas. Hope Lange, who had made a Hollywood splash onscreen with Lana Turner in *Peyton Place* and Joan Crawford in *The Best of Everything*, took over the role of Roxane to give the show an extra hit of good ol' American star power.

My big scene in the first act was a sword fight – a duel with Cyrano. It was a great sword fight, splendidly choreographed by an exceptional fencing master named Paddy Crean, famous in show business for doubling for Errol Flynn in all his big swashbuckler hits. Chris and I had been rehearsing with lightweight rapiers, but when we got to rehearsal on this particular day the real swords had arrived from Canada, and they were Spanish, and considerably heavier than the ones we had been rehearsing with.

The rehearsal studios on Second Avenue were all humming with activity that week. Down the hall from us, Greer Garson and Douglas Fairbanks Jr. were rehearsing for another classy TV series, *The DuPont Show of the Week*. When we bumped into each other in the corridor, Chris introduced me, and Fairbanks, whose father had been the most famous screen swashbuckler of them all, told us that he was looking forward to seeing our sword fight on camera.

I smiled. What a gracious thing to say.

Chris smiled too. "In that case," he added, "would you like to see it now?"

Fortunately there were no cameras rolling in the hallway, because the look of panic on my face would have been a dead giveaway.

Fairbanks joined us in the rehearsal hall, and we did the sword fight on the spot, with the heavier Spanish swords. I was so out of sync that Chris must have thought he was duelling with Buster Keaton. After we finished, Fairbanks allowed that he had never seen anything quite like our version. God knows, neither had we.

I was somewhat chagrined because I had messed up a few moves, but I was perfect on the night we went to air. Ironically, Chris, who was flawless for Fairbanks, missed a couple of moves on show night. (Yes, it happens in the best of families.) Normally I would have been all over myself, cocky and confident and insecure and terrified about doing live television from New York. But all I could think of was getting home to Toronto and Charm. We were married on November 2, 1962. Barbara Hamilton was Charm's maid of honour. Barbara's main squeeze, Ken James, was my best man.

Where did we honeymoon? In Niagara Falls. For forty-eight hours. After which we quickly came back to work. We were actors, first and foremost, and we were grateful to be working.

working man

MAYBE IT WAS DUE TO MY NEW MARITAL STATUS, AS I
had just married my very own lucky Charm, but whatever the
reason, suddenly my prospects seemed to jump from famine
to feast.

After my stellar performance as a tree in his Stratford production of *The Tempest*, George McCowan gave me new roots
with a running part in his trailblazing series *Scarlett Hill*, the
first daytime soap opera ever produced for Canadian television. Then I scored another TV job in a children's series
called *The Forest Rangers*. It was the first Canadian series produced in colour, and the executive producer was a trailblazing
lioness named Maxine Samuels, who also liked working with
George McCowan.

As one of the adult leads I was fairly comfortable playing
second fiddle to the kids, who were the real stars of the show,
mainly because I was in over my head. Everyone I was working
with seemed contentedly outdoorsy, while I by now had become
a full-fledged city boy. Meetings to discuss the trappings for my
role only added to my anxiety. Should the young RCMP officer
I was playing, Sergeant Scott, ride a horse? Drive a car? Have a

dog? Wear the Mountie red tunic? When asked for my opinion, I graciously acquiesced to theirs. "Whatever serves the
story best," I murmured magnanimously. Besides, since I
couldn't ride a horse or drive a car, and was easily intimidated
by even a sleeping dog, I was personally rooting for the red
tunic. Quintessentially Canadian and all that.

Happily they decided to scrap the horse and the dog,
probably for budget reasons. It was all settled then; Sergeant
Scott would drive up to the fort in a brand-new 1962 Ford,
which may or may not have been tied to a sponsorship deal.
And by the way – did I have a preference for standard or
automatic transmission?

"Standards are my great love," I lied. "But since we're going
to have the Junior Forest Ranger kids in the car from time to
time, better make it an automatic. Safety first," I added
thoughtfully. "Safety first."

The second assistant director took the car down to a dip in
the road, not visible to the fort, where I would start my run.
The third A.D. stood by, out of camera range, ready to give
me my cue. The director himself, the ever-prescient George
McCowan, instructed his first A.D., Peter Carter, to move the
rest of the crew inside the fort.

"Yes," said George, nodding sagely. "I think we should go
inside now." Because he had asked me if I could drive a car, and
of course I had said Yes. And George could tell when an actor,
whether he was on stage or off, wasn't telling the truth.

I got my cue, put 'er in Drive, hit the gas pedal, and proceeded to careen through the dust storm I was creating, coming
to a smart halt only inches away from the fort.

"Cut!" yelled George. "And print!"

I slid effortlessly out of the driver's seat, strolled over to my trailer, and threw up behind it, causing the youngest member of the Forest Rangers to announce, "Sergeant Scott just puked!"

All in a day's play.

When I wasn't on set I devoted a fair amount of time to stalking one of the country's hottest directors. During Paul Almond's directorial reign on the Canadian film scene, it would always be a badge of special merit for an actor to have worked in an Almond production. When one was first appearing on the scene, and haunting the director-producer floors of the CBC, one soon discovered some offices stood out as most impenetrable – Paul's being one of them.

The first trick was to catch Paul en route from elevator to office door. Birdlike, he was. Definitely in flight. This is not to say I was dismissed by him or by his angel girl Friday who, if I'm not mistaken, bore the name Olwyn Millington, but rather that he was, for one thing, taller and loftier than I, and clearly on his way to or from something far more elevated than the points on the landscape I frequented, I, fresh off the Rock, unable to tell the difference between an iambic pentameter and a fish cake, and now one of the Toronto acting rabble, clattering up his pathway, always close enough to smell the warm odour of a script fresh off the mimeograph machine.

I was about to say I had never had the pleasure of being under his august guidance in one of his productions, but that would not be entirely true. He and I shared wasp bites on an episode of *The Forest Rangers* – he as director, and me as the questionable Mountie, Sergeant Scott.

When I wasn't on one set or another, I was working on stage. The prolific playwright Bernard Slade, a personal friend, was constantly honing his craft, and constantly coming up with wonderfully original ideas. By the end of the decade his resumé would be awash in hit TV series – *The Flying Nun*, *Bridget Loves Bernie*, *The Partridge Family* – and by the end of the seventies he would be a bona fide Broadway baby, breaking box office records with *Same Time Next Year*, *Tribute*, and *Romantic Comedy*. But Bernie was brilliant even back then, so it didn't take much persuading to get me back on stage in Winnipeg to do his new play, *A Very Close Family*, with Bud Knapp and John Vernon for the MTC's 1962–1963 season. I played the family's youngest son, who happened to be gay. And even though the play was still a bit rough around the edges, CBC bought the rights to it and televised it the following season in the network's most prestigious series, *Festival*. It proved to be a career highlight for me, because Charm was in it too – one of the few times we would work together onscreen. The cast included Tom Bosley, who would one day become famous as Howard Cunningham, Ron Howard's father on *Happy Days*, and Jill Foster, a natural comedic talent who never seemed to be "acting" and who by now had become Mrs. Bernard Slade. An unexpected bonus, particularly thrilling to me, was the casting of Melvyn Douglas as my father. Granted, he was considerably smaller than when I had last seen him, looming large up on the screen at the Nickel in Grand Falls. But for me this was a close encounter of the best kind. I was sharing the screen with the man who had made Garbo laugh. Even Flossie Cooper Pinsent knew who Melvyn Douglas was, and when the neighbours asked her which role I was playing, my mother replied, "The son who doesn't like girls."

I was doing *The Forest Rangers* when I was asked to meet with a couple of gentlemen at a favourite CBC watering hole, the Four Seasons Motel on Jarvis Street. One was Julius Rascheff, a cinematographer, who was also the producer and one of the writers for a movie they wanted to make in Greece. The other was the director, a man named Cedric d'Ailly. This was all very new to me, meeting people who made independent films. They wanted me for the lead, and I thought, *Oh, so this is how it works. They see you on TV, and they like you for something they are planning, and you get to try something new.*

At the time it seemed to be too good a thing to turn down. And Charm felt the same way about it, even though it meant we'd have to be away from each other for a while. Rascheff and d'Ailly allowed that it was an independent film, not a big studio movie, and they didn't have much money. They offered me the princely fee of one thousand dollars. And the trip, of course. And they said it would be fun, because they had a lot of connections over there.

I said Yes.

So I flew to Greece, and we were housed in a private home in Athens, down the road from the summer palace of the young prince Constantine, who would ascend to the throne the following year. It was a very nice spot, but it was nothing grand. A meagre breakfast, a meagre lunch. They provided the meals, but they weren't great, and it wasn't like I was getting paid all this money so I could go out and buy better meals. I never even made it up the hill to the Hilton. We filmed first in Athens, then shot more stuff in Piraeus with all the boats. We filmed mostly in Hydra. The whole shoot was a horrible experience, mainly because there were just not enough funds. A few years earlier Melina Mercouri had made *Never on Sunday*, and that tune was still playing everywhere we went. And the place was alight with Greek character and fury and dancing and singing, and because it got so hot so early in the day we had to get up at 4 a.m. to start shooting. Then we'd have to come back and try to sleep in the afternoon.

Trouble was, I couldn't. I simply could not fall asleep. I was so sleep deprived that I actually thought, *I'm not going to make it through this.* I could have had a better time over there if I'd just been a young bachelor, but I wasn't, and my thoughts were with Charm, who was in Toronto. I wasn't a kid actor. I wanted to make sure that I did the job that I had set out to do; I wasn't there to party. And the partying went on and on and on, and I didn't want to become part of that. But it was wicked. I had at least five nights in a row with no sleep. And I hated cats at that time, and Greece was full of them, clawing at your ankles to get food while you were sitting at an outdoor café, trying to have dinner, or even just trying to relax. Charm had a cat she loved, named Clea, after one of the novels in Lawrence Durrell's *Alexandria Quartet*. Clea was not my greatest fan, nor I hers, and here I was, sleepless in the Hellenic Republic, surrounded by mewling cats. I had never taken a sleeping pill, but I was ready to. But the production doctor hadn't arrived yet.

By the end of the shoot, I hated everything about Greece. One night I was sitting in a taverna with a group of Americans, including a leathery old lady who was wearing a lot of diamonds, a lot of bling. She was from New York, and apparently wintered every year in Greece. And for some reason the main topic at the table was astrological signs.

"What sign are you?" she asked me.

I answered her with a stoney stare.

"What day were you born?" she persisted.

"July 12," I said, hoping that would satisfy her curiosity.

"Oh, Cancer," she said. "My husband and all my boyfriends were Cancers."

"I can't help that," I said wearily, and I stood up and left the taverna. I think that if I had been older, or disappointed in life, I would have considered committing suicide, because it was that bad. I had lost the language of sleep. I just couldn't do it. It was totally impossible for me to nod off.

I heard footsteps behind me. The woman from New York had followed me. She said she had something at home that would help me sleep. She rented an apartment close to the place where Leonard Cohen used to stay every year. And when we got there she poured me a glass of local Greek wine that made retsina taste like Pouilly-Fuissé.

She also had three cats. One of them had only three legs. Another had only one eye, which was constantly draining.

"I really have to go," I announced. "I've really got to try to get some sleep." And after I was out the door I took my boots off, because it was late and I didn't want to disturb anybody, and walked through all the donkey shit back down to the port where I was staying. I'm sure I was really something to see. And when I got home there was a whole mess of cats in my bed, and I had to heave them all out onto the roof.

The next morning, when I was having coffee down at the port, the woman from New York came by again, and after she left I asked someone who she was.

"That lady," they said, "is the woman who wrote 'Que Sera, Sera,' and she's been living on royalties ever since."

"I don't think so," I said. I was pretty sure Jay Livingston and Ray Evans had written "Que Sera, Sera." But after five nights without sleep, what did I know?

Not sleeping is not good. It was hideous. And I'm sure they thought I was just a giant pain in the ass. They couldn't understand why the Canadian guy kept complaining about Greece. But it wasn't Greece that I was complaining about. Years later I went to a psychologist who hypnotized me. And he said, "Don't think of that place as being awful. Think of it as being a treatment room."

The movie was called *Lydia*. I was playing an American who was dying of a fatal disease, and most of the time I felt like I was. I was also advised that the leading lady was a personal friend of the producers, but they couldn't have been all that friendly, because we weren't even halfway through the film when they tried to replace her. When they couldn't do that, they decided to hire another actress to re-voice her part. So after we finished in Greece we had to go to Rome, to Cinecitta, to do that. It was just fucking endless. And all I wanted to do, of course, was go home. And go to sleep. Mostly in that order.

On the plane back to Toronto, as I dozed on and off, I thought of some of the jobs, both real and imagined, I had turned down so I could be in a movie, just like all my black-and-white heroes who sparkled on the big silver screen at the Nickel. Thanks to my sleepless nights in the Aegean, the glamorous world of film-making had never seemed less appealing, and I fell into bed the moment I got home.

"You've had a terrible time," Charm agreed. "Just awful. But the next time will be better. And the time after that will be better still. You'll see."

And then her cat jumped up on the bed.

As it turned out I went right into what turned into another movie.

George McCowan cast me as a pre-*Columbo*, raincoat-clad detective named Grainger, five years ahead of Peter Falk, in a two-part episode of Maxine Samuels' weekly dramatic series *Seaway*. Stephen Young and Austin Willis were the leads, and the cast for this special two-parter included, among others, Ivor Barry, Sean Sullivan, Murray Westgate, visiting U.S. glamour girl Lynda Day George, and Ms. Charmion King as Anna Amorest.

It was all a bit incestuous, because Maxine Samuels' partner and co-producer was Michael Sadlier, Kate Reid's first husband. So he had lots in common with *Seaway* star Austin Willis, who was also an ex-husband of Kate's and the father of her two children. Ironically, the only one who wasn't on the set glaring at someone was Kate; I think she was in Hollywood with Natalie Wood, Charles Bronson, and Robert Redford, shooting the screen version of Tennessee Williams' *This Property Is Condemned*, after her new fan "Tom" (a.k.a. playwright Williams) had recommended her to sophomore director Sydney Pollack.

In any case, the episode was called "Don't Forget to Wipe the Blood Off," and the two parts were later edited together and released, not once, but twice, as a ninety-minute theatrical film, first as *Affair With a Killer*, then as *Don't Forget to Wipe the Blood Off*.

(I can't honestly remember if we even knew that we were going to be seen on the big screen too. I doubt it. I'm sure we would have asked for more money!)

It was good to be back home again, especially when the phone rang. Producers were pitching projects to be part of a CBC Television summer series called *The Serial*, which was designed to showcase new dramas. Would I like to play a rookie MP in one of them?

I said Yes. And my life ever so quietly shifted on its axis.

The show – actually a series of six half-hour shows – was called *Mr. Member of Parliament*, and I played a naive young MP who arrives in Ottawa and quickly learns that he is a very small fish in a very big pond. One great thing about the character, whose name was Quentin Durgens, was that although he was full of piss and vinegar, he wasn't full of himself. So as he learned, we learned. Which we all thought was a pretty good premise.

What we didn't realize right away was how many Canadians would be interested in sharing that learning experience with him. Happily for me, the executives at CBC quickly saw the show's potential – their vision no doubt assisted by dynamic *Mr. MP* producer-director David Gardner – and ordered a winter series to complement their first hour-long drama, *Wojeck*, which featured John Vernon as a crusading crime-fighting coroner who bore more than a passing resemblance to a real-life headline-maker, Toronto coroner Morton Shulman. Network brass ordered only eight episodes of our new series, but we would become CBC's second hour-long drama, and we would also return with a new name: *Quentin Durgens, MP.*

Because the priority mandate of the Canadian Broadcasting Corporation was to bring Canadian stories to Canadians "from coast to coast to coast," most TV directors and writers had cut their teeth on news reporting and documentaries. These talents were fully exploited in our story lines, which more closely resembled reality than fiction. Freshman MP Durgens waded recklessly into such thorny Page One issues as pornography, violence in minor-league hockey, gender discrimination, and religious tolerance, all within the context of his struggling to learn the inner workings of power and how the backroom deals were made. It was a groundbreaking show, and we knew it. It was the first time anyone in Canada had seen their own government portrayed on a weekly drama series. The series was giving Canadian viewers an inside look at their own politicians, and even though the politicians were fictional, it was very important storytelling, and most of the time we had the freedom to do it the way we wanted to. Writing from the Parliamentary press gallery, Peter C. Newman noted that on Tuesday night CBC telecast new episodes of *Quentin Durgens,* "and on Wednesday morning Ottawa MPs go to work with an extra spring in their step."

Quentin Durgens was also giving me the kind of public profile that I had secretly dreamed of. My pal Perry Rosemond had already directed profiles of Oscar Peterson, Arthur Hailey, and Donald Sutherland for CBC's popular *Telescope* series, and persuaded series creator Fletcher Markle that he should do one on me. So off we went to Newfoundland, to shoot in Grand Falls. We had a lot of fun doing it, even though the weather was, as usual, predictably unpredictable. We took Perry to meet all the relatives, and to all our favourite haunts, and he somehow learned to keep screech down. At one point the whole family came over to my brother Harry's place, and I chided Perry because he couldn't remember whom he met minutes after he met them.

"There's a good reason for that," he assured me. "When your family gets together, we are talking about a crowd which is roughly the size of the population of New Hampshire."

We were shooting a sequence on the cliffs behind our house when it started to rain. Perry and the film crew loved it, because in daylight rain diffuses the light and looks great on camera. Meanwhile, I was getting wet. "Here," Perry said, and against his better judgment handed me his good suede jacket to wear. Clearly, he really wanted that shot.

My brother Harry watched the whole scene – take one, take two, take three, and me standing in the rain, in a good suede jacket – and just shook his head.

"So, Harry," said Perry, "what will Grand Falls think of your kid brother now?"

"Well," said Harry, "they won't think he's learned much on the mainland, coming out on a day like this!"

I spent three years in Parliament as Quentin Durgens, MP. It was the kind of role, and the kind of reaction, that made me think I might have a future in this business after all. We didn't get huge numbers, but the show became very well known very quickly. I went on the road to promote the second season. Alberta was going through a dry wheat problem at the time, and one day when I was signing autographs in Calgary, an old farmer came up to me and asked if I could help him.

"Because I saw what you did for the Indians last week," he said, "and the teachers the week before. I was hoping you might be able to do something for us."

He thought I was a real MP.

"Could you come out and look at it for me?" he asked. And I had to say, "No, I'm afraid I can't." But it broke my heart to say so.

Another lesson in the power of television.

Quentin Durgens, MP ran only three seasons, but its impact was undeniable. One night Perry threw a going-away party for himself, because he was leaving to try his luck in L.A., and I guess the theme was White, because I remember I was all decked out in white – white sweater, white pants, white shoes – I was even driving a white car! I also remember overindulging in a number of white bourbons. I left the party early – well, early in the morning – and was on my way home when I was pulled over by the police. Minutes later, there I was, an inebriated vision in white, quite unsuccessfully attempting to walk a straight line.

A senior officer sidled up to me, clearly disgusted.

"You ought to be ashamed of yourself!" he scolded. "A public servant like you!"

I blinked.

I performed.

"I know, it's a terrible thing!" I told him. "One of my constituents was extremely depressed, and he needed someone to drink with, so he could get his problem out. So I had to join him in the drinking."

The senior officer frowned. "Yes, but still," he began, shaking his head.

And after another scolding and a stern warning, they let me go.

Another lesson in the power of television. And how easy it is, intentionally or accidentally, to abuse it.

One of the greatest things about playing Quentin Durgens for three years was that I actually impressed both my biggest fan and my greatest critic: Charm. She candidly told one interviewer that before she saw me in the series, she thought I was "a darling actor and a good leading man – a good *young* leading man. But when I saw him do *Quentin Durgens* I thought no, this is it, this is big-time. This boy's a star. And I hadn't seen that before."

Charm hadn't seen me as a star. She hadn't seen me as the President of the United States, either. But she was about to.

Colossus: The Forbin Project was stylishly scripted by James Bridges, who would go on to pen *The Paper Chase* and *The China Syndrome*. The story was a cautionary tale about the potential perils of creating artificial intelligence, no doubt inspired in part by the unhinged H.A.L. in Stanley Kubrick's big box office hit from the previous year, *2001: A Space Odyssey*. In Bridges' scenario, scientists join an American supercomputer with a Russian supercomputer to form one brilliant colossal computer to benefit both nations. Unfortunately, the Colossus decides to take over the planet, and the scientists who created it are forced to go underground to fight it. The tagline said it all: *We built a super computer with a mind of its own and now we must fight it for the world!*

A year earlier, in 1968, Bobby Kennedy had been assassinated. An American producer had seen an episode of *Durgens* and thought I had a Kennedy look about me, so he cast me as the young U.S. president. I went down to Hollywood and we shot it on the Universal back lot. I played the understandably perturbed but undeniably Kennedy-esque leader of the free world; old pro Bill Schallert played the head of the CIA, and the supporting cast included Marion Ross, who would go on to play Ron Howard's mother for ten, yes, *ten* consecutive years on *Happy Days*.

The two leads, the actors playing the American scientists, were Eric Braeden and Susan Clark, both contract players at Universal Studios, and I enjoyed working with Susan again. Susan was a seasoned CBC veteran who had starred in a number of classical productions for the network's prestigious *Festival* series. We had worked together on *Taming of the Shrew*; Larry Dane and my friend Kenneth Welsh appeared with her in *Hedda Gabler*. She was also an accomplished stage actor, but there was no doubt that her great face and her great voice were made for film. She was also the last of the Universal players. She had signed a ten-year contract, considered a "slave contract" in Hollywood, after studio scouts saw her do *Abelard and Heloise* on CBC's *Festival*. Susan had only two or three years to go on her contract, but she never stopped working, or learning. She had already worked with Clint Eastwood and Robert Redford when the studio cast her in this one. (Eastwood and Burt Reynolds had also been Universal "slaves" until the studio, seeing little hope for their future as screen actors, fired them both.) She made at least twenty movies for Universal, but ironically it was television where she would really shine, first as track-and-field Olympian Babe Didrikson Zaharias, then as controversial aviatrix Amelia Earhart, and then in her own hit comedy series, *Webster*, with her husband Alex Karras and diminutive scene-stealer Emmanuel Lewis.

Susan's co-star was not a happy camper. Despite winning plaudits in earlier appearances in TV series like *The Rat Patrol*, the studio had made him change his name from Hans Gudegast ("too German!") to Eric Braeden for this film. *Colossus: The Forbin Project* was his first leading role. Ten years later, with no major screen roles coming his way, he would reluctantly agree to join the cast of a U.S. daytime soap called *The Young and the Restless*. And the rest, as they say, is history.

Shooting my scenes on *Colossus* took me twelve weeks. I loved working in Hollywood. The whole place was steeped in history and legend. It didn't take much to please my eye. I could be happy just looking at ceilings. Even when I could see only the tops of buildings I could still tell when they were built. The sidewalks were filled with careers that had gone well and careers that had not gone well. Every time you turned a corner in Hollywood, there was more history waiting for you, if you truly wanted to see it. And I wanted to see it.

Maybe I could do both. My friend Larry was doing both, and our pal Al Waxman was doing both. They were always

jumping in their cars, going back and forth, from Toronto to
L.A., from L.A. to Toronto.

At home the phone was strangely silent. *Durgens* was over,
and other producers were pitching other new series to take its
spot on the CBC schedule, with other up-and-coming actors
looking for their big break.

Charm had decided to put her career on hold for a while to
focus on our greatest production, our brand-new baby daughter Leah, and her joyful gurglings filled our days and nights
with delight and wonder. I was thrilled to be a father again, but
anxious, too. I knew I would have to wait a while, most likely
quite a while, before I would be offered another series. So we
decided to take on Hollywood. We packed our bags, and our
toddler's toys, and set out for California.

hooray for hollywood

———◦◉◦———

ALL THOSE YEARS OF BEING SEDUCED BY THE IMAGES
on the silver screen had given me an encyclopedic knowledge
of American character actors. Everyone knew who the stars
were, but Porky Pinsent knew the names and credits of every
key supporting player. These men and women were household
faces, yet remained mostly anonymous to everyone in both the
public and, with the possible exception of casting directors, the
industry. And they were exceptionally approachable, of course,
because they were not hounded for autographs; off-screen they
were hardly ever recognized, even on Hollywood Boulevard.
So if you went up to them and introduced yourself, and told
them how much you admired or appreciated their work, their
reaction was truly something to see.

"Look, there's Dick Foran!" I exclaimed to Perry one day in
L.A. He followed my gaze to a man crossing the street almost
a full block away and shook his head in amazement.

"Jesus, Gordon!" he cried. "Where does *that* come from?"

I just grinned. I was probably more impressed by Hollywood
than some, because I knew so much about it. I remember seeing
Huntz Hall, from the Dead End Kids, sitting at a drugstore

[97]

counter having a coffee, and no one paying any attention to him whatsoever. Because of course they didn't know who he was, let alone who he had been. And I kept thinking, *Omigod, it's* Huntz Hall!

I remember walking in to the Cock 'n' Bull on Sunset with Larry, and there was Sonny Tufts, sitting at the bar, telling these wonderful stories to the bartender, who was clearly bored to tears. And I was there another time when Marlene Dietrich came in, so tiny, hiding behind these big shades.

One time, when I was working at Universal, the man putting on my makeup was one of the Westmore brothers, and on one of the shelves behind him were the plaster-cast makeup heads they used for Bogart and all these other stars. In some ways, especially at moments like this, Hollywood had a lovely small-town familiarity for me. It was comfortable for me at the beginning. To be in the history. Because in my head I *was* Hollywood. No two ways about it. And they treated me professionally. They had great respect for Canadians anyway, and wondered where we got all this experience that we've got. That was a nice feeling, that I wasn't really starting at the beginning again.

I was also dazzled by the crews. Hollywood film and television crews were amazing. I remember in one of the things I was in, one of those weekly series, that the makeup guy went all the way back to *Juarez*. I can't tell you how much I loved it, how thrilled I was to meet him. When I was doing *The Forbin Project* this fella kept coming up and standing next to me, an old guy with a little hat on his head, and he said, "You got a double yet?" And I said, no, I don't. "I'll be your double. My name is Mickey." And suddenly they would start calling for him: "Where's Mickey? Where's

Gordon's double?" And he was always over in the corner, playing cards with the crew. Because they had all known each other forever, and Mickey went all the way back to *King of Kings*. The *first* one.

That was wonderful. To sit in a car with the crew, being driven to the Mojave Desert at six in the morning, with guys who did every movie you ever wanted to see. And they all talked about it. "Remember Robert Preston? Remember that time when he did all those stunts?" "Yes, he was real good. But not as good as the guys in *Gunga Din*, they really gave them a run for their money."

I had chills.

I knew Brando's makeup man too. He had been John Barrymore's makeup man. And the stretch from one to the other took decades and decades of film history.

I think I was working with Burt Reynolds on *Dan August* when I was asked to report to the continuity woman for something, and she was sitting there with this big leather folder, a very large folder, and inside it was the current script we were shooting. And later I learned that she had done continuity for *Gone With the Wind*, and the big leather binder she carried was the same one she had used then, when she was working for Selznick. *Oh. My. God.*

I loved that stuff. I fell for all of it. Working on *The Forbin Project* had given me a taste for feature films. I wanted to do more of them.

Getting settled in Hollywood was an experience in itself. Fears that Martin Luther King's funeral the previous April would set off more riots proved unfounded but were frightening nonetheless. Friends of ours had gone to their local liquor store to pick up some wine for dinner when they heard a voice commanding them to fall on their knees. The man who was talking to them pointed a gun at their heads and said, "Kneel down for Martin Luther King." And they did. And they looked up a minute later, and there was no one standing behind them. So they got back up on their feet and scurried out of there as fast as they could.

Charm and Leah had just flown in from Toronto and I had insisted on meeting them at the airport – I wanted to show off for Charm, show her I knew my way around. But I was never a great driver. On the way in from the airport I missed the turn at La Cienega Boulevard, and I kept driving, and driving, and driving, and I started to notice that the farther we drove, the more black people there were on the streets. So finally I said, "Charm, in case you're wondering, I've taken you this way because I thought it was important for you to see Watts." And she just rolled her eyes, of course, because she knew I was lost. We could still see traces, lots of traces, of the riots that had decimated that neighbourhood three years earlier.

We had rented an apartment in Blair House on Roscomare on the outskirts of Hollywood, close to Bel Air, so we'd have a home base while we went house-hunting. One of my most vivid memories of our time there is of Charm making us a wonderful chicken dinner. She wouldn't let me help. She wouldn't even let me in the pokey little gallery kitchen. "Don't bother me, Sir Raleigh! Go to sea! I'll call you when it's ready." So Leah and I played games until Charm summoned us to the table.

I don't know what it was that she did with that chicken. Maybe it was something as simple as a pesto – I can't really tell you. But it was sensational.

By now Leah was enrolled in day care, and shortly after we arrived Charm did a quick guest shot as an exchange teacher on an episode of *Room 222* with Michael Constantine and the talented Denise Nicholas, who I would end up working with a few years later. But the role she most wanted to play, much to the delight of Leah and myself, was wife and mother, which is probably why I can look back at my Hollywood years today without shuddering. Charm made a home for us wherever we happened to be.

At times I didn't appreciate that as much as I should have. Especially on weekends. My pal Larry Dane and I suffered from the same affliction. We hated holidays and weekends. On Friday at five o'clock, casting directors and agents went home, and we knew that the phone wasn't going to ring for the next two days. And it was horrible, and we couldn't wait until Monday at nine o'clock, when something, *anything*, could possibly happen.

I had applied for my green card in Los Angeles when I was hired to play the president in *The Forbin Project*. My application was approved, and I picked it up in Massachusetts when I flew to Boston to shoot *The Thomas Crown Affair*, the original *Thomas Crown*, with Steve McQueen and Faye Dunaway and Christopher Chapman's brilliant kaleidoscope images, for Norman Jewison. Then, as now, Norman was always looking to showcase Canadian actors in his films whenever he could. But I wasn't happy with my work in the film, and I suspect

Norman wasn't all that thrilled with it either. I had made the mistake of being too prepared. I was playing Faye Dunaway's boyfriend, an insurance salesman, and I thought that the role was underwritten, so I arrived with a character delivery of my own, which maybe wasn't the best plan. Should have left it entirely up to the director. Still, now I had my green card.

I had come to Hollywood to do movies. However, first and foremost I was a product of television, and Canadian television at that. On American television established American stars got the leads. You could guest star as the villain, which I did in a number of series. When my phone rang, which was not nearly as frequently as I would have liked, it was mostly for guest spots, playing that week's bad guy on someone else's series.

"They're not calling you as frequently as you want them to call you," said Larry, "because they don't see you as a villain. They see you as a leading man. You need to nail a series for yourself." One studio – I think it was Screen Gems I met with – liked the *Durgens* series and wanted me to do an American version called *The Senator*. This was a few years after Richard Crenna had played a state senator on *Slattery's People* and a couple of years before another Canadian, Daryl Duke, picked up an Emmy for directing Hal Holbrook in a dramatic series called *The Senator*. But an American version of *Durgens* never happened.

Back in Toronto, CBC was telecasting an ambitious anthology series called *Program X*, produced by Paddy Sampson and George Jonas, with such directors as David Cronenberg, Lorne Michaels, and Jonas himself contributing their talents on a weekly basis. Producer Herb Roland persuaded them that I should do a one-man show, *Bits & Pieces of Gordon Pinsent*, a mix of dramatic readings, some of my poetry, and even a few tunes I'd come up with, accompanying myself on guitar. I wrote an excerpt of what would become *John and the Missus*. I did a bit of *Cyrano*, and an excerpt from *Durgens*, and that's when I wrote "Easy Ridge."

> *I need no rock to rest upon,*
> *I need not be at home on time*
> *No need to sing my distant song*
> *in any other time but mine.**

I flew home to do it, then returned to L.A. I had talked myself into doing an episode of *It Takes a Thief* in fervent hope that I might get to work with Robert Wagner's co-star, the legendary Fred Astaire. But unbeknownst to me, Fred had made an exceedingly elegant exit after the first five episodes – had he, I wondered, danced on the ceiling on his way out? – and I never even got to meet him.

CBC called again. Would I come back to Toronto to guest star in a new series? I said Yes, and played a reckless priest who wants to test his faith by shooting the rapids in an episode of *Adventures in Rainbow Country*.

Back in Hollywood I did a TV movie for the director Leo Penn, later famous as Sean Penn's father. Talk about eclectic casting: Sharon Farrell, Sam Jaffe, Terry Moore (who was secretly married to Howard Hughes at the time, apparently), and Greg Mullavey, among many others, in a story about a

* From "I Spent a Day on Easy Ridge," by Gordon Pinsent.

family of doctors (Gary Collins, John Dehner, Susan Howard, and me) who suddenly find themselves up against a cholera epidemic and a movie star who refuses to accept treatment. The movie was called *Quarantined*, and it probably should have been, except for the fact that one of my cast-mates was the mercurially brilliant Wally Cox, who was about to be our new neighbour. We had found a wonderful house up in the hills, off Mulholland Drive, with a spectacular view of the San Fernando Valley, and Charm was already deep in the process of transforming a house into a home.

The idea of working, of being busy, of being in demand, was slowly turning into a new kind of challenge for me. Suddenly I could find merit in a mediocre script if I thought it could be a legitimate stepping stone to my goals. And each film and TV series I did gave me fresh and frequently unwanted insights.

I had a wonderful publicist. She was Glen Campbell's publicist too. Thanks to her efforts I was chosen Newcomer of the Year by *Modern Screen*, the monthly movie magazine that also served as the home base of Louella Parsons. On another occasion she positioned me next to another Hollywood gossip queen, Sheilah Graham,* at a luncheon honouring veteran producer Hal Wallis. Elizabeth Taylor and Richard Burton were at the head table with Wallis, but otherwise most of the

---

* Gossip columnist Graham was already a Hollywood legend, but not for her columns. In *Beloved Infidel*, the 1959 screen version of her book about her affair with F. Scott Fitzgerald, Deborah Kerr played Sheilah and Gregory Peck played Fitzgerald.

tables in the hotel ballroom appeared to be populated by managers, studio executives, and bankers.

Miss Graham, who was clearly a fan of my publicist, was not shy when it came to expressing herself. "You're the only *actor* in this room," she noted pointedly. "I hope you appreciate that."

I did.

I had four agents. I changed them like shirts. My favourite was a great fellow named Bill Barnes. He was wonderful, all long fingers, a character right out of the fifties. His face looked fat because his shirt was too tight, but he was a gentleman of another era. His favourite line was "Get out your paper and pencil. Take this down." He had credentials, too, of sorts. He was Ryan O'Neal's agent before (but, alas, not after) Ryan hit the jackpot with the TV series *Peyton Place*, and at one time he had also represented Sue Lyons, the young actress who played Lolita with James Mason and Shelley Winters and who attempted to lure Richard Burton away from Ava Gardner and Deborah Kerr in *Night of the Iguana*.

One day Bill took me to the MGM commissary for lunch and showed me Spencer Tracy's and Katharine Hepburn's old parking spots. I thought I'd faint. "There was a time when I could just walk through the front door of this place," he told me, his voice tinged with sadness. Which, in hindsight, was definitely an indication that this man might not be the answer to my prayers.

We did a bunch of meetings – I remember waiting for an answer on a Kirk Douglas movie – and he got me to do a screen test over at 20th Century Fox with Debbie Reynolds for a new TV series she wanted to do, produced by Jess

Oppenheimer, who was a key player in the phenomenal success of *I Love Lucy*. Debbie was auditioning actors to play her husband, and while we were waiting for them to finish lighting the set, she told me that they were shooting the notorious Gore Vidal novel *Myra Breckinridge* on the same lot, with Raquel Welch and John Huston and Rex Reed, and that they had constructed a special dressing room for Mae West.

"C'mon, Gordon," she insisted, "we've got to see that dressing room." So off we went, and found it easily, two sound stages away. Debbie was thrilled, because she was genuinely fascinated by Hollywood history, even back then. And then we did the screen test, which seemed to go all right, and she said, "How do you feel about doing a series, Gordon?"

"Well, to be honest," I said, "I just came off one, so I don't know if I want to go back to one so soon."

Suddenly the air seemed to get a bit cooler, and I was going to say more, to explain that I'd really come to Hollywood to do feature films; but I had to stop, because I was giving Bill Barnes a heart attack. And I liked him too much for that.

Up on Mulholland Drive my indefatigable Charm had worked her magic with our house in Sherman Oaks. I was not a great swimmer, but I loved having a swimming pool. Wasn't that what Hollywood was all about? Sunshine and swimming pools and California bungalows perched precariously on the sides of sunburned, brush-covered hills, overlooking stone canyons and lush green valleys. Oh yes, the hills were alive, all right, but not with music. With Charles Manson and his disciples and whoever else had become unhinged by this crazy life around them. And you didn't have far to go down the hill to get to 10050 Cielo

Drive and the house Doris Day's son Terry Melcher had rented with his girlfriend, Edgar Bergen's actress daughter Candice. Manson had a grudge against Melcher, but unknown to Manson and his followers, Melcher and Bergen had moved to another location and the landlord had rented the house to director Roman Polanski and his wife Sharon Tate. A horrible nightmare of a night. And right after that, the LaBiancas – they lived on Waverly Drive, and the Manson tribe had killed them the next night – and you had the awful feeling that these people, and other people like them, were crawling through your neighbourhoods in the middle of the night, and that no one was safe. And right away, before we even really knew who they were, the iron gates went up everywhere, new security systems were installed, and attack guard dogs were the order of the day.

I was working on *Dan August* with a seasoned Hollywood veteran, Richard Anderson, and Richard invited Charm and me to dinner at his place. After work I picked Charm up at our new house.

"Do they live very far away?" she asked me. Going to a friend's house for dinner in Los Angeles would often involve a forty-five-minute drive.

"No, just down the hill," I replied. "We'll be there in less than five minutes."

"Well, that's handy!" she said, laughing. I didn't tell her that Richard and his then-wife Katharine lived on Cielo Drive.

The episode of *Dan August* that I shot with Richard and Burt Reynolds was called "Epitaph for a Swinger." Burt was pretty excited about having his own series – he had just come off *Gunsmoke*, where he played the blacksmith – and did most of his own stunts, which made him one of the most respected players in Hollywood. Film crews loved him, because he took as much pride in his work as they did in theirs. Burt was still under contract to Universal, and so was Julie Adams, who was a regular on the series. On one lunch break the three of us were walking along, and he had been asking about me and Canada. Julie, who had sort of a schoolteacher-ish thing about her, was between us, and Burt was being naughty, because he loved to tease her.

"Gordon," he said, "you must get a lot of fan mail in Canada!"

"Yes, a fair bit," I said.

"In Canada," he said, "what do the girls send you in the mail? . . . nice things?" Julie shot him a don't-go-there look, and he shrugged. "I just want to see if it's the same as the stuff they send me."

A minute later we went into a store where he insisted on buying each of us a copy of *Screw* magazine. "Here's one for you, Gordon. Here's one for you, Julie. Everyone should have a copy of *Screw* magazine."

Burt was good. I was amazed at his athletic ability. He did superb work. He was chasing me, and I was going upstairs, then running across a corridor, and he did a running, jumping, flying leap over boxes, onto other boxes, onto the ledge and railing and climbed up and dealt with me. There is that thrill that the actor gets, if the actor can be that athletic, because it comes under the heading of showing off, and showing the crew and everybody else around you that you are right for this job. And he was marvellous. I played the villain in that episode of *Dan August*, and after we wrapped he sent me a note:

Gordon, you're a terrific actor.
Just don't forget to pick up
the latest copy of *Screw* magazine!

Some jobs were boring. Some were downright discouraging. When I got hired to do an episode of *The Young Lawyers*, I was in awe of Lee J. Cobb. But then, who wouldn't be? He had done it all, on stage, on film, on television. Studio One. Playhouse 90. *On the Waterfront. Twelve Angry Men. The Brothers Karamazov. Exodus.* He was the original Willy Loman when *Death of a Salesman* opened on Broadway in 1949; Arthur Miller said he had written the role with Cobb in mind. On *Young Lawyers* he played an attorney named David Barrett, and when we weren't shooting I don't remember ever seeing him smile once. He walked around the set like he was slumming, like he'd somehow mistakenly taken this giant step down, and had not landed where he believed he should have.

When they say there are only seven scripts in the world, they must have been referring to those days in Hollywood, because every show looked the same. All the series that were being turned out looked the same – trashier, in various ways, but the same.

I played a German general with Bob Crane in *Hogan's Heroes.* "*Sitzen sie!*" That was all the German I was required to learn. "*Sitzen sie!*" The series was on its last legs; they had only one more episode to go. I had scenes with Bob Crane and of course with Werner Klemperer, who played the POW camp commandant Colonel Klink. What a strange fellow he was. Before he was cast in *Hogan's Heroes* he was regarded principally as a serious actor. Onscreen he had worked for Hitchcock and Stanley Kramer, and even played Adolf Eichmann. But he became famous playing a bumbling coward on television.

While we were shooting my episode, 20th Century Fox was hosting a big premiere for *The Poseidon Adventure*, and during a break I remember hearing Bob Crane on the phone – "So you've got the tickets, great, yes, I can be ready for a seven o'clock pickup."

Klemperer heard him too, and was going out of his mind. "What is he saying? Has he got tickets for the *Poseidon* screening tonight? I want to go to that!"

They were all so jealous of each other. This series was all but over and they needed to be seen, they needed to be out there. When I look back on it now, and the tragedy that lay ahead for Crane, I wonder how many of us were busy keeping junk and throwing all the good things away.*

I had a lot of down time in L.A. For many actors down time is treasured time off between movies or plays or television series. But I wasn't so much between things as looking for things to be between.

Like most young actors trying to make it in Hollywood, my pal Larry Dane had leased a wonderful apartment for himself. And, like most young actors trying to make it in Hollywood, Larry couldn't afford to furnish it. So he had started building furniture, and once I saw what he was doing, I thought, *I should be building furniture too*. So he would come over to the house and together we would build these massive pieces, and he still

---

* Bob Crane was found beaten to death in 1978 in Scottsdale, Arizona. His murder remains an unsolved homicide.

talks about the wonderful weekend dinners that Charm would create for us when we had finished our work for the day. In our dreaded down time Larry and I built a massive, majestic table and two wonderful cathedral chairs, and I tried to live up to that table, by imagining myself as the head of Viking royalty. Leo Penn came to dinner and sat at the table. So did Susan Clark and Pat and Wally Cox and Nancy and John Vernon. Leah remembers "lots and lots of parties," with Pat and Wally, John and Nancy, and many more. She remembers Leslie Nielsen standing at the buffet, pointing to a bowl of Brussels sprouts is a seriously sinister way. "Y'know what's in those, kid?" he whispered. It would be years before she was willing to try them again.

Because I appreciated the history of Hollywood, and admired the men and women who had made that history, I didn't have much time for those who just wanted to slip in and slide out again, without any regard for what had been achieved and accomplished before they arrived. I'm sorry to say John Vernon was one of them. But he had a couple of good contacts – Don Siegel, the director, and a couple of others – so he did all right.

Wally's pal Marlon Brando walked out to the patio where we overlooked the valley and said, "You've got the best view of any of us!" And I thought, *Well, then, I must be a success. So why am I still doing crap?* And then Charm would say, "Oh Gordon, get over yourself!" and bring me back down to earth again.

Still, I spent more time playing with Leah than I spent in front of the camera, and when I did get in front of the camera, I frequently wished I was back at the house playing with Leah instead. In her early years she thought of me more as a playmate than a parent. Leah remembers the house mainly by what happened there. She remembers the landslides and worrying that our house was going to topple over the edge and slide down the hill, which is what Charm and I were worrying about too. She remembers the earthquake, and me and Charm jumping out of bed in the middle of the night to grab her so we could all take shelter under the heavy dining room table.

That incident also lives in her memory, she insists, because it was the first and only time she ever saw her father naked. (Well, yes, I did jump out of bed in a hurry.) She also remembers that we didn't send her back to school for quite a while, because we had determined that if we were going to go down in an earthquake, we were all going down together.

Hollywood isn't like any other place. You find a house you want and buy it. Life revolves around that. It revolves around the place you buy, the time you spend on the phone, the jobs you take or you don't take. And you sit a lot, and wonder where you're going, and wonder if you're living their career or yours, and wonder if you're becoming part of a yellowing kind of system where you are the tenant, not the landlord.

Your neighbours aren't like everyone else's neighbours. Leah liked to visit a neighbour a few doors away from us, a sweet old lady who liked Leah to read to her. The sweet old lady was Joan Blondell, the same Joan Blondell who had starred with James Cagney in *The Public Enemy* in 1931 and kicked up her heels with Dick Powell and Ruby Keeler in *Gold Diggers of 1933*.

And yes, we had a swimming pool. But everybody had a swimming pool. What I really wanted was a shot at something good. *I gotta make it happen here, so I can prove myself on another level, an American level.* But the work was simply not there. Those were awful times, when you weren't sure if anyone believed in you and you weren't sure you believed in yourself. And then every once in a while, a ray of sunshine, a brighter day.

I had a good time making *Chandler*, not just because it was a feature film. *Chandler* was an odd picture, something a little different. Chandler was a detective played by Warren Oates. I played a mafia mobster and Leslie Caron played my wife. Michael Laughlin, her husband at the time, produced it. And what a cast. Gloria Grahame, Scatman Crothers, great character actors. I loved being around them. Loved doing something different, too. But then James Aubrey, the executive John Houseman had dubbed "The Smiling Cobra," took over MGM, and he personally re-cut the picture. Ruined it, in my opinion. It was no longer something different. In fact, it wasn't much of anything by the time he got through with it. Two of the actors, Royal Dano and James Sikking, weren't even in it anymore. So much for creative integrity.

will power

―◦―

I spent a day on Easy Ridge
Not nearly long enough for me
And with myself, I waited
For the light so I could see

I need no rocks to rest upon
I need not be home on time
No need to sing my distant song
In any other time but mine

Confusing how my childhood
Comes around again and round again
And no amount of strangers now
Can take what I had then*

DESPITE THE DOWN TIME THAT KEPT GETTING ME down, we pressed on. Looking back now, I remember being furious most of the time. Furious about the stuff I was not

* From "I Spent a Day on Easy Ridge," by Gordon Pinsent.

Standing on my own (almost), thanks to my sisters and the branches of an unsuspecting tree.

Haig, Lil, and me, Porky, on a summer afternoon.

My sisters Lil and Hazel (my champion) and me, absolutely standing on my own at 15.

Pvt. G.E. Pinsent reporting for duty.

Horsing around with Haig, while our sister Nita ignores us.

Faking it as an Arthur Murray instructor in Winnipeg.

With the girls with the "binoculars" in *Death of a Salesman*.

Rehearsing *Glass Menagerie* with Ramona McBean and director John Hirsch at the Manitoba Theatre Centre.

I don't know how viewers felt about it, but this "live" CBC-TV prison drama in Winnipeg made a big impression on my beautiful co-star. (In time she forgave me.)

With Lillian Lewis in *Two for the Seesaw* (right after my notorious "guest" shot as Ernie in *Mr. Roberts*).

Playing Marlon's role in *Guys and Dolls* for John at the MTC, with Judy Armstrong.

With Miss Charmion King in *Madwoman of Chaillot* at The Crest
– the first (but not the last) time I would whistle for her.

In summer stock
in *The Long, the
Short and the Tall*
with the Straw
Hat Players.

With Melvyn Douglas. When we shot *A Very Close Family*, my
mother told her friends that I played "the son who doesn't like girls."

As *Quentin Durgens,
M.P.* I said Yes, and
my life ever so quietly
shifted on its axis.

My favourite picture of Charm and me. Guess who was making us laugh? Newspaper columnist George Anthony, who made me laugh again, a lot, when we worked together on this book.

being offered and furious about the stuff I was being offered. Stuff I normally wouldn't touch. And Charm watched it happen, watched me deal with it, sometimes badly. Washing down lunch with a couple of Scotches. Yes, it was only two o'clock in Los Angeles, but it was cocktail hour in Toronto.

Thank God for Wally.

"Do you hike, Gordon?"

"Hike?" I asked.

"No, hike is what I said. You have to say something else."

Wally Cox was witty and brilliant and kind and funny. The first three qualities alone were enough to make him virtually shunned in Hollywood.

"We're going to go hiking," said Wally. "Unless you have something better to do."

I didn't.

Wally had become a household name in America in the fifties thanks to an NBC sitcom called *Mr. Peepers*. He had done guest spots on dozens of other sitcoms, usually playing the milquetoast character he had perfected. Entranced by his quick wit, producers sought him out as a panelist on such shows as *What's My Line?* and, especially, *Hollywood Squares*.

"I'll pick you out a nice snake stick," said Wally. But after he saw the look on my face – had he not in fact just said the words *snake stick?* I was fairly sure I'd heard him correctly – he explained that on the ridges where we were going to go hiking, snakes would come out of the bushes to bask in the sun in our path.

Nor would we be hiking alone. He had also invited a friend, possibly his best friend, to join us. Years ago they had been roommates in New York, trying to eke out a living while they were studying acting with Stella Adler, and their friendship had never waned.

"What's his name?" I inquired, so I wouldn't forget it after we were introduced.

"Marlon," said Wally.

You could have baked a pie in my mouth.

Surely I would not be climbing local ridges with Terry Malone from *On the Waterfront*. It would be like being in a film without having to audition.

Marlon, said Wally, was getting ready to do a movie over at Paramount for Francis Ford Coppola,* and thought a hike or two with Wally might help him get in shape.

"Listen," he added, "he's going to try to make us think he's been running all the way from his place on Mulholland. But he's just parked down the slope."

Unlike Marlon, off camera Wally was strong and athletic and, as I soon learned, Wally's idea of a "'hike" was my idea (and Marlon's) of a "climb."

Wally's so-called hikes soon became the highlight of my weeks. We would travel off Mulholland into Bel Air, and down into this special area that defied you to see any other part of the city. And in this "escape" you'd come upon a series of ridges. Wally had named them A, B, C, D, and E. A was for astronauts; B was for bulldozers; C was for Captain America; and D was for Democrats. He had named E as Easy, as this one could be scaled in minutes, making it possible to return to the house for a drink.

* Yes, that one – *The Godfather*.

The practice was to peel off our shirts, make belts out of them, and, armed with our snake sticks, simply scale the easiest of the five ridges. Wally went first, "Gordo" next, with "Marl" following behind. Oh yes, I was *Gordo* now. Wally loved to play with words, on any and every occasion.

He said his name was Gordo
and he had a Gordo face
But what was Gordo doin'
in this godforsaken place?

On one excursion I had diligently sharpened my snake stick to a fine, sharp point, while "Marl" had invested his time and energy decorating his forehead with a leather band, worn warrior-style. It made me wish I had one too, so I could feel that we had both come out of Western Costume together.

Out on the trail Marl's grunting made me think he was impatient with my progress up ahead of him, but thankfully it turned out to be plain old everyday grunting, brought on by his own estrangement with the art of climbing.

Wally didn't have to turn around that often to know that his friend Marl had not got off to a good start, and could read this from Brando's heaving (compared to my own wheezing).

After five minutes of Edmund Hillarying, I noticed that Marlon had stopped altogether.

In a pose that suggested he had plenty more in him, he had bent over, ostensibly quite taken with a wildflower.

"Hey, Wally!" he shouted.

"Whaddyawant, you fat bastard!"

"Wassa name o' this flower?" asked Brando.

Replied Wally, without a second's hesitation: "It's called *an excuse for stopping!*"

Climbing a hill with Wally Cox was sort of amusing. Climbing a hill with Terry Malone from *On the Waterfront* was quite something else.

The next pause came in the form of Wally's surprise engagement with the mother-in-law of all rattlers, shooting out from between some rocks at him. "SNAKE!" cried the famous comedian, bolting straight up and back onto, guess what, my trusty well-sharpened snake stick – "FUCCCK!" – propelling him forward into snake territory again, where he was in a much better position than the hugely talented Marlon Brando or myself to nail the bastard with a whole lot of rocks till dead. This done, he cut off its head, informing us that the head is the most dangerous part for anyone else to pick up.

Later, when we were putting our feet up at Wally's, his wife Pat asked what had happened.

"Everything was fine," said Brando, "until Gordie the Newfoundlander stabbed Wally with his snake stick!"

Now I was *Gordie.*

On another occasion Marlon raced into Wally's house, ran right past us into the kitchen, ripped open the fridge door, grabbed a chunk of chocolate cake, squashed it onto his face, and flopped into the nearest chair. Deciphering Brando wasn't the easiest chore at the best of times, but when spoken through a mouth full of pound cake, his speech became a linguist's nightmare.

"Whergumblskeelatembo?"

"No, I'm not going to a movie with you, you fat bastard!" Wally replied. Brando grunted. Wally shrugged. "Take Gordo, if he wants to go."

"Wanna go to a movie, Gordie?" asked Fletcher Christian.

We went to a double bill at a theatre in the San Fernando Valley, where we saw two of what were surely the longest MGM movies ever made, *The Brothers Grimm* and *How the West Was Won*. On the way there we stopped to pick up Marl's wife, Tarita (from *Mutiny on the Bounty*,) who was still nursing their daugher Cheyenne at the time, and two of his other children were there as well, Christian and Miko, wild kids, both of them. We sat there for 300 bum-numbing minutes, and every time another big-name actor came onscreen – Marlon was practically the only big-name actor who wasn't in one of those two films – he'd snort dismissively. Jimmy Stewart appeared onscreen, and Marlon snorted. And then Lee J. Cobb came on. Marlon had worked with him in *On the Waterfront*, of course, and I had just worked with him on a series.

"There's your friend!" I said.

Marlon stuffed more popcorn into his mouth.

"The trouble with Lee," he said, "is that he has this awful voice." Which was pretty funny considering Marlon was unintelligible most of the time.

After *The Godfather* came out, a story started circulating that I was the one who suggested Marlon stuff his mouth with cotton to play Don Corleone. Oh sure. *More cotton, more cotton, we can still hear you!* The story was very amusing, but of course it wasn't true. Yes, I had talked to Marlon about *The Godfather*. I asked him why he had chosen to do this particular film, and he said, "The banks, the banks." I think his island retreat in the South Seas was in deep financial despair, and he needed to make some money to bail it out.

I think he accepted the role of Jor-El, *Superman*'s father, for the same reason. The producers came to see him, all sweaty and nervous, because they were about to meet Marlon Brando. And he said, "I want to play him like a bagel," and they just looked at each other and then back at him – and he could out-stare you for weeks – and they said, *Okay, all right, sure.*

Over time I did some sketches of Wally, and a couple of Marlon, and Marlon wanted them, so I gave them to him. And at the end, after he died, they were put up for auction with the rest of the stuff that he had diligently squirrelled away.

Leah remembers going hiking with Marlon and me as a little girl and how he kept trying to get her attention, especially when she seemed to be ignoring him, which she did most of the time, she admits, because she thought he was a bit creepy. Marlon was outrageous, but in a different kind of way. He asked a lot of questions but never answered any. And he was a bit of a coward. But it was still exciting to be around him. I taught Marlon to sing "Danny Boy." He always asked me to sing it, and I don't think he even had a copy of my album.

Your album? you ask, as well you might. Yes, my album. It was called *Gordon Pinsent: Roots*, with a particularly piquant photo of me on the album cover. I look like the father of *The Brady Bunch*. In deference to celebrated Canadian entrepreneurs Michael Budman and Don Green, I should hasten to add that the title of the album, *Roots*, had absolutely nothing to do with their now-famous Canadian clothing label. Nor did it have anything even remotely to do with Edward Albee's play, which we had performed at the Crest, or the Alex Haley mini-series of the same name. All the tunes on the album came from my roots on the Rock: "She's Like a Swallow," "Cod Liver Oil," "Barbara Allen," "Foggy Dew," "Let Me Fish Off Cape St. Mary's" – perhaps the most lyrical song in the collection – and, of course, "I's the B'y." It was released (some say escaped) by Arc Records in 1968, as a twelve-inch vinyl LP, and thanks to YouTube, some audio tracks still haunt me to this day.

But, I digress.

Life in L.A. wasn't all rainbows, but it wasn't all thunder-storms, either. *Invitation to a March* was a very elegant TV movie, with a very elegant cast. Arthur Laurents had adapted his play for television, with Marvin Chomsky directing, and they assembled a company they knew they could count on. Blythe Danner, Rosemary Murphy, both Broadway veterans; Patricia Quinn, who had played Alice in Arlo Guthrie's movie of *Alice's Restaurant*; Michael Sacks, who had played the lead in *Slaughterhouse Five*; Cliff Potts, who was so good as Bruce Dern's partyboy sidekick in *Silent Running*. And one of the producers, Norman Lloyd, was himself a working actor. Not only was he one of the original players in the John Houseman–Orson Welles Mercury Theatre, he was also a favourite of Alfred Hitchcock, who had hired him to act in, produce, and direct select film and television projects. Norman, in fact, had played the spy who had slipped from Robert Cummings' grasp in Hitchcock's 1942 thriller *Saboteur*. It was fun to be spending some time, on and off stage, in such good company, however briefly.

Down time again. And then, more down time. And I was trying to keep my brain alive, trying to remind myself that I was still an artist. Wasn't I? Was I? I was still sketching, and I was painting now, watercolours, oils. And building more furniture.

By now it seemed I could only run on two speeds – when I was performing and when I was not performing. I seemed to be doing an awful lot of waiting. Wondering, wishing, hoping that things would work out, hoping that good scripts would start to come to me, scripts with blood and flesh and bone. My whole life was tied up in it. If I'd only had the sense to see the waiting and the wondering as only part of my life, not all of my life. But I couldn't, not then, and I gave myself over to it, almost to a dangerous degree. And then one day it suddenly didn't seem all that mysterious. The writing was right there on the wall. If I wasn't going to be offered the very best things, or at least something better than the kind of thing I'd been doing, well, then, I'd better start looking elsewhere.

I knew I couldn't build a movie the way I built furniture. I knew I couldn't sketch a movie, or paint a movie. But maybe, just maybe, I could write a movie. I had reached a critical point where I realized I had to take my career into my own hands. I had to write something. Something good.

Larry used to say that to make it in Hollywood you had to be in the right place, at the right time, with the right thing. And if you're not, then you have to create the right place, the right time, and the right thing. *Your* thing. So that's what I would attempt to do. I would write a movie about a character based on me – the alternate Porky Pinsent, in a fictional parallel universe. Same guy, sure, except this time he never leaves the Rock, never has to seduce tough Canadian customs officers, never joins the army, never . . . never becomes Gordon Pinsent.

I started typing.

The words started coming.

The central character, Will Cole, has his own philosophy: "Seduce it if it moves and drink it if it pours."

This is not bad, I think.

I rewrite the first act. Yes. Much better.

Second act, and we're wondering how long Will Cole can get away with being Will Cole.

Third act, and Will's world is starting to fall apart.

I think this is – dare I say it? – pretty good. Maybe.

Life starts coming back into focus.

Larry reads it. He loves it. He announces that he personally wants to produce it.

"You're an actor, Larry," I tell him, "what do you know about producing a movie?"

"Gordon," he says, "what does *anyone* know about producing a movie?"

I love Larry, but I'm highly dubious. Still, Larry is one of the very few people I know who seems to understand that "show business" is two separate words. He knows all about Show. He believes his Lebanese heritage has given him an innate sense of Business. And he's also kept his eyes open, and has observed how business, especially the movie business, is currently being conducted in Canada.

"Let me see if I can raise the money," says Larry.

"Okay," I reply. "Sure. Why not."

I consult with my agent-du-jour, who reads it, loves it (what else is he going to say?), and cheers me up considerably when he says he thinks the studios "could really go for this one!"

Turns out he's right.

"It's really offbeat, different from all the other stuff I've been reading," says one studio exec. "What do you hope to do with it?"

I tell him.

"You want to do it *yourself?*" He shakes his head in disbelief, then shrugs his tailored Saville Row shoulders. "You're never going to do it yourself. You'll never get it made."

Another exec at another studio has connections. Major Movie Star connections.

"All right, I'll tell you this much, Elliott Gould has expressed some interest in it as a producer. And I can probably get this to Steve McQueen. But why do you have to do it there, in Newfoundland? We can do it right here," he says, with a sweeping gesture, "right here on the back lot." He too shrugs. "Never mind, we'll get beyond that. In the meantime, do you want to sell it?"

And I do, really badly.

And I would, if I just had one other good idea – just *one* – for myself.

So for once I don't say Yes. I don't "do a deal."

I pick up my script and go home.

Back on the hill overlooking the San Fernando Valley I pour myself another Scotch and whine to Charm about my day.

The next morning I look in the mirror and discover that I have a paunch, a protruding lower abdomen, which is no doubt one of the dividends paid by too much down time and too many Scotches. I get out the old weight belt and strap it on. And resolve to start drinking more water and less Scotch. Someday very soon.

Charm is eyeing me suspiciously. I am also aware that she is keeping Leah well away from me, in case I might do something . . . *strange*.

The next afternoon the phone rings. I've been wearing the weight belt for about four hours. Charm answers the phone.

"It's Larry, calling from Toronto," she informs me.

I pick up the phone.

"We've got the money," he says simply.

Not only does he, do *we*, have the money, we actually have the money to shoot *in Newfoundland*.

A shoestring budget? Bloody right. Maybe only half a shoe-string. But, *we have the money*.

We make plans to make plans, but I still make him tell me three more times before I let him hang up. And then, giddy with joy, I jump fully clothed into our Hollywood swimming pool – and sink right to the bottom.

I am still wearing the weight belt.

Not a strong swimmer at the best of times, I unhook the belt and slowly fight my way to the surface.

I am going to star in a movie I've written, in the outlandishly beautiful place where I was born, in a feature film for theatrical release. And my dear friend Larry is going to produce it.

We are going to make *The Rowdyman*.

lovely, tell your mother

Making *The Rowdyman* in Newfoundland was a frustrating, exhilarating, terrifying, joyful, exasperating, and richly rewarding experience. As always, there were a number of bumps along the way. Larry had miraculously raised the money from a group of people, and we were already in Newfoundland scouting for locations when one of them pulled out. Finally his R.C.M.P. mentor, veteran film producer Budge Crawley, came to the rescue. When Budge became our executive producer, we started to make it happen. But it was seldom a smooth ride.

Onscreen we cast for chemistry, and we got it. Frank Converse was a handsome, stage-trained leading man who was more interested in playing meaty character parts, so he was happy to be playing Will's somewhat reluctant sidekick. Linda Goranson, who was playing Will's suicidal love interest, had made her screen debut at eighteen, playing Rita Tushingham's sister in *The Trap*. And Will Geer, already a legend in American theatre, squeezed us in between working with Robert Redford and director Sydney Pollack on one of their frequent collaborations, *Jeremiah Johnson*, and shooting the first season of a soon-to-be-historic TV series about a mountain family called *The Waltons*.

Off-screen, in my opinion, our casting was not nearly so successful. Our director, Peter Carter, had worked with Paul Almond as an associate producer when Almond directed Geneviève Bujold (at that time still his wife) and Donald Sutherland in *Act of the Heart*. When Budge Crawley launched a TV series called *R.C.M.P.*, Peter graduated from unit manager to assistant director, and by the time *The Forest Rangers* rolled around he was a good, solid first A.D. He put in two years on *The Forest Rangers* and then another year on *Seaway*, and then producer Ron Weyman gave him a break and let him direct one of the episodes in the second season of John Vernon's high-profile series *Wojeck*.

I believe Peter Carter was born to be a first A.D. As a director he was unsure of himself, and his insecurity produced an anxiety that took its toll on the production. He had actors slotted, pigeonholed in a certain way. If you had wakened him at three o'clock in the morning I don't believe he could've told you what he was going to be doing that day. Because he truly didn't know. So he would yell at you, and swear at you – although never at me – but, if you drank beer with him, or played cards with him, you could get by quite handily. It was like there was a private A.D. school in itself, and Peter ran it, and he made sure he ran it.

He would show up in the morning hung over, with his hair uncombed. He was held together by a few jokes and knowing when to laugh when the boss told one. There was never a thought of him becoming a director; far from it. One day he decided he wanted it. And it was terrible watching him, yelling at children, treating them so badly. He had this funny thing, that if someone was telling a story, and you were listening to the story, he'd be watching you, as if he'd heard it before, which he hadn't, to see if you were going to laugh, so he would know whether to laugh or not.

The Rowdyman was his first film as a director. And Larry and I were so tight on this project; it was near and dear to our hearts, and we'd put so much into it. On the first day of shooting I went down to the tracks at St. John's. The CNR had temporarily restored service on a passenger train so we could shoot a travelling scene. I wasn't needed right away, but I wanted to be there. Dawn Greenhalgh was on the train, ready to shoot the scene. She said, "Have you seen Peter?" I hadn't, but she had, and he had come to work drunk, on the first day of principal photography. I looked down the track and there he was, standing there, with his legs far apart, like the Lord of the Manor. It was very disheartening.

After we screened the first dailies I said, "I want to talk to someone."

He said, "Talk to me, Gordie."

I said, "Peter, what colour are my eyes?"

"Blue," he said.

"That's right," I said. "So why can't I see my eyes on the screen?"

"Oh, don't worry about that," he said, a bit anxiously. "We can always shoot some close-ups."

Great. We've just started shooting, and already we're doing patch-ups.

I never said so at the time, and I haven't said so up to now, but I don't think he was at all suited for that role. A good director sees a good story and all the wonderful places it could go.

In my experience, Peter was far more interested in finishing whatever job he was on so he could get to the next job, whatever it might be, than he was in investing any time looking at where he might be able to take the story. For the most part you couldn't get him into a decent, lengthy conversation about anything.

Producers like to hire directors like Peter because they get it done fast. But directors like George McCowan got it done fast too, only George got it done fast because he had worked it all out, first in his head, and then on paper, and then with his crew and his actors, before he ever started to roll film.

Peter had done a tour of duty with the British Army in Korea, and I think he was carrying a lot more emotional baggage than he or any of us knew. Sometimes he would go into his own world and you'd have to pull him out again. But when he got it, he got it, and captured it onscreen. And brought the film in under budget, at $320K. And there were some good times too, when we had fun. When the mood was right, we did have some laughs. So it wasn't a nightmare. But it should have been a dream, the way, Larry and I had dreamed it, and Peter was not a dreamer.

In all fairness to Peter – or P.C., as he liked to be called – the Rock was not overtly film-friendly. The people were wonderful, but the weather was, well, Newfoundland weather. "Gordon, you come from here!" he would wail. "Can't you do something about these goddamn winds?" In the morning we would shoot a scene when the clouds were moving so fast it was impossible to match the shot. We'd get to a location and it would be sunny, but by the time we set up it would be cloudy, and by the time we finished rehearsing the scene for camera it would be raining, and by the time we were ready to shoot the scene it would be hailing. So we would break for lunch, and it would be sunny again.

We had to wait eight hours to shoot one scene because the rain was so heavy. On another shoot a local fisherman took me out in a little boat, ostensibly for a beauty shot, but halfway across the bay the boat began to sink. So they brought me back in and tried again, and this time the oarlock broke. "Fuck it!" said Peter, and we abandoned the scene. On another occasion Eric House, a wonderful actor, flew in from Toronto to do this one big scene where somebody's home burns to the ground. I thought the scene looked great on film, but it still ended up on the cutting room floor.*

There's no denying we were a pretty rowdy crowd. One crew member got so drunk one night that his mates rowed him out to a little island opposite the Holiday Inn where we were staying in Corner Brook – the island was a little bird sanctuary of sorts – and when he woke up the next morning, he found himself on this little patch of dry land, surrounded by water and exceedingly cranky swans. So there were more than a few glasses being raised, by all of us, and more than a few pranks being played, on all of us.

Because we couldn't afford to fly in as many actors as we wanted, we had to rely on both the talents and the generosity of Newfoundlanders – and for me and Larry, part of the dream

* Film history aficionados say the house-burning sequence still exists, in a making-of documentary shot at the same time as they were shooting the film, called *Action, Cut and Print.*

came true. The guy who played the Constable was actually the head of the Newfoundland tourist bureau. Will Cole's sister was played by an old school friend of mine from Grand Falls. The local Kinsmen Club organized the picnic scene in the film, with booths, decorations, even a girl's school band. And when there wasn't enough of a crowd to shoot a crowd scene, we sent out an SOS on radio, and the residents poured out of their homes to help us. By the end of the shoot we had used almost one thousand local residents as extras in street scenes. And one of the crew, boom swinger Deryck Harnett, sat down and wrote the tune that became the signature song for the film, using one of Will Cole's favourite expressions, "It's a Lovely, Tell Your Mother Kind of Day."

By the time *The Rowdyman* was ready to be seen I had also completed the book version, and went on the road to promote it. In the pre-Internet seventies, going on the road meant flying from city to city to chat up every newspaper columnist and radio and/or TV talk show host who would have you, and at the time we believed that the only way to cope with the ongoing buzz in your ears from those seemingly interminable Air Canada flights was to inhale a few highballs per flight. However, as the combination of alcohol and altitude frequently produced unexpectedly high spirits, you often arrived far more cheerful on landing than you were on takeoff. We all drank hard liquor in those days, but never as much as we inhaled on those flights. Still, you had a job to do, promoting your series, promoting your book, whatever it was, and sometimes that's just what came with it.

Consequently I was very happy, and more than a bit cheerful, when my *Rowdyman* publicity tour took me back to Winnipeg, my old stomping ground and one of my favourite cities. By that time I had toured half the country, starting in Newfoundland, doing interviews and talk shows and telling anyone who would listen that there was a book coming out. In Winnipeg I went through the usual string of print interviews – the *Winnipeg Tribune*, still going then, and the *Winnipeg Free Press* – as well as a lot of television and radio interviews, selling my *Rowdyman* book.

The book itself was not exactly heavy-duty. As I recall it may have been seven or eight pages long – well, something like that, you get the idea. Not a huge tome. However, there I was, trying to sell the book and the movie, of course, at the same time. And by the time I got to Winnipeg, flying across the country from city to city – well, let's just say there was a fair amount of medicine being taken. By the time I got there, to a territory very well known to myself – my old haunt, really – I couldn't stand up some of the time. I remember doing one interview where I. Measured. Every. Word. And. Spoke. Just. Like. That. Almost slipping off the chair while I did it. Two questions later, I'd used up all the time they had allotted. Because I was in that state where you're not really fit for anything except maybe embalming.

As it turned out, I was staying at the Winnipeg Inn. Also staying at the Winnipeg Inn were Don Harron and Catherine McKinnon and Catherine's sister Patrician. I'd just checked in when I got a call from Don, who said he and Catherine and Trish were going out to see Sammy Davis Jr. Would I like to join them, as Trish's "date"?

Well, *sure* I would! I'd said Yes to everything since I was a boy. I wasn't about to stop now.

That day I went to see Irene's brother, my ex-brother-in-law Billy Reid, and we had a few drinks, and in the late afternoon I did a few more interviews, a couple in bars. By the time I got back to the hotel I wasn't really in the mood for much. I just made it down the hallway, and I remember that I fell flat on the bed, just as the phone rang, and I rolled over to the other side of the bed to answer it. That would be the sum total of my rest for the day.

"Yes, Don, of course, where are you? Oh, you're down in the lobby, waiting for me. You thought we'd have dinner first. Yes, of course, be right down."

I roll off the bed, and out the door, and down the hall, ricocheting off the walls, and just make it to the elevator, when the elevator doors open and two people step out, and one of them says, "Oh look, it's Gordon Pinsent!" – at which point I fall flat on my face right between the two of them. So now I'm getting pummelled by the elevator doors, which are trying to close, despite the fact that my prostrate form is blocking them. Finally I get inside, and down we go to the lobby, where the doors open wide again, and out I go, staggering forth, right into a large green fern the size of a small tree, crawling out the other side of it in full view of all the guests who are just signing in at the front desk.

Somehow I get to dinner, and somehow I get through dinner – "Yes, sounds lovely, I'll have that too!" – making small talk that makes absolutely no sense whatsoever. And after dinner we're crossing the lobby and don't you know that someone is handing out splits of champagne. "Look!" I say, "champagne splits!" So now I'm drinking champagne, on top of quite a lot of everything else. Then we go to see Sammy Davis Jr., and he comes out and starts to sing, and then he takes his very last final bow, and I realize that I have missed everything in between. And as we're leaving someone says that Sammy is now going to be singing on this boat that goes up and down the Red River, and that we are all invited.

We're now in Elmwood, where I had lived, and we're approaching the boat. And the captain has this huge mastiff dog, which he wears as part of his professional persona. Other people are already onboard, but we make it to the boat, and Patrician is wearing this gorgeous dress, and as soon as we step onboard, this mastiff, this huge dog, jumps up on her and knocks her to the ground. He's now on top of Trish, and of course I should be helping her. But in my present state I think this is the funniest thing I've ever seen. No question about it, I was born for these moments. The captain hauls the dog away and apologizes profusely, and the boat shoves off, and we go downstairs, below deck.

"It's awfully stuffy down here," says Trish. "I think I'll go back upstairs."

"Good idea!" say I, and follow her. She walks out on deck, in that gorgeous gown, looking like Kate Winslet in *Titanic* long before Kate Winslet was Kate Winslet, and she is looking out at the shores of Elmwood, where I had lived, and I say, "Oh look, there's –" and heave. And my hurl sails right past her, just catching the edge of her dress, and right over the railing of the ship. And to this day neither Don nor Catherine has ever mentioned it. Not once. All those years ago, and not once. Maybe they were so embarrassed for me they just want to pretend it never happened. And Trish, the poor darling! First the dog, and then me!

Never mind. With a little help from our friends – or to put it more accurately, with a *lot* of help from our friends – we tried to give the film a proper launch. If we'd made *The Rowdyman* in 1992 or even 1982, I'd probably be telling you how we had to fight to get a gala screening at the Toronto International Film Festival. But this was 1972, and the film festival was barely a glint in its founders' eyes. And since we had almost no budget for promotion, we needed to be as Creative as possible.

In one such burst of Creativity, Larry and I go to Boston, where more than two hundred thousand Newfoundlanders had gone before us, to launch the picture there. We have no money so we order little printed decals to stick on car windows: *The Rowdyman's Coming to Boston Looking for Trouble.*

Once we arrive we go to rent a couple of tuxedos for the evening show. When we get to the shop we are waited on by a very nice gentleman, a lovely man, and we try on a couple of tuxedos.

I study myself in the full-length mirror. "I don't know, Larry, what do you think?"

The salesman looks around, to make sure he can't be overheard.

"Take 'em! Take 'em!" he says. "I'm quitting here tonight."

Pardon?

"Oh yes!" he says. "I'm going to be working across the street tomorrow."

Larry and I are now running down the street with two tuxedos. Two broke Canadians, running down a street in Boston clutching free formal wear.

Couldn't wait to get back to the hotel.

That night we have bagpipers marching across the street to the movie house, we're all dressed up in our tuxedos, and the manager, who loves the movie, is telling people, "If you don't like this movie, I'll give you your money back!"

Unfortunately, we're not the only hot ticket in Boston tonight. The Red Sox are also in town, and our opening night fails miserably. And of course there's an opening-night party, and Larry and I are all decked out in black tie, and someone says, "Gordon, to commemorate the film coming to Boston, you should present something to the Mayor onstage."

"Sure," I say. "but what am I presenting?"

I get up onstage to greet the mayor, but it's not the mayor, because the mayor couldn't make it. He's probably watching the Red Sox. So I'm about to present whatever I'm going to present to the assistant mayor, or vice-mayor, or whatever he's called. And they hand me what I'm going to present. It is a lump.

Really. A *lump.*

"What is it?" I ask the organizer.

"It's a walrus, curled up sleeping."

"It is?"

Mustn't laugh.

Must *not* laugh out loud.

"Where are the tusks?"

"Oh, the tusks came loose, so we've taped them on underneath."

"Oh yeah," I reply half-heartedly, nodding my head. "That makes a difference, I guess."

The mayor's understudy comes on stage to get his lump, and I have never before or after seen such a funny look on a man's face. So *The Rowdyman* found trouble in Boston after all.

Months later I receive a phone call from a young woman who says she works for a formal wear shop in Boston and that the store owner wants his tuxedos back. Her voice sounds vaguely familiar but I can't place it, so I immediately call Larry, who confesses that he persuaded his current girlfriend to make the call to me. Back then, as now, Larry loved playing pranks. Especially funny ones. And especially on me.

The Rowdyman is invited to the reasonably prestigious Karlovy Vary International Film Festival in Czechoslovakia, which at this time is still one country and still firmly tucked away behind the Iron Curtain.

At Karlovy Vary, justifiably more celebrated for its spa than its cinema, there is one central meeting place, the theatre where the films are screened, which also has its own café, dining room, and bar. Each country has its own table, distinguished by the presence of a small replica of its own flag. My table is the size of a school desk, because I am the only one at it. I am particularly drawn to the East German delegation, who are followed everywhere by men in black. I join them for drinks and dinner, and we keep our voices low, because we know we are all being monitored.

The café is a bit of a throwback to black-and-white Hollywood melodramas of the fifties, with the East German delegation noisily holding court at their own table, which appears to be somewhat larger than the rest. The café itself features, among other things, a poorly dressed crooner whose sister walks around him dancing in fishnet stockings while he sings. At one point he sings a German song, playing up to the German table, until a delegate from Poland jumps to her feet and cries out, "Stop singing that! You're singing that just because there are Nazis in the room! You are Polish. Sing in Polish!"

Which is a bit shocking for the rest of us. But my new comrades assure me she is right about the Germans. One of them says he went on a tour of the area with them, and claims that they were pointing out places where they had shot Czechs and Poles during the war.

One night we stay until the café closes, which drives our minders crazy; they are very anxious to get us back to our hotel, so they can wash their hands of us. So we let them take us back to our hotel, and I quietly let it be known that I am hosting an open bar in my room. The East Germans aren't allowed to leave their rooms, but all our rooms are in a row. So they climb over the balcony railings, balcony by balcony, until they reach my room. They want to know all about Hollywood, and I tell them some of my Hollywood stories, and they are absolutely enchanted.

Before the screening of *The Rowdyman* I might as well be invisible. I am simply the foreign guy who seems to be part of the East German delegation. After the screening there is applause from all the tables, and suddenly I am a somebody. Of course I have no idea what my hosts actually think of my film, until one night an Oscar Holmoka–type at the bar introduces himself to me in halting English, saying something like "Me, jury." Suddenly I am face to face with a real live jury member. Before I can ask him anything, he volunteers: "Me, *Rowdyman*."

I am thrilled, of course, but surprised that a juror at the Karlovy Vary International Film Festival would declare himself to me before the final day.

"Well, thank you!" I say, as modestly as I can manage. "I'm glad you liked *The Rowdyman*."

Mr. Jury Member looks puzzled, and then consults with his interpreter, and then nods, finally grasping what I just said to him.

"No, no," he says, shaking his head. "No like *Rowdyman* movie!" He leans forward, just to be sure I understood. "Me, I *am* a rowdy man!"

Probably.

After I get back to America – which isn't a moment too soon for me – I write a script inspired by my adventures in Karlovy Vary. It is called *Melancholy Buns*, and I tuck it away somewhere for safekeeping.

Now it's so safe that even I can't find it.

When we premiere the movie in St. John's, we bring the house down. Literally. The roof falls in on the Paramount Theatre. Fortunately it happens overnight, when the cinema is empty. Structural weakness or some such thing. Happily, we manage to pull off our big opening night, with lineups that stretch all around the block, without inflicting any serious injuries.

When we premiere the movie in Ottawa, I am seated next to Pierre Elliott Trudeau. My seatmate, the Prime Minister of Canada, has already finished his bag of popcorn during the trailers. The lights dim, the screen flickers, the music starts, and hey, there we are, up on the big screen, upside down.

I find myself wondering if Peter Carter's heart is going to blow.

"It's upside down, sir," I tell Trudeau, hoping he will not conclude that I think him incapable of figuring that out all by himself. "I'm sure they're working on it."

Canadian film.

Government money.

What could be better?

The Rowdyman is a success.

Better than that, it's a bona fide hit. A mini-hit, yes, a Canadian hit, yes, but a hit nonetheless.

In his review in the *Los Angeles Times*, film critic Charles Champlin notes that "this rogue is part of an unfamiliar and beautifully observed setting. The environment helped make him, and the movie reveals them both." Champlin finds our whole ensemble, particularly Frank Converse and Linda Goranson, to be fresh, attractive, and notably gifted. He loves Will Geer's performance too, and displays impeccable taste, keen insight, and great wisdom by stating, quite unequivocally, that my performance is "excellent and charismatic."

God bless the *L.A. Times*.

Refreshed and renewed, I return to Hollywood. Everything will be different now. I may even get offered a serious film – maybe even a film that dares to take a fresh look at the lives of our beleaguered African-American neighbours. Something movie audiences have never seen before. A story with a clear, unmistakable moral.

Be careful what you wish for.

home to the hill

No sooner had we arrived back at our house in the Hollywood Hills – had we even unpacked our bags? – when the phone rang. My agent-du-jour was calling with an offer for a fairly substantial role in a new movie. And not just any movie. No, this would be a film that dared to take a fresh look at the lives of our beleaguered African-American neighbours. Something movie audiences had never seen before. A story with a clear, unmistakable moral.

The story, what there was of it, was about an African prince who gets bitten by a nobleman from Transylvania – yes, *that* nobleman – and then gets locked in a coffin for two hundred years until two L.A. antique dealers buy the coffin and open it, thereby unleashing Blacula – yes, *Blacula* – on the City of Angels.

Not quite the serious drama I had in mind. I suppose you could call it a period piece, in as much as they never should have made it, period. But somebody had to play the police lieutenant, and after *The Rowdyman* my bank account definitely needed a transfusion.

I said Yes.

As sorry as I was feeling for myself I felt even worse for William Marshall, Vonetta McGee, and Denise Nicholas (Charm's cast-mate in *Room 222*), because they were the leads, and they had to carry the movie. A year later the Academy of Science Fiction, Fantasy & Horror Films in the U.S. gave *Blacula* their Golden Scroll Award for Best Horror Film of the Year, but none of us rushed to include it on our resumés.

What a comedown – not to mention a letdown – after shooting *Rowdyman* on a mere fraction of the budget they were spending on this piece of crap. *Never mind*, I told myself, *no one you know is ever going to see this*. And to this day, by and large, that's still true.

There were more letdowns waiting in the wings – a series of disappointments that could only serve to feed my growing discontent. I started writing again – this time a play about a Newfoundland couple who are forced to move off the land they love when the mine shuts down. The more I wrote, the less like a play it seemed. No, I thought, *this is not a play, and it's certainly not a movie. It must be a novel.* So I tore it up and started all over again.

Charm could see how restless I was, and she understood it, not only because she knew me better than I knew myself but also because she was getting restless herself. Her friend Kate now had her first hit movie, *The Andromeda Strain*, for *Sound of Music* director Robert Wise, and was in London shooting the screen version of Edward Albee's *A Delicate Balance* with Katharine Hepburn and Paul Scofield. Her friend Barbara had just wrapped a six-part mini-series, *Anne of Green Gables*, and the writers were already dreaming up new scenes for her in a sequel to be set in a picturesque Atlantic town called Avonlea. When Charm was asked to join Rock Hudson and Susan Saint James on an episode of *McMillan & Wife*, she was relieved and delighted to do so.

Rock Hudson was a widescreen action hero who had learned his craft on the job, and surprised everyone, including himself, by becoming the best romantic comedy actor since Cary Grant. When Hollywood started to lose interest in him, Hudson had turned to television, where he and the gifted Ms. Saint James could give each episode the playful light touch it needed, and where he was instantly a top draw.

Similarly, George Peppard had turned to television after a promising film career stalled and fizzled. Vincente Minnelli had introduced Peppard to moviegoers in a 1960 potboiler called *Home from the Hill*, and Peppard had followed up with a string of hits (*Breakfast at Tiffany's*, *How the West Was Won*, *The Victors*, *The Carpetbaggers*). For whatever reason, he consequently chose a series of action roles that made few demands on him creatively, and after a string of B-movies and a sudden dearth of offers, he discovered that television audiences were less picky about plot and character development. I first met him when I did a guest shot on his sporadic dramatic series, *Banacek*, in which he played a Polish-American detective. Between takes George sat on a tall director's perch, made of leather, not canvas, literally looking down on us, the rest of his cast, as we sat in the standard folding chairs. Some actors found this somewhat off-putting; I found it funny, and tried not to crack up every time we had to sit down at the same time. I don't think his two *Banacek* sidekicks, Ralph Manza and

Murray Matheson, found it quite as amusing as I did, but George seemed to think it was funny too. George was still drinking then, still smoking two packs a day, and yet, with the help of five devoted wives – he had just been divorced by second wife Elizabeth Ashley – he would in time conquer his alcoholism and keep himself and his career going for another two decades.*

Keeping a career going, for any actor, is no small accomplishment. On a film called *Incident on a Dark Street*, Bill Shatner was billed fifth, Gilbert Roland was billed seventh, John Kerr was billed eleventh, and I was way down at the bottom of the list – twenty-ninth, or something like that. I played the mayor, a glorified bit part, and as usual I found my cast-mates far more interesting than the script. I was fascinated to see Gilbert Roland in the flesh. He had started making movies in the twenties – he was about sixty-five now, still full of energy, with no intention of retiring. His film credits were dazzling, from playing The Cisco Kid to major roles in major movies like *The Bad and the Beautiful*. He'd worked with all the greats, from John Huston to John Ford, and had seduced more than a few of his leading ladies. Even now, he was still seducing the camera, and would continue to do so for another decade or more.

The real shock for me was seeing John Kerr so far down on the totem pole. *Eleventh* billing? How could that be? Twenty years earlier he had co-starred with Deborah Kerr (no relation) on Broadway in Maxwell Anderson's *Tea and Sympathy*. Directed by Elia Kazan, he had won the Tony Award for Best Actor, and then reprised his role onscreen for director Vincente Minnelli.

* George Peppard died of lung cancer in May 1994.

Two years later he was on movie screens all over the world as Lieutenant Joe Cable in the screen version of Rodgers & Hammerstein's *South Pacific*. But despite those blazing big-screen moments he supported himself mainly by acting on television, at first at such auspicious addresses as the Hallmark Hall of Fame and Playhouse 90, and then by doing guest shots on the high-ratings TV series of the day – *Gunsmoke*, *The Virginian*, *Wagon Train*. He did them all, from *Alfred Hitchcock Presents* to *Peyton Place*. Even while we were shooting this TV movie for director Buzz Kulik,* Kerr had already started to play recurring characters in two of the top drama series of the day, *Police Story* and *The Streets of San Francisco*. He was interested in directing, too, and was apprenticing with Leo Penn. From what I could see John Kerr loved acting, especially in courtroom dramas, and he loved being on camera. Perhaps he too was addicted to saying Yes, and like me, determined to make the most of whatever opportunity came his way. In his so-called spare time he had graduated from UCLA Law School and was now a bona fide Beverly Hills lawyer, and although he couldn't always commit to new film projects, he seemed to enjoy living in both worlds. .

I could relate to that, in some manner, because I felt that I was also living in two worlds, with one foot dragging me through Hollywood and one foot somewhat insecurely planted in Toronto. But I happily put both feet on an Air Canada

* Buzz Kulik had just come off a monster TV movie hit, *Brian's Song* with James Caan and Billy Dee Williams, and would soon direct Susan Clark in *Babe: The Babe Didrikson Zaharias Story*.

plane when the Canadian Film Awards were announced. *The Rowdyman* lost the Best Picture statuette to a dark little film by Bill Fruet called *Wedding in White*, which featured Donald Pleasence and a frighteningly shy performance by a nineteen-year-old slip of an American actress named Carol Kane. Best Actress went to Micheline Lanctôt for her stunning work in Gilles Carle's wonderful *La vrai nature de Bernadette*. And Best Actor went to Porky for *The Rowdyman*. Needless to say I was delighted, and then delighted all over again when I was asked to host the second-ever ACTRA Awards.

Over the years I had discovered that I enjoyed hosting on camera. The first time I had ever hosted anything was before I left Winnipeg – a CBC musical show called *Music for a Quarter*. Why? Because it was fifteen minutes long. (I spoke faster then!) A lot of networks were running live-to-air fifteen-minute music shows back then. Eddie Fisher did one twice a week sponsored by Coca-Cola, *Coke Time with Eddie Fisher*. Dinah Shore did one too, before she took over Sunday night on NBC. Bands on fifteen-minute music shows were comprised of some of the best musicians on the planet; Lenny Breau was one of ours, and you couldn't get a better musician than Lenny.

In all, I hosted the ACTRA Awards about three times, I think, once with elegant trailblazer and renowned broadcaster Barbara Frum. I hosted the Genie Awards too, once in white tie and white tux, leaning on a white piano, singing something I can't quite recall, and once with Dawn Greenhalgh and Ted Follows's daughter Megan, still known all over the world as the quintessential Anne of Green Gables. On that one I finger-synched rocking out on an electric guitar. We assumed everybody would know it was a gag, until one Calgary reviewer commented, "You think he can act? Just wait 'til you hear him on electric guitar!" So maybe I was just a little too convincing.

Back in 1973 the offer to host the ACTRAs was a welcome respite from the B-movie life I felt I was living in Hollywood. The awards had started quite modestly one year earlier, and sculptor Bill McElcheran had created the corpulently voluptuous statuette who had been nicknamed Nellie, possibly after Nellie McClung. (Most of us always thought it looked more like Barbara Ham. Including Barbara Ham.) I sang a song I had written, "Children of the Thirties," and had a bit of fun with Kate Reid and Pierre Berton. Pierre was nominated that night, and Kate, notorious for her offstage binges, was conspicuously absent, having begged off with the flu.

"One of our leading ladies couldn't be here tonight," I said, "because she has the flu. As a matter of fact I understand she had several gallons of flu last week." Which drew nervous titters and appreciative guffaws. And then, looking around the room: "My God! Just look at this crowd! There's more wall-to-wall talent in this room . . . and more tinsel . . . and more glamour . . . and more ego . . . than when Pierre Berton dines alone!"

A 1972 ACTRA winner himself, Pierre couldn't wait to corner me as I came offstage.

"Who did you get that line from?" he demanded.

"Made it up on the spot," I lied.

"You got that from somewhere!" he insisted. "I know where you got it from, and one of these days I'll remember it!"

All in all I had a very good time, and so did my peers, which made it somewhat easier, and somewhat harder, to return to

Hollywood. But return I did, to Charm and Leah and the house off Mulholland Drive, and a stint on another weekly cop show, *Cannon*, which turned out to be memorable for all the wrong reasons.

William Conrad had played Matt Dillon in *Gunsmoke* on radio, and he played more than one hundred "heavies" on television before he actually got the lead in his own television series. And there he was now, bored to tears – he'd already done maybe thirty episodes of *Cannon* by the time I did one – and I could hear him approaching, grumbling. I was playing the villain again, and I was married to Susan Oliver, and the two of us were in this trailer travelling across the United States. And I could hear him coming – this was day one – barking at the first A.D.: "Okay, what's this episode called? Which one is this?" There was no sense of, Hey, this is *important*, we've got to get this *right*. From what I was observing he had already tired of the show, and didn't want to be doing it. But of course he didn't want anybody else doing it.

"Well, obviously I haven't read it," he told the first A.D., "so you'd better get out the cards." And he played all our scenes together looking over my shoulder to the cue cards the A.D. was holding up behind me.

At one point he said, "Do you know George McCowan?"

"Yes, I do."

"He's a queer one, isn't he . . . a strange one!"

"I like George McCowan," I said. "He's one of my favourite people."

"Is he!" he said. "He could be brilliant, you know."

"Yes, I know," I said.

That was the kind of conversation you would have with Conrad. He seemed to like making you squirm. We had this fight scene, between two cars, and he said, "I don't want a stunt-man, do you?" I said, "Nah!" And he pinned me up against this Cadillac, the one with the wings, and I had to go to the nurses' station before the end of the day.

He was one of those people, like certain other people in our business, who learned just enough about it all to get what they wanted – and they knew what they wanted. Just wanted a pay-cheque and a few other perks. I wanted a paycheque too, but not at that cost. If you're in a series, and you're bored to tears, you still aren't doing anything else, because there isn't time to do anything else – no time to read a book, to think about a scene, to think about how you might play it differently, to think about the different shades you could bring to it. You just get up the next day and do it all over again.

You can't have it all. If you're in a hit series – and who doesn't want to be in a hit series? – you're picked up every morning at five and brought back home every night at seven, and if you're in a hit you could be doing this for six or seven years, and you have no time to learn about the world. And you get so bored with it. And that apathy is absolutely killing after a while. Even when I was doing *Quentin Durgens* and, later, *A Gift to Last*, there should have been enough there to keep me interested. And there was, and I was. But I couldn't help thinking that there could be other wonderful things waiting for me, and that I was losing time. And I was starting to come into more significant birthdays, because I wasn't a kid anymore. A few years ago I told Leah, "I'm so glad you didn't end up in a series like *Charlie's Angels*. Because you would have had no time to learn what you know now."

Remember Robert Young? I had grown up watching him on the big screen and the small screen, when we still believed the lie that *Father Knows Best*. What I didn't know, what none of us knew, was that his acute anxiety fuelled his days and nights, and he was still engaged in his thirty-year battle with the bottle when I played a "guest doctor" on his hit series *Marcus Welby, M.D.* As one of Hollywood's leading men he had romanced Claudette Colbert, Joan Crawford, Katharine Hepburn, and Loretta Young on the silver screen, but was painfully shy in real life. His shyness had propelled him from social drinker to alcoholic in his MGM years, and despite all his later success with *Father Knows Best*, first on radio and then on television, his raging insecurity required that crutch to get him through the day.

It wasn't for lack of trying. He had initiated a ritual at the start of every day on the set of *Marcus Welby* where cast and crew would join hands for a minute of silent prayer or meditation, and I later learned that he often held AA meetings in his home. He would be in his seventies before he managed to stop drinking once and for all, and despite being beset by Alzheimer's and heart problems, he would live to ninety-one.

A lot of actors I have appreciated have gone to the funerals of their livers long before their time; not having, to a large part, fairly lived up to the promising quality of their organs. Perhaps I should have been disturbed to discover that so many of the silver screen heroes of my youth had feet of clay, but instead I felt a surprising sense of relief. I wasn't the only one with anxieties. I wasn't the only one drinking Scotch in the middle of the day. And then I realized that staying any longer would be the fastest way to the graveyard for me as a creative individual. A fair-to-good actor in Hollywood, trying to get established, will be only too happy to get himself a long-running series. It's better than driving a truck or digging a ditch. But I felt I was being taken over – quite easily, in fact. And I was growing more restless and more impatient.

My pal Perry Rosemond had come to Hollywood before us and would stay longer. We spent a fair bit of time in Los Angeles together. "Gordon," Perry would say, "we are strangers in a strange land. In Canada you can act, write, direct, produce. In America, if you do fenders, you don't do hubcaps."

I made up my mind that I was just not "right" for Hollywood, not in the usual sense. Yes, with the vast numbers of shows being done, I would fit somewhere, but I was not a "natural," I was not Rock Hudson, I was a character actor with a leading man's face, with the good stuff underneath the makeup.

I've always felt that. You can go through four lifetimes in Los Angeles and never get the best material, never get the opportunities you seek. So if things go funny you've got to remember who you are, so that when you leave the house you take *you* with you. You don't leave *you* behind. You don't go out in the world to impersonate. We've got impersonators. We don't need any more.

What you do need to do is be yourself. Because that may be the richest thing you have, and that may be the thing that they are looking for as well. Or not. But in the meantime, the clock is ticking. Because you use up a lot of time there. I wasn't in line for the good material, unless I happened to luck out. The bigger stars were coming from the movies and going into television. So the things that came around were not really my idea of where I wanted to go. And that could have gone on forever. I remember the health club in Encino, all these aging actors with old faces and young bodies, all waiting for the phone to ring. I took a lesson from that, too.

I had sent my novel to McGraw-Hill in Toronto, who agreed to publish it. Two years earlier, when I had needed to generate work for myself, I'd sat down and wrote *The Rowdyman*. Now I needed to get moving again. Now I needed to start writing again. And finally it came down to where I wanted to work – and Hollywood wasn't it.

My novel was published. It was called *John and the Missus*, and after it came out, I read it again and shook my head.

"What's wrong now?" asked Charm, with the patience of a saint.

"I think I was mistaken. I think it will work better as a play," I replied somewhat tentatively.

"Then write it as a play," she said with a shrug.

We sold the house in the Hollywood Hills to Perry, who inherited what absolutely everyone, including Marlon Brando, said was the best view of the San Fernando Valley they'd ever seen. Perry was happy, and so were we.

We had been there almost six years.

We packed our bags and headed home.

comeback

———◆———

Returning to Toronto I couldn't wait to tell every producer, director, and casting agent I knew (or had even heard of) that I was back in town and raring to go.

One of the first jobs I landed was hosting a weekly drama series, *The Play's the Thing*, on CBC Television. Next came a National Film Board movie shoot in Montreal. In *The Heatwave Lasted Four Days*, I played a TV news cameraman who accidentally photographs an escaped convict, played by Larry. It was fun to do – imagine, having fun making a movie. I'd almost forgotten it was possible – and Alexandra Stewart and Domini Blythe played the brainy female eye candy, and gorgeous eye candy they were. Much to Larry's chagrin, Alexandra Stewart was preoccupied, and Domini Blythe was seriously involved with another actor, the charismatic Richard Monette. "Two beautiful girls, and neither one of them on the market," Larry sighed. "What a bummer!"

In Hollywood George Peppard was about to shoot *Newman's Law*, a movie about a cop who uncovers an international drug ring involving some high-ranking police officers. My phone rang again, and I added one more Hollywood film credit to my bio. And best of all, when I was wrapped I got to come home to Toronto and work on a musical version of *The Rowdyman* for the Charlottetown Festival, which was hoping to come up with another monster hit besides *Anne of Green Gables*. Could a musical *Rowdyman* be the answer? We'd soon see.

Herb Roland was producing a weekly soap opera for CBC called *House of Pride* and asked Charm to play Mary Kirby, one of the key recurring characters. Bud Knapp and Cec Linder were already cast as Pride family scions, and now that Leah was safely enrolled in the Bishop Strachan School, a fairly rigorous private school for girls in Toronto – the same one her mother had attended – Charm felt free to do it.

"I wonder if Cec will wear his suit," Charm mused. Cec Linder had been given the stylish suit he'd worn in *Goldfinger* and had cleverly recycled it, donning it for at least a dozen onscreen performances since then. "I don't know," I said, "but I won't be wearing mine!"

I was about to play my first priest, in a TV movie called *Only God Knows*. Paul Hecht was the rabbi, and John Beck was the minister, and we were stealing from the Mafia to keep a young people's home going. Mia Farrow's sister Tisa was in it too. And Larry, who also produced it. At the time it seemed like a natural for a TV series spin off, but it didn't happen. Still, it gave me a taste for playing a man of the cloth, one that I would tuck away and use thirty years later as Father Fitzpatrick in *Saint Ralph*.

After *Only God Knows* I was offered a great part, playing Phillip Stockton in *Horse Latitudes*. Of course I said Yes. Stockton was an egocentric yachtsman determined to sail in a non-stop race around the world who realized he couldn't win and decided to fake the race. But between his own feelings of guilt and his fear of getting caught, he ended up hallucinating himself into his own private hell. So it was a great part, but *Horse Latitudes* was hard to make, because I had also taken over from Brian Bedford at Stratford in a show called *Trumpets and Drums*. So I was doing that at night and shooting *Horse Latitudes* on Lake Ontario in the morning, which was very tricky in a trimaran. A trimaran is easier to work on if the water is rough, because it can be quite unstable in smooth water. But we got it done, and it was a fascinating study of a man so desperate to be noticed that he eventually sailed himself into madness and suicide. At one point, when I saw the quality of work that the young director Peter Rowe was getting, I asked him to consider shooting an additional fifteen or twenty minutes so it could qualify as a feature film. But it never happened.

The musical version of *The Rowdyman* opened at Charlottetown. I had written the book and the lyrics; musical wunderkind Cliff Jones had taken over composing chores from Charlottetown contributor David Warrack. It was all very pleasant but decidedly lightweight, and I realized quite quickly that I should have devoted far more time to it than I did. I had worked diligently on it, but at a time when I clearly had too much on my plate, none of which I was prepared to give up. The end result was a lacklustre event for both the Charlottetown Festival and me. Another lesson learned the hard way. Maybe one day I would be able to learn things the easy way, whatever that was. But that day was probably still a long way off.

Donnelly Rhodes, one of our original Winnipeg gang at the MTC, was doing a weekly series with Jonathan Welsh called *Sidestreet*, so I was happy to do a guest shot. Donnelly and I also ended up in the same movie, a thing called *Drága kisfiam*. In English it was called *His Mother*, and it was based on a *New Yorker* short story by Mavis Gallant, and it was my first "Euro-pudding." That's what they called them, back in the day – co-productions with international co-producers who could access tax benefits and local production funds. *Drága kisfiam* was a Canadian-Hungarian co-production, a movie for television with most of the funds coming out of Hungary. Donnelly shot all his scenes in Canada; I shot all my scenes in Budapest. I played a Hungarian, and Iréna Mayeska played my Canadian wife. Hungary was still state-run, and we were paid in their currency, forints, of which there seemed to be an endless supply. Only catch was, they had to be spent before leaving the country. Which was a pretty big catch. Oh well. Another day, another *forint*.

I loved acting, and it was still my first priority, but by now writing was a passion for me, superseding sketching and painting and almost any other creative endeavour. I decided to write a Christmas special, set at the turn of the nineteenth century, called *A Gift to Last*. The story was told by Clement Sturgess, an elderly man who looked back on his childhood Christmases with especially fond memories of the family hero, his uncle, the colourful and irresponsible Sergeant Edgar Sturgess of the Royal Canadian Regiment. CBC liked it and liked the idea of me playing Edgar. I had actually fashioned it for Douglas Campbell, but Herb Roland, our producer, insisted.

Before we started shooting *A Gift to Last* I decided to give my novel one more shot, this time as a two-act stage play. *John and the Missus* had its world premiere at the Neptune Theatre in Halifax and was warmly (read, kindly) received. I'd written great parts for all the actors, of course, including and especially me. For me that's what it was all about. But it was clear to me that as a play *John and the Missus* still needed work.

Back in Toronto I proposed a bit of offbeat casting for *A Gift to Last*. I liked the idea of enlisting Melvyn Douglas, whom I'd worked with when I first came to Toronto, to play the family patriarch Clement Sturgess. My old ally, producer Herb Roland, helped make it happen, and Douglas showed up for work like a pro. Like the rest of us, he was now ten years older, but still a wonderful actor, and I loved working with him again. But the unsung heroes of the show were the people behind the scenes, literally. I loved the crews, the crafts-men of the CBC – they were proud of their work, and they should have been. They did wonderful work. They were remarkable. And they were so attuned to the material, which made them even more terrific.

When December rolled around, *A Gift to Last* stood out from all the other Christmas specials. It was a big hit – so big that CBC asked me to spin it off into a weekly dra-matic series.

I said Yes.

I started working on the scripts with Peter Wildeblood, who had come over from *Upstairs, Downstairs* as head editor and ended up writing a couple of episodes. Peter was a man whose colourful past made him an astute observer of human behaviour,* and in the next twenty-one episodes we would trace the family's history (and in doing so, our own) in small-town southern Ontario from 1899 to 1905.

Meanwhile, it soon became apparent that some viewers saw Edgar, the character I played, as the father figure they'd always longed for. One of them, watching from the other side of the country, was my daughter Beverly. Beverly was particularly smitten with my handlebar moustache. My first wife, Irene, had remarried, and Beverly and my son, Barry, were living in Vancouver with their mother and their stepfather. But I didn't know that then.

I was writing too, but between drafts of episodes I managed to sneak in a few guest spots on Bruno Gerussi's popular series *The Beachcombers* and even did a turn in Allan King's screen version of W. O. Mitchell's *Who Has Seen the Wind*. It was Allan's first feature film, and Charm did a bit in it too. I played Gerald O'Connal, Charm played Mrs. Abercrombie, and we were part of a strong ensemble cast, including Patricia Hamilton, Chapelle Jaffe, Helen Shaver, Cedric Smith, Gerard Parkes, and José Ferrer.

Mitchell was a wildly eccentric guy. When he came to dinner he brought his own spittoon. He was always chewing

* Peter Wildeblood was a British-Canadian journalist, novelist, play-wright, and gay rights activist before that term was coined. He was one of the first men in the U.K. to publicly declare his homosexuality and was imprisoned for it. In 1955 he published *Against the Law*, a significant account that detailed his experiences, brought to light the appalling conditions in British prisons, and campaigned for prison reform and acceptance of homosexuals in society.

and spitting and chewing and spitting. He was, without a doubt, memorable. I was hosting the ACTRA Awards when the picture was nominated, and Bill Mitchell was in the audience, of course, and I said, "Let's go out behind the shed and play W. O. Mitchell." I wish I could tell you that he had roared with laughter, but he was not amused.

Who Has Seen the Wind was a seminal book and in some ways a seminal film, but that title was too much fun to resist. Because Mitchell's work was still such a part of our *zeitgeist*, Second City got a lot of attention ten years later when they called one of their shows *Bob Has Seen the Wind*.

The Christmas special *A Gift to Last* had inspired viewers to write letters, and a lot of fan mail was coming in. CBC would send the letters to us, so Charm and I could go through them. One said something like, *My mother said I could look you up one day*. I passed it over to Charm. I didn't think anything of it.

Charm was far more astute. "Guess what?" she said, handing back the letter I'd already read. "That's your daughter."

My mother said that when I was old enough I could write to you and perhaps meet you. I am twenty-seven now. I have thought of you so often and can't wait for the opportunity for us to get together. If this is impossible, please tell me, and I won't pursue it further. If nothing happens, I will at least be satisfied I have been in touch and opened the door a little at least in our getting to know each other again.

I answered the letter, and a few months later Beverly knocked on my door – I was staying in a hotel in Vancouver – and there was this girl with this terrific face, this sweetness, whom I hadn't seen in eighteen years. A new beginning. A second chance. A silent vow to do better by her this time.

Much as you'd expect, Charm and I were concerned about Leah's reaction to finding out she had a sister. We needn't have worried. When she was little Leah used to call herself "a lonely child," and Charm would gently correct her.

"No, Leah," she would tell her, "you're an *only* child."

"No, Mom, I'm a *lonely* child," Leah would insist, because she had always wanted brothers and sisters. And suddenly, at long last, she had one.

The first season of *A Gift to Last* was warmly received by viewers even when we killed off Harrison Sturgess, played by Alan Scarfe, in the first episode. His survivors included his wife Clara, played by Janet Amos, their children Clement and Jane, played by Mark Polley and Kate Parr, his mother Lizzy, portrayed by Ruth Springford, and his brothers, the meek and conservative James, played by Gerard Parkes, and the rowdy, high-spirited Edgar, played with unabashed enthusiasm, relish, and delight by yours truly. The central episode of the series, which won an ACTRA award as Best Television Program of the year, was the one in which Edgar finally married Sheila, the Sturgesses' maid, who was wonderfully well played by Dixie Seatle.

By the final season, the now-married Edgar was serving in the militia, and Clara, suffering ill health, succumbed to consumption. Why did poor Clara have to die of consumption? So Janet Amos could be written out of the script for eight episodes while she toured the U.K. with Theatre Passe Muraille. We were, all of us, first and foremost creatures of the theatre. While I was toiling on set on *A Gift to Last*, Charm was originating the role of the indomitable actress Jessica Logan in David French's madcap comedy *Jitters*, first onstage in Toronto at the Tarragon Theatre, and then in New Haven at the Long Wharf. She was spectacularly good in it, and she knew it. And I was itching to get back on stage again.

On hiatus from shooting *A Gift to Last*, I slipped back into cleric's garb again, doing a bit in a CBC Newfoundland project called *Up at Ours*. I call it a Newfoundland project because that's what it was – a project designed to stimulate and showcase some of the considerable talents on the Rock. A twelve-episode dramedy series about the disparate residents of a Newfoundland boarding house, it was produced in St. John's and directed by Newfoundlanders, with scripts from such noted Atlantic writers as Walter Learning, Michael Cook, Alden Nowlan, and me. Mary Walsh played the owner of the boarding house, Ray Guy played her long-standing lodger, Janis Spence played the lady who lived next door, and Kevin Noble played a myopic taxi driver. In my episode I played a parish priest who found his faith tested, then reconfirmed, by his encounter with two young women.

The second and final season of *A Gift to Last* was a bit of a stumbling block for everyone but me. In addition to its high ratings at home, the series had been sold by the CBC to television stations in the States and to networks in Belgium, Australia, Ireland, and South Africa. In South Africa we were more popular than *Dynasty*.

(Sorry, I had to say that!)

(Sorry for saying sorry.)

Little did I know that the pilot Christmas episode of the

series would soon be adapted for the stage by Walter Learning and Alden Nowlan. As it turned out, *A Gift to Last: The Musical* was destined to become a perennial Canadian Christmas favourite in regional theatres across the country, including the Gryphon Theatre in Barrie, the Persephone Theatre in Saskatoon, the Neptune Theatre in Halifax, and the National Arts Centre in Ottawa. Thirty years later the show would still be playing to Christmas audiences – but all that was yet to happen. In my present-tense meanwhile, it had taken two seasons to tell the story I wanted to tell, and to get the series established. And then the story was told, and as far as I was concerned, it was time to end it.

I may have been quite popular with the viewers, but I wasn't very popular with some actors, especially when they realized I had pulled the plug on the series. I remember going to a party at Herb Roland's house and Dawn Greenhalgh was there, and she said, almost spitting out the words, "Gordon! What have you done?" And she wasn't even in the series. But people like Ruth Springford, and a lot of the actors I had cast, were very unhappy about the decision to end the series, and Peter Wildeblood was just as shocked as the others.

"Gordon, it's a hit show!" he protested. "We must continue! That's what you do with a hit show!" But I had so many other things I wanted to explore and needed to try. Our final episode of *A Gift to Last* was telecast on a Sunday night in December 1979, and a few days later I looked up from my typewriter at the calendar and the seventies were over.

Did I mind? Not one little bit.

Looking back now, I think I was just getting warmed up.

let us now praise famous men

———◆———

WHEN YOU KICK-START YOUR SCREEN CAREER BY
playing fictionalized versions of Canadian MPs and American
presidents, or characters who at first only exist in the minds of
novelists and screenwriters, playing real-life, flawed, flesh-
and-blood civilians like bogus sailor Phillip Stockton is an
irresistible challenge to an actor. Over the years, between
guest appearances on almost every dramatic series shooting on
a sound stage or location near you, I was lucky enough to play
a lot of them. First up? Bill Gates.

No, not that one.

Rowdyman director Peter Carter was whipping a mélange of
Jack London stories into a feature film called *Klondike Fever*,
with young Jeff East playing Jack London. Surrounding the
innocent lad onscreen were all the characters London had
described so vividly – Rod Steiger as legendary scoundrel
Soapy Smith, Angie Dickinson as saloon siren Belinda McNair,
Lorne Greene as Sam Steele of the Northwest Mounted Police,
Lisa Langlois as Diamond Tooth Gertie, Barry Morse as out-
doorsman John Thornton, and yours truly as Swiftwater Bill
Gates, known simply as Swiftwater Bill. Given his personal

background and his penchant for research, Canada's most entertaining historian Pierre Berton knew a lot more about Swiftwater Bill than I did and documented some of his antics in his book *Klondike*. Suffice it to say that Bill was a rogue, albeit a lovable one, and we had a good time making the picture. Ron Steiger's character, Soapy Smith, was an American gangster, an ex-priest who was perhaps the most famous confidence man of his times. He was credited with organizing organized crime in Colorado and Alaska. Rod was having a lot of fun playing him. Not that he was even the slightest bit like him, of course!

We shot the movie up in Revelstoke, and whenever we got to a new location Rod Steiger would tell the producer that he and I needed a two-hour lunch, so he could try out the local restaurants. We went to this one place, still in costume, and he was standing in front, to negotiate the best table, and I was standing behind him, in my Swiftwater Bill wardrobe.

"Hello, my dear!" Ron said to the young lady who greeted us. "We're here for lunch."

"Oh, I'm sorry, we don't serve lunch!" she said with a sad little smile. And then she happened to see Swiftwater Bill standing behind him.

"Ooooh!" she cried, "*Gordon Pinsent!* What are *you* doing in town?"

Steiger didn't move a muscle.

"Ooooh!" she cried again. "Oh I think we can serve *you* lunch!"

And then she took us in and sat us down, and Steiger kept staring at me with those eyes of his. Years before he had been introduced to me by Norman Jewison, but he didn't really know me, except as this guy who was working on this movie with him. At which point another woman from the kitchen came out and said, "Oh my God, it *is* you!"

I looked at Rod's face, which was about to ignite.

"Yes, and *Rod. Steiger.* is here too!" I said.

"Oh!" She smiled politely. "Hello, Ron!"

"Pinsent," said Steiger, "this is the last fucking time I'm buying you lunch. The next one is on you. And I want two bottles of Pommard to go!"

We were all housed in the same motel, and Rod couldn't resist sharing his impression of Lorne Greene with us, usually whenever Lorne was within earshot. Trouble was, Rod did him rather well. "Here. Comes. *Mister. Bonanza!*" he would proclaim, prompting gales of laughter. Lorne did not appear to be as amused as the rest of us.

I loved working with Angie Dickinson on *Klondike Fever*, and I suspected the feeling was mutual. But I knew it was when she told me about her next project, a TV movie about a woman whose husband, a college professor, kills himself, leaving her with guilt, shame, and an angry teenaged son.

"Gordon," she added pointedly, "you've got to do this film with me."

I said Yes, of course!

Back in Toronto, while waiting for Angie's film to happen, I jumped at a chance to direct Charm in *Once*, a TV drama about an older woman who has an affair with a younger man. I needed to find some subtle way to let the audience know that when they made love the young man was giving her a level of sexual pleasure she had never before experienced. Happily, I found it. In the bedroom scenes I worked with the lighting director to bring the lights up and down, with increasing rhythm, to convey moment-to-moment orgasm. It worked, thanks to CBC technical expertise and Charm. Making *Once* work inspired me to take on another directing assignment, this time for the prestigious CBC series *For the Record*, guiding Richard Monette and Mary Ann McDonald through a ninety-minute drama called *A Far Cry from Home* with Louis Del Grande and Gerry Salsberg. Monette played a middle-class businessman who was battering his wife, a gym teacher who couldn't seem to see herself as anything but a victim, played by McDonald. It was a taboo topic at the time, not one that was widely discussed, but the show was a big hit when it aired, drawing 1.5 million viewers and an 81 percent EI (Enjoyment Index). So we must have done something right.

It was time for me to go back to being on camera. The day I showed up for work on Angie Dickinson's movie I sent word to her that I had arrived, and when she heard I was on set she flung open her trailer dressing room door, opened her arms in a big embrace, and purred, *"Swifty!"* – which delighted me and probably mystified everyone else. And although we shot it after we wrapped the Jack London movie, *The Suicide's Wife* aired before *Klondike Fever* opened, creating a kind of reverse reunion for us onscreen.

In 1980 the forty-year-old Canadian Film Awards were remounted as the Genie Awards, and *Klondike Fever* went on to earn nine nominations, including nods for Best Picture and Best Director. So Peter Carter had certainly earned his stripes on that one. (As it turned out, the Best Picture award went to *The Changeling*, and Best Director went to Bob Clark for

Murder by Decree. The only prize given to *Klondike Fever* was the Genie for Best Actor in a Supporting Role, and I was pleased and happy to accept it.)

Playing a Canadian ambassador wasn't a very exciting prospect – unless the ambassador was Ken Taylor. Previously faceless to the public, Ambassador Taylor became a national hero after he and his crack Canadian Embassy staff in Teheran hid half a dozen American embassy staffers during the Iranian hostage crisis. Risking his life, he cleverly smuggled the same Americans out of Iran safely, in full view of the internal Iranian security forces. *Escape from Iran: The Canadian Caper* had a stellar supporting cast, including Bob Joy, Jimmy Douglas, Julie Khaner, Carl Marotte, and R.H. Thomson, and Ambassador Taylor seemed to get a kick out of seeing a pivotal moment in his life on the screen. He told me that one time in Ottawa a woman in an elevator told him, "You look just like that actor!" And whenever we would bump into each other after that he would always make some reference to it. "Gordon, are you still getting my calls?" he would tease. "Because I'm still getting yours!"

Back on Air Canada, back to L.A., this time to take a meeting with Shirley MacLaine. We met for dinner at Wolfgang Puck's newest Hollywood oasis, Spago, just off Sunset Boulevard. An outspoken and independent woman herself, Shirley was fascinated by the story of another female maverick, Betsy Bigley, a notorious turn-of-the-century Canadian con woman who had relieved a string of amorous millionaires of their fortunes. Shirley's mother hailed from Nova Scotia, and Shirley liked to say that she and her brother Warren

Beatty were half Canadian. "In Warren's case, it must be the top half," she would add, eyes twinkling. In any case she thought Betsy's story had the makings of a wildly entertaining feature film, one which could be shot in Canada, and she wanted to meet me to discuss my possible participation as one of Betsy's husbands. It was a tasty meeting – Puck's *nouvelle cuisine* Italian innovations were delicious – but nothing ever came of it – at least, not for me and Shirley. A few years later Jennifer Dale would make a splash playing Betsy Bigley in a TV movie version called *Love & Larceny*, directed by Rob Iscove, which proved so successful that a few years after that she starred in a sequel, *Grand Larceny*, directed by Stephen Surjik. So clearly the enterprising Ms. MacLaine had been on the right track.

That first winter of the new decade I made another movie for my *Who Has Seen the Wind* director Allan King. Ellen Burstyn had held the option on *The Silence of the North* for six years and came to Canada to get it made, with producers she didn't really know, and a group of actors she didn't know, except for maybe Tom Skerritt. She didn't know Allan either, and quite understandably she was very protective of the project. It was based on the true story of Olive Frederickson, a woman who braved the northern wilds during the early part of the twentieth century, and I got to play another real-life character, her husband John Frederickson. The producers had hoped to sell it as an exciting adventure set in the beautiful Canadian wilderness, but moviegoers stayed away in droves. All four of us, Burstyn, Skerritt, Allan King, and I, were later nominated for Genie Awards, which also eluded all four of us. We heard that one studio exec at Universal referred to the film as *Silence at the Box Office*, but years later it became a cult favourite, and I'm told Ellen Burstyn still gets asked about it today.

Meanwhile, back in semi-civilized southern Ontario, there was everything *but* silence at the King-Pinsent household. Leah announced that she had decided to follow in our footsteps and become an actor. I was appalled at the very idea. My sweet little girl, barely a teenager, so bright in so many other ways, wanted to go into show business? Not on my watch.

"Say something!" I barked at Charm, looking for support.

"Oh, for God's sake, Gordon, get over yourself!" Charm barked back.

Did I mention before – I believe I did – that this was the Era of Hard Liquor? Oh sure, it's all white wine spritzers and SATC Cosmos now, but back in the eighties the only time we drank wine was at weddings. I had grown extremely fond of Scotch whiskey, and Scotch had grown extremely fond of me. And Charm, Kate, and Barbara Ham, in their time, were justifiably proud of the fact that they could drink any man under the table and, given the somewhat more relaxed traffic regulations of the era, drive him home when he was too inebriated to find his own car.

At sundown Charm and I would indulge in a cocktail or three before dinner, followed by a couple more with our meal, which always prompted what I still prefer to remember as lively debates and spirited exchanges of ideas. We both had big voices, we both had a flare for the melodramatic, and neither one of us was ever accused of being even remotely reticent, let alone shy. Leah remembers our debates somewhat differently. She reminds me, gently but succinctly, that one of our friends who was a frequent witness to our verbal battles at the dinner table used to call us George and Martha, an homage of sorts to the married protagonists in Edward Albee's classic *Who's Afraid of Virginia Woolf*. When she was a teenager, Leah would often leave our nightly dinners in tears, which is something I still regret. Charm kept telling me I was being too overprotective, and I didn't want to admit it at the time, but yes, of course I was. I've met a lot of fathers over the years, and it's a common trait in all of us. Rodgers & Hammerstein got it absolutely right in *Carousel*; you can have fun with a son, but you've got to be a father to a girl. Which necessarily calls up your personal definition of fatherhood. And this was the little girl I taught to foxtrot to Sinatra records. This was the little girl who would sing with me when I played the guitar. This was the little girl who would help me learn lyrics when I was doing musicals like *Guys and Dolls*. Of course, this was also the little girl who had grown up at Fenton's and the Celebrity Club with Anna Cameron and Kate and Barbara Ham. I didn't want my little girl setting herself up for a vocation of rejection and disappointment, but there was more to it than that. I was still carrying a lot of the guilt I felt for not being there for Beverly and Barry when they were growing up. With Leah another thing took hold. I came on strong. I wanted her to come to *my* senses, but of course I couldn't see it at the time. I didn't see myself in that role until after the fact. And then I kept asking myself, Why was I being so rigid? Why did I keep trying to direct her, to steer her path?

Happily, Leah didn't listen to me, and followed her dream. Apparently Father doesn't always know best.

———

By now, of course, audiences had seen my daring heroics as ambassador Ken Taylor. I'm pretty sure my role as a Canadian who rescued Americans in peril didn't hurt my reputation in Ottawa or Washington, because when Pierre Elliott Trudeau decided to stage a glamorous gala to welcome visiting U.S. fireman Ronald Reagan, he asked me to host it.

I said Yes, of course; I was honoured by his invitation. And when I walked out on the Opera House stage at the National Arts Centre on that night in March, I thought that since this was their first visit to Ottawa, it might be appropriate to give the Reagans a geography lesson.

"Here in North America," I began, "it might be said that we all live in one big house. Welcome to the attic."

It was a great night, with the Irish Rovers and the Shumka Dancers, Anne Murray and Ginette Reno, Rich Little (who of course did spot-on impressions of both Ronnie and Pierre) and many others, and I quite enjoyed the splendour of it all. My only disappointment was that, due to a previous commitment, Charm was unable to be there with me.

The next morning I got a call from the Prime Minister's Office asking if I would like to sit in the Speakers' Gallery to hear Reagan's speech to the Senate. *Sure!* What a splendid way to finish up the trip!

Except for one little detail.

"The thing is," I said, "I'm afraid I didn't bring a tie with me, only the black tie for last night's gala. And I know you need to wear a tie to get into the Speakers' Gallery."

"Oh, that's no problem," said the voice on the other end of the line.

All right, then!

I showed up outside the Speakers' Gallery as requested, and Trudeau's sons were there, and his sister, and Robert Charlebois, and quite a few security people. And of course I still didn't have a tie. There was someone else there, too, a lovely young woman with an impressive connection to the arts. And why not? This was the post-Margaret era, and Pierre Trudeau was known all over the world as an extremely eligible bachelor leader.

A woman came out to tell me that the Prime Minister would like to see me in his office and escorted me in.

Trudeau looked up from the papers on his desk. "How are you, Gordon!"

"Fine," I said, "but I don't have a tie."

Trudeau turned to the woman who had brought me into his office. "Give Gordon my Emergency tie."

Off she went, returning no more than a minute later with this green job, with a big Windsor knot, bigger than I've ever seen him wear, with a few coffee spots on it.

"You don't really wear this, do you?" I said.

He shrugged. "Sometimes."

And then, as we were leaving his office: "And you'll join us for lunch?"

"With pleasure!" I said. And I thought, *What fun! I'm so sorry Charm is missing out on all of this.*

So we listen to Reagan's address to the Senate, and after his speech the limos are waiting, and off we go to Sussex Drive to have lunch. As it turns out I'm seated next to the aforementioned lovely young woman, who is absolutely charming, and everyone at the table is speaking English and French, and Trudeau, who is a wonderfully gracious host, is repeating everything to me in English, because he knows I'm not fluent in French. And after lunch he says, "Gordon, I have to get back to the House, but I can drop you at your hotel on the way."

Now the three of us are in the car, Trudeau and me and the lovely young woman. And I hear him say to her, as I pretend to be looking out the window in the opposite direction: "Well, you don't have to go home this evening, do you?" And realize why I'm along for the ride. I have been cast by Pierre Elliott Trudeau as the beard.

(No, not the Bard – the Beard.)

The limo took us to our hotel, where there was champagne waiting for us, just another layer of icing on the cake. So we had a little champagne, and I don't know if the lovely young woman ever got on her plane, but I got on mine. And two weeks later Charm and I saw the Prime Minister at the Genie Awards in Toronto. As he walked in he was immediately surrounded by fans and admirers, but at one point he looked up and saw me.

"Where's my tie?!?" he inquired playfully, cocking his head to one side.

"You'll get it," I assured him. "You'll get it."

As it turned out, I spent a fair amount of time in Ottawa that year. The National Arts Centre's own theatre company staged a revised version of *John and the Missus* for Ottawa audiences, with a wonderful cast including Edward Atienza, Wayne

Best, Neil Munro, Gerry Parkes, and Florence Patterson as my Missus. Because I was working with actors of that calibre, I couldn't wait to go on stage every night. John Wood, the director, was able to bring some new ideas to this production that he'd been unable to achieve when we'd premiered the play in Halifax five years ago.

"Well?" said Charm. "What do you think of it now?"

"I think it's a film," I said. Which of course I had wanted it to be all along.

The following year, when Pierre Elliott Trudeau brought our Constitution back to Canada from Britain, I sent his Emergency tie back to him in an envelope with a personal hand written note:

> *Please, don't thank me.*
> *It's the least I can do.*

Back in 1952, the big news was the escape of the Boyd Gang from the Don Jail in Toronto. It was the second time they'd escaped.

I remembered reading about them when I was in the army. Their leader, Edwin Alonzo Boyd, had been jailed for robbing banks in 1950 and met two of his future gang members, Willie Jackson and Lennie Jackson (who were not related) while doing time in the Don. The three of them broke out of jail with a hacksaw concealed in Lenny's artificial leg. After adding an ex-musician, Steve Suchan, as their fourth member, the "gang" went on a bank-robbing spree that ended tragically when Suchan shot and killed a policeman. All four were arrested and, by some twist of fate, all four were locked up together in an empty death-row cellblock at the Don Jail. On September 7, 1952, they managed to escape for a second time with the help of another saw blade smuggled in by a lawyer. The following night, the CBC's first television newscast, anchored by Lorne Greene and produced by Harry Rasky, detailed the escape, and it was pretty riveting stuff.

Lennie Jackson and Steve Suchan were found guilty of murder and were executed in a double hanging at the Don Jail that December. Willie Jackson was sentenced to thirty-one years. Boyd himself was sentenced to eight life terms plus twenty-seven years concurrent in Kingston Penitentiary, but was paroled ten years later. After serving another four years for parole violations, he moved to the West Coast, changed his name, and started a new life.

The Life and Times of Edwin Alonzo Boyd was an ambitious, stylish project – a faux documentary narrated by me as Boyd, whom I also played onscreen. The stellar supporting cast, especially Jean-Marc Amyot, Domenic Tudino, and Jack Langhorn as the other three gang members, were not overly familiar faces, which gave the story that much more credibility. After I wrapped my part in the Boyd Gang saga, I teamed up with director Allan King again to shoot *Ready for Slaughter*, a fifty-five-minute drama for *For the Record*. We must have been doing something right again, because *Ready for Slaughter* took the highly coveted Best TV Drama prize at the Banff Television Festival, and I myself was nominated for two ACTRA Awards that year, one for *Boyd* and one for *Slaughter*.

Years later I was in Victoria, staying at the Empress with Charm and Leah, when the concierge called up to say that a man was waiting for me in the lobby. I explained that I was not expecting anyone, and asked if the man had identified himself.

"Yes," said the concierge, "he says his name is Edwin Alonzo Boyd."

I could see a glint of mischief in Charm's eyes. "Bring him up for tea," she suggested.

I went down to the lobby and greeted him with outstretched arms. "Eddie!" I cried. He hesitated, but only briefly, before shyly returning my embrace.

We had tea with Edwin Alonzo Boyd.

"I've got four copies of that film!" he confided, munching on a cookie. "Y'know, all that criminal stuff aside, I see it as my biography."

No kidding.

More than twenty-five years later Scott Speedman played him in *Edwin Boyd: Citizen Gangster*. The film premiered at the 2011 Toronto International Film Festival and was chosen as one of the Ten Best Canadian Films of the Year. Boyd didn't get to see that one. He died in 2002, half a century after his headline-making second escape from the Don Jail.

After playing Boyd I played another real-life character – prolific journalist and war correspondent Quentin Reynolds – for director Eric Till in a TV movie version of Louis Nizer's *A Case of Libel*, his personal account of Reynolds's celebrated lawsuit against newspaper columnist Westbrook Pegler. The names were changed, not only to protect the guilty but also to protect Nizer, who had won the case for Reynolds, from more lawsuits. *A Case of Libel* had started as a book, then became a play, and then became a movie, twice. Our TV movie remake pitted *Mary Tyler Moore Show* alumnus Ed Asner, as Nizer, against fellow Canadian thespian and *Klondike Fever* alumnus Robin Gammell, while I played the Quentin Reynolds role and Daniel J. Travanti of *Hill Street Blues* played the Westbrook Pegler role. Larry was in it too, so it was not a dull shoot.

Back on the boards, I was at the Vancouver Playhouse, playing Prospero in *The Tempest*. I was in my dressing room between a Saturday matinee and evening performance when I heard a slightly tentative knock on my door. When I opened it, the young man looking back at me from the hall was, well, me. It was like looking at an old eight-by-ten of myself. It was ghostlike. Amazing.

"I'm your son," he said.

No kidding.

"Your son Barry," he added a bit shyly, perhaps concerned that I might confuse him with my imaginary sons Larry, Moe, and Curly.

Despite his sister's Beverly's assurances that I did not in fact have two heads, he had waited another eight years to contact me, he would later explain, "just in case you turned out to be an asshole." He was a jet pilot and a soon-to-be published novelist and would eventually enjoy new success as an actor (*hello!*) and, toughest of all, as a stand-up comedian.

It was a wonderful first visit. There would be many more ahead. More new beginnings. More new chances to take a crack at finishing unfinished business. My own loose ends were slowly disappearing in the mist. Charm thought I looked more relaxed when I came back from Vancouver, and she attributed it to Barry's visit. "Because now you have children you love who love you, so you don't have to pretend that none of that ever happened."

I was growing up.

Back to work, and another real-life character, for *Sam Hughes' War* and CBC. Sir Sam Hughes was Canada's maverick Minister of Militia and Defence from October 1911 to November 1916, and the driving force behind Canada's early war effort. Controversial and incorrigibly irreverent, he was as pugnacious as a pitbull, constantly scrapping with his superiors, whom he clearly did not respect as such. By now a thorn in the government's side, Hughes was finally dumped by Prime Minister Robert Borden, but he is still regarded today as the single most important figure in organizing the first Canadian war effort. And I got to play him flanked by a top-drawer company including Douglas Campbell, Richard Donat, David Fox, Christopher Newton, Douglas Rain, and Tony van Bridge.

In Hollywood, award-winning Canadian director Daniel Petrie had become famous as an actors' director. On television he had guided Sally Field to greatness in *Sybil* and Jane Fonda to new heights in *The Dollmaker*. He was also the man behind Paul Newman's startling performance in *Fort Apache, The Bronx*, and Sir Laurence Olivier's terrific star turn in Harold Robbins' *The Betsy*. Born in Glace Bay, Nova Scotia, Dan wanted to come home to make a Canadian film. He'd already written the screenplay, and the film he wanted to make, *The Bay Boy*, would provide two second-generation film talents with memorable screen debuts: Kiefer Sutherland, son of Donald Sutherland and Shirley Douglas, in the title role, and Leah Pinsent, the teenaged daughter of Charmion King and Gordon Pinsent, as his love interest. Kiefer was wonderfully appealing onscreen, and so was Leah, and I don't think either set of parents could have been much prouder. When the Genie Award sweepstakes were announced, *The Bay Boy* had racked up eleven nominations, winning Best Picture and best screenplay for Dan. Five cast members – Kiefer, Leah, Peter Donat, Jane McKinnon, and Alan Scarfe – were also nominated, but only Scarfe took home a golden statuette. Kiefer lost to Gabriel Arcand in *Le crime d'Ovide Plouffe*, and Leah was trumped by Linda Sorensen in *Draw!* Nonetheless, both Kiefer and Leah had made auspicious screen debuts that would serve them well in the future.

Meanwhile, the 1985 ACTRA Award recipients were announced, and I was asked to present the very first Jane Mallett Award for Best Radio Actress to the enduring Canadian show business survivor Charmion King.

"*Quelle surprise!*" said Charm as she accepted the award. "I have waited all my life for this kind of recognition for my work. I really appreciate this. It's an honour to be the first recipient of the Jane Mallett Award. Jane has been a role model for all of us. She had the spirit that we all need and I loved her very much." She held up her cherubic Nellie for all to see. "And of course it's a great pleasure to receive this from someone who will be as happy as I am that at last I got one of these fat little darlings of my own!"

I renewed my efforts to make *John and the Missus* sing as a screenplay, interrupting the process just long enough to do guest shots on Louis Del Grande's hit comedy mystery series *Seeing Things* on CBC and Nicholas Campbell's engaging detective series *Diamonds* on Global.

I received a call from Michael Levine, the country's top entertainment attorney, the man who represented such renowned authors as Mordecai Richler and Peter C. Newman and such renowned broadcasters as Brian Linehan, Patrick Watson, and future Governor General Adrienne Clarkson. Would I like to do a talking book?

I said Yes.

I'd never done an audio book before, but sitting in front of the microphone for a few hours, reading someone else's prose, didn't sound particularly arduous. Unless, of course, the book you were hired to read was Peter C. Newman's *A History of the Hudson Bay Company: Volume One: Company of Adventurers*. All 650 pages of it. A perfect tape for your car, for a long, long, long, long drive. Or perhaps for the half-frozen passengers of a downed northern bushplane out of Nunavut. Never mind – a gig is a gig. I spent something like sixty hours in a sound booth. Went mad for a period of time, but the director, who'd flown over from the U.K. to supervise the taping, waited patiently for me to get back my bearings, which I did, and he was soon able to fly home again, head still held high, with all eight audio cassettes.

Charm's old friend, Arthur Miller favourite Kate Reid, was back on Broadway, co-starring with Dustin Hoffman in an acclaimed revival of *Death of a Salesman*. "When I get back to Toronto," she told Charm, "you and I have *got* to do a play together!" Meanwhile, Charm had been conscripted to appear in the new screen version of *Anne of Green Gables* with Dawn Greenhalgh and Ted Follows' daughter Megan. When Charm finished filming her scenes she returned to the stage in an audience-pleasing revival of her David French play *Jitters* at the Tarragon Theatre in Toronto. As it happened, *Anne of Green Gables* was a huge hit, and Charm happily returned to the soundstage to shoot a sequel.

I was on a soundstage too, doing my first and only CBC music special. It was originally planned as a concert of Irving Berlin songs, but as I recall, the executors of Berlin's estate were not as thrilled with the idea as we were. So the thrust of the show was switched to Hollywood songs – "Puttin' on the Ritz," "Tea for Two," "Fascinating Rhythm," and a pleasing collection of more golden oldies from the silver screen. My producer, Lorraine Thompson, had wisely surrounded me with a trio of musical crowd-pleasers – Kerrie Keane, Jeff Hyslop, and Peter Appleyard. Unfortunately, I was suffering, and I do mean suffering, from a pinched nerve in my groin, which made most dance steps excruciatingly painful. Did I say dance? I could hardly stand. I asked Lorraine to delay production. Which she did, but not long enough for me. I had originally wanted Lorraine and Alex Barris, the writer on the special, to let me slide in and out of the show in a guest spot. (Imagine, an actor asking for *less* attention!) I did not want it to appear that we thought I was the best all-round vocal purveyor of Astaire songs; for one thing, Tony Bennett was still working. But, producers don't always listen to the on-camera talent. And Lorraine and Alex had other ideas.

"I can write the review for you right now," I warned them.

"Gordon Pinsent hosted his own special last night. He also sings a little."

Most of the reviewers were kinder than I was. Suffice it to say that Fred Astaire had nothing to worry about. Granted, I might have had a step or two more in me, if I had been able to walk. Turns out I had to sing all those songs instead. So I just sat there in front of the curtain and surprised everyone by staying on key. But no one, including and especially me, suggested we should do this again sometime. Ever.

Bringing *John and the Missus* to the screen – finally! – presented its own special set of challenges. It was an important story, to me and to many Newfoundlanders who had faced the same reality. My character, John Munn, refuses the paltry amount of settlement money offered by the government when the copper mine – his town's only source of income – is closed, because he doesn't want to leave the land of his ancestors. In truth, things pretty much go downhill from there; when the town turns against him, he literally uproots his house and sails away. But the story is filled with heart and pain and some very "big" moments that need to be played very small, so I was especially happy to be directing it myself. My producers, Peter O'Brian and John Hunter, were the current young lions of the Canadian film industry. They had recently won Genie Awards (for Best Picture and Best Screenplay, respectively) for *The Grey Fox*. Blessed with thirteen nominations, they had gone home with seven statuettes. Composer Michael Conway Baker had won a Genie for his stirring score, and Jackie Burroughs had picked up the Best Supporting Actress award.

I had first met Jackie in my salad days with the Straw Hat Players, a Muskoka summer theatre company created and sparked by the same group of Hart House alumni who had founded the Crest – Donald and Murray Davis, their sister Barbara Chilcott, and of course Charmion and Kate Reid. I was doing something called *Wedding Breakfast*, a three-act comedy set in New York in the fifties, and Jackie was doing all sorts of things. There was no real work for her there, so she was painting scenery, sweeping the stage, doing whatever needed doing, because she wanted to be part of it. Later our paths crossed many times. We had shared the stage at Stratford in *Trumpets and Drums*, and at any number of events over the years – by now she had dozens of television and film credits, in which she successfully portrayed independent women from twenty-six to eighty-six – but I had never thought of her as someone who could play the Missus to my John. However, my producers were so keen on her, based on their *Grey Fox* experience, that we offered her the part, and she accepted. And once she decided she was doing it, that's all there was to that. Her understanding of it, her homework, was incredible. She did incredible homework. And for a mainlander she displayed an uncannily deep understanding of the situation. "It's a pretty simple story," she told one reporter. "Plain folk. Small town. But what's underneath is that all their lives are at stake. Not just their possessions, but their pride, and their dignity, and don't you damn dare play with that! And to me," she added, "that's like Gordon."

I was impressed, and so were the members of the Academy of Canadian Cinema and Television, who nominated her for Best Actress of the Year. All in all we picked up six Genie nominations, but at the end of the day we were gently trounced by

Denys Arcand's *Decline of the American Empire*. Our only two wins were for Michael Conway Baker, who composed another Genie-winning score for us, and for myself, for Best Actor. Backstage I held up the award proudly. After all its incarnations, after all those investments of time and money and talent, *John and the Missus* was finally paying dividends.

"What do you think, Charm?" I asked her, grinning like a schoolboy.

She rolled her eyes in mock disdain, then laughed and gave me a peck on the cheek. "I think," she said, "you should build a bigger mantel."

Unfortunately, there were no glittering red carpet premieres when it opened stateside, which film critic Janet Maslin was quick to point out in the *New York Times*. "Despite its terrible title and the complete lack of fanfare with which it arrived at the Quad Cinema yesterday," she wrote, "the Canadian film *John and the Missus* is a fine little sleeper." It's still a gorgeous-looking film, just a knockout visually, and I always thought Frank Tidy should have won the Genie Award for Best Cinematography – but he wasn't even nominated.

I know, I know, it isn't personal. But some days you don't win.

Charm was busy again, doing a guest shot on *Twilight Zone*, playing a recurring character on a series about a canine crime-fighter called *Katts and Dog*, and starting a new TV movie with Chris Plummer, Shirley Douglas, and Brent Carver called *Shadow Dancing*. I was back behind the camera again, this time directing John Vernon and Jan Rubes in *Two Men*, Anna Sandor's touching screenplay about the waking-nightmare existence of concentration camp victims. John and Jan played the survivor and the war criminal, respectively, and I also got a chance to direct Lila Kedrova, who had recently emigrated to Canada. The irrepressible Kedrova had won an Oscar for playing Madame Hortense in *Zorba the Greek* in 1964, and twenty years later won a Tony Award for playing the same role in the Broadway musical version, *Zorba*.

We'd graduated from ACTRA Awards to Geminis and I'd been nominated for a guest shot on one of the most popular dramas on television, *Street Legal*. The actual nomination sounded much more important: Best Guest Performance in a Series by an Actor or an Actress. The award itself was very attractive, and I decided there and then that I wouldn't mind owning one. But I was sad to see Nellie relegated to the wings, and expressed my feelings in a cover story of our union magazine. *Nellie*, I wrote,

You graced our gatherings, enlivened our lives, and brought us closer together than we'd ever been. Even if there are many impressions of you, you still have a way of telling each of us with your beamish saucy smile that you are truly an original. Your steadying belief that you could easily get off the ground told us we could do the same. It was as if you were giving a bit of ourselves back to us.

You can have your Junos, your you knows, your Genies, your weenies, your Oscars and things. There is nothing that fills the hand and delights the eye as does yourself when the light is right.

You couldn't have been more real to us or had more spirit, more charm or pure beauty if you'd walked and danced among us. Even as you were, you could have been Prime Mistress of Canada. And we are

going to miss you, Nellie. You were on a pedestal for good reason. And now, on your much deserved sabbatical, be assured you will not get dusty on my mantel nor tarnish in my heart.

Meanwhile, three bright, young, talented entrepreneurs had started a successful Canadian animation house called Nelvana and scored a huge hit with their *Care Bears* movies and TV shows. The trio – Michael Hirsh, Patrick Loubert, and Clive Smith – had made an animated movie about one of childhood's most endearing heroes, Babar the elephant, and asked me if I would like to voice the role of King Babar himself. I thought it was a charming idea, and the fastest way to make money short of inheriting it. So I said Yes, voiced the role of the King, and thought no more about it. But the movie was such a hit that Nelvana asked me to voice sixty-five new episodes for television. I loved doing it, because I'd grown very attached to Babar and my role as the royal father elephant. I loved the cheques, too.

Another awards show, another black-tie evening. "And the Gemini goes to . . . Gordon Pinsent for *Street Legal!*"

My first Gemini. I promised myself it would not be my last.

Before the end of the decade I got word that the New American Library would be "paperbacking" the two earlier books: *The Rowdyman* and *John and the Missus*. Would I come to a book fair in Halifax to promote them? Yes. But when I arrived at the bookseller's booth I was advised that I was one of two authors they would be featuring over the two-day period. The other author would be arriving momentarily.

Curious, I skimmed to the bottom of the press release, and there found the identity of my "companion" with whom I'd be doing the necessary press, radio, and TV interviews. And just as I came to her name, I felt what I imagined was a minor seismic shock overtake us all. This was answered by the entrance of my publishing handler's second author, and my "date" for the next forty-eight hours, the inescapable Xaviera Hollander, a Dutch treat if ever there was one. For those too young to have shared the planet with the lady at the time, she was a marvel at being larger than life in all ways, may I say. She had written an international bestseller about her life. It was called *The Happy Hooker*, and Xaviera was enjoying every minute of her notoriety, making splashy entrances for press photographers everywhere.

Coming face to face with me, and having spent the last few minutes waiting for her trailing tiger-tail, she smiled and blinked her mighty lashes, daring me to keep my balance. We could have re-read both our books in the time it took for her to fold her lips around "'Hello!," causing my usually lyrical lower baritone to sound like Doris Day, for all the world. Xaviera was about to autograph my forehead when she was informed that I was her date for the event, which would start with an introductory cocktail party. At the appointed time I picked her up at her room, and we swished down the corridor, the two of us, and made our entrance; she and her "Eunuch." I might as well have been holding her two pet cheetahs on leashes, I was that useful.

All heads turned. The entire convention, grabbing each other for support, drinking everyone else's martini. My mind went immediately to Charm's face back in Toronto, seeing cozy photos of me and Xaviera at a Halifax soiree.

Not to worry. Within minutes Xaviera had grown young men on all parts of her, to prevent her from catching boredom.

Next time she saw me, she didn't know me.

I pointed to her autograph on my shirt, and was rewarded with a flicker of recognition. Nevertheless, our hosts seated us at separate tables for dinner, so we could entertain two different groups, and we had just finished our entrees when I was advised by one of the publisher's reps that they had bumped me up to First Class for my flight home. I was grateful, and frankly a bit relieved. Charm was coming to meet me at the airport, and Xaviera, who would be seated several rows behind, would be getting off the plane several minutes after the First Class passengers disembarked. It was all good.

Xaviera, at the other table, was apparently blessed with stereophonic hearing. "If Gordon is going home First Class, I want to go First Class too!" she said, pouting. Next morning there we were, side by side in First Class on the Air Canada flight from Halifax to Toronto, while she engaged me with an endless tale from her early life, to do with a bathtub, a rubber duck, and a lot of Spaniards.

I could be wrong about the duck.

When we landed, the very first face I saw was Charm's. Charm always insisted on being there the second I came home, warming my arrivals from anywhere. I sort of trusted my new Dutch friend to see the oncoming impasse, and to slide her arm out of mine. After all, anyone could tell that we, Xaviera and myself, had been no more than travelling companions . . . who looked as though they had swallowed Monaco!

And then – about to reach Charm – I opened my mouth, to introduce the leopard-skirted woman who had apparently grown out of my hip, when suddenly Xaviera swung loose, veering off to parts unknown, leaving her farewell phrase to die on the wind – "Goodbye, Gordon! Keep in touch with the Dutch!" – in a voice that could have passed a Broadway audition.

I couldn't have thanked her enough.

Playing one role consistently, as I had done in *Quentin Durgens* and *A Gift to Last* and even *Babar*, could be very satisfying, as long as you could keep discovering more and more about your character. Playing many different characters, in movies, TV movies, and TV series, was more challenging for me as an actor, and it was a challenge I relished. But as time went by, it also became more of a challenge to some viewers. One night, while whetting my whistle in a pub in St. John's, a fellow imbiber approached me.

"Gordon," he said, "can you clear up something for me?"

"Happy to help if I can," I replied.

"The thing is, the other night I was watching you and you were a lawyer. But I fell asleep, and when I woke up, you were a doctor!"

I had to break the news to him that he had been watching two different series.

all in the family

───◦◉◦───

IF YOU, YOUR WIFE, AND YOUR DAUGHTER ALL SPEND your days waiting for the phone to ring, you must be in show business.

By the early nineties Leah had a few more TV movies behind her, including a bit in *Glory Enough for All*, a dramatized account of the Nobel Prize–winning discovery of insulin at the University of Toronto by Frederick Banting and Charles Best, with R. H. Thomson as Banting and Robert Wisden as Best, and she was starting to get calls for both new and established series, including a stint with Angela Lansbury on *Murder, She Wrote*. She had also met a talented actor from St. Louis, Michael Capellupo. A few years older than Leah, Michael was a charming fellow who was waiting for the phone to ring like the rest of us, and was now thinking he could cast himself in better roles by writing them himself. (Sound familiar?) Michael and Leah were married in 1991.

Charm and Kate were finally working together again on stage, in a revival of *Arsenic and Old Lace* at their beloved Hart House Theatre. Not to be outdone, I had been persuaded, without too much arm twisting, to play Matthew to Barbara

Ham's brilliant Marilla in a revival of *Anne of Green Gables* at the Elgin Theatre in Toronto. Coming on stage every night, it was a delight to go home to Charm instead of an empty hotel room, and I savoured every moment of it. I had turned down the same role twelve months earlier, but now I felt ready to play Matthew, ready to do him justice, and strong enough to hold my own on stage with Barbara. The audience and the critics seemed to agree, and a few months later I would win my first and only Dora.* (So far.)

While I was on stage at the Elgin, I was still looking for my next truly memorable role. Offstage I was having fun jumping from series to series, and promoting my first attempt at a memoir called *By the Way*. I had an onscreen reunion with Chris Plummer on *Counterstrike*, did a showy turn with Sara Botsford on *E.N.G.*, and played a recurring role on *Street Legal* with Cynthia Dale, Eric Peterson, and newcomer Albert Schultz. I even had a reunion with *The Missus*, Jackie Burroughs, on *Road to Avonlea*, while *Avonlea* resident Barbara Ham kept us laughing between takes. I did an episode of *The Hidden Room* with Lara Flynn Boyle, and I did an episode of *Kung Fu: The Legend Continues* with David Carradine and Neve Campbell. Neve was very shy. I think it was probably one of her first acting roles, because she had started out as a dancer and was trying to make a new name for herself as an actor. She didn't smile at all, which was fine. We were both struggling a little bit with our

---

* The Dora Mavor Moore Awards, named for the beloved theatre pioneer, are presented annually in Toronto and are the Canadian equivalent of Broadway's Antoinette Perry (Tony) Awards.

Australian accents – why we had Australian accents I can't remember – but Carradine was going around asking, "How many bars are there in this area?" and I determined, once again, that if I wanted a great part, I would have to write it myself, because no one out there was going to hand it to me.

Seldom if ever have I been so happy to be wrong.

Steve Smith had already created Red Green as a character, and now he wanted his friends to play other characters on his new show. Steve had snagged my future son-in-law, Peter Keleghan, to play Ranger Gord, and seemed to know instinctively that trained actors who traditionally worked in drama could bring his quirky characters to life in a uniquely believable way. Hence he had cast, among others, Graham Greene as an explosives expert who was clearly unsuited to his vocation, Wayne Robson as a light-fingered ex-con still on parole, and me as Hap Shaughnessy, a guy who never met a story he couldn't tell better with a few highly distinctive embellishments of his own. When I read the part for the first time, I was almost on the floor laughing, and Charm was too. "My God, this is funny!" she said. So I figured, if I can keep a straight face, I can get it done.

Hap called himself a water taxi captain when in fact what he had was a raft. He would stop whatever he was doing to tell a really long story that would always bore the hell out of Red Green. And of course I grew to admire Hap; I thought he was terrific. With any luck he could tell you this tall story, and you might believe him. "Oh yes, yes, I was part of the Rolling Stones. You know, whenever Keith Richards had a little too much and couldn't go on." I just loved the guy. I remember sitting around the table at one read-through where Hap said he had worked as a foreman of a tiger rodeo – a *tiger rodeo!* – and I only got through three lines before I just burst out laughing. Hap claimed to have been an astronaut, too – "One small step for Neil Armstrong, a piece of cake for me." We did one on ice fishing, too, with me and Steve in a boat, and I just couldn't look at him, because I knew if we made eye contact I would never ever get through it. I think my very favourite was when Hap tells Red about his mother, who sold chips in Port Alberni but was really Anastasia, the daughter of Czar Nicholas – "Grandpa Nick" – who had smuggled her out of Russia in a giant Fabergé egg.

"After she grew up," Hap continues, "she married Ernest Hemingway."

"You're not telling me that Ernest Hemingway was your father!" says Red incredulously.

"Sure," says Hap. "That's why Margaux Hemingway and I couldn't ever get married. Because our kids would be idiots!"

Steve has a great talent for picking characters. Peter's character, Ranger Gord, who lives by himself in a tower in the woods and keeps insisting he isn't lonely, is a classic as far as I'm concerned. Because it's just so real.

I was on the first season of *Red Green*, and most of the others, I think. I just loved it. What I didn't love, soon after we started shooting, was learning that ACTRA had voted me the 1992 John Drainie Award for Overall Contribution to Broadcasting. John Drainie was an esteemed colleague, of course, so I was gratified to receive a prize bearing his name. But I didn't like the sound of it. It had that "Lifetime Achievement" cachet and that peculiar perfume of early retirement. As far as I was concerned, I was just getting the hang of it. Bowing out was simply not an option.

"They think I'm finished in the business!" I whined to Charm.

"Oh Gordon, for heaven's sake!" she sighed. "Get over yourself!"

I did. And quickly, too, the moment we learned that Kate Reid had been diagnosed with brain cancer. She died in Stratford, near the Shakespearean theatre she loved, on March 27, 1993. She was only sixty-two.

As always, it was a relief to go back to work. Charm did a bit in a Harlequin Romance movie, and I did my second Euro-pudding, a less-than-epic mini-series called *Les amants de rivière rouge – Red River Love Stories*, as it were. It was a western, with absolutely no relation to the classic western directed by Howard Hawks in 1948, and I can assure you that neither John Wayne nor Montgomery Clift was anywhere in sight. It wasn't being made for consumption in America. It was being made for Europe. Which was a good thing, because it could very well have spelled the end of my career. I played the father of three girls out on the prairies. Unfortunately, my three girls couldn't speak English. I spoke English to them; they delivered their lines in Italian. Nick Mancuso was also there for a while; he was a favourite of the director, Yves Boisset. I wasn't, I guess, because Yves never said one word to me. He was one of those snooty guys who like to comment on other people's films. "What a dreadful piece of work!" he would say, but then everything was dreadful as far as he was concerned, unless it was something he was working on. So there I was with my three daughters, and I said, "I'm sorry, we're trying here, we really are." But I couldn't understand what they were saying, and they couldn't understand what I was saying, because they hadn't put any real system in place to make it work. And I had really been looking forward to it, because I thought it was going to be a real western. The only thing that made it bearable was the arrival of my daughter Beverly, who had wanted to visit me on a movie set. Bev is a horse person, so she had a great time, because of course there were plenty of horses in the production. So she had a better time than I did.

I had to miss a few *Red Green* episodes because I was doing other things. Happily, some of the "other things" served to reassure me that despite my John Drainie Award I was not finished in the business. Best of the bunch for me was the pilot for a new TV series called *Due South*. *Due South* was a wonderfully fresh look at the core values of the RCMP, as personified by Benton Fraser, an officer whose RCMP father had been murdered on the job. Part of what made the series such a delight was Benton's relationship with his dead father, whose ghost became a central character in the story. I knew Paul Gross first as an accomplished playwright, and then as an accomplished actor – I had even directed him in the eighties, in an episode of a Roberta Maxwell series called *Air Waves* with Tabby Johnson and Ingrid Veninger. Even then he was a man of ideas. He was already writing and producing. And I thought it was perfect casting, because he was spectacularly good as Benton.

The series was created by Paul Haggis, who went on to win Oscars for writing *Million Dollar Baby* for Clint Eastwood and writing and producing *Crash*. Both Pauls were convinced that I was the guy to play Fraser Sr., and who was I to argue? It was supposed to be a one-shot deal, with Fraser Sr. getting killed at the top of the pilot and then appearing to Fraser Jr. as a wisdom-provoking ghost. The image that seemed to stick with people the most was of the two of us sitting across from each other, with Paul in his Mountie hat and me in my sawed-off Stetson. Before we shot that scene I had to wear it quite a few times before I could stop laughing. In the scene we're sitting across from one another at a table, talking, and Paul asks me, "What's wrong with your hat? . . . You only have half a hat." And I say, "That's how they buried me." Or something like that. Because that's how they were able to put Fraser Sr. in his coffin in full uniform, by sawing off the back of his hat.

Another favourite scene was when Paul's character is in a pool, getting physiotherapy. And I float by on my back, in full dress uniform, with the hat, too, of course. And when we were shooting I surprised them by breaking into the first verse of "Rose Marie."

Rose Marie I love you . . .
*I'm always thinking of you . . .**

We shot my big death scene in Skagway. It was very snowy in Skagway, close to a whiteout, and there was some real

* From "Rose Marie," music by Rudolf Friml and Herbert Stothart, lyrics by Otto Harbach and Oscar Hammerstein II, from the operetta *Rose Marie* (1924).

concern that we might not be able to get the shot. But it cleared just enough, so we did. It was a great scene. I was standing at the edge of a cliff, and I turned to the camera – the camera representing an unknown assailant – and I said, "You're going to shoot a Mountie? They'll hunt you to the ends of the earth!" It was a great set-up for the series.

Paul Gross remembers it slightly differently. He remembers a blinding snowstorm that persisted until I took my place on the edge of the cliff. "At that moment," he told one Ottawa audience, "the snow stopped, the skies actually parted, radiant sun filled the landscape, bears crawled out of their dens, trees suddenly burst into full bloom, and I could swear I heard a choir singing."

That's not quite the way I remember it, but I like his version better.

While I was in Skagway I saw a statue of a woman that inspired me to sketch her. More of a monument than a statue, really, with a bust of a woman on top. The woman had apparently helped the miners and their families going to Skagway on their way to and from panning for gold, and she was really regarded as the Saint Anne or Saint Therese of the North. And if you walked around to the back of the statue you found another inscription by a man who was now the mayor of Seattle. Turns out that man had always been in love with her, and more than once had asked her to marry him. She was murdered, by a lover or someone who was jealous of her. But then there was no shortage of gold rush stories, as Pierre Berton so often reminded us.

We finished shooting the pilot for *Due South*, and went for drinks at the end of the day. Paul Haggis was already saying, *C'mon Gordon, of course you want to play this guy, we just have to bring him back.* And I was happy as hell, because I'd wanted to do another series, especially one I could phone in! I liked *Due South* a whole lot. It was like walking into the centre of television at its best. It seemed so right, so real, so expertly done that you wondered where these people had come from.

Paul Gross took me out to dinner to ask me to do the second season, and while we were talking I suggested that he consider using a clothes closet as a portal into the past – that when Benton Fraser opened the closet door he would see clothes on hangers, but if he pushed the clothes to one side he would see into his father's old office, with his father still sitting behind his desk. He thought that was good, so we went with that. As it turned out my idea worked rather well, and Paul, very graciously, always gives me the credit for it.

Paul is a worker, and boy, was he good! He did a lot of stuff on that show. And he always had his laptop handy. So he wrote, and checked, and added, and took away from the stuff that was already on the page and from new stuff he wrote himself, always to make it the very best it could be. And I took particular pleasure in amusing him.

One day Paul walked into our house, saw me working on an oil painting, and looked at me wide-eyed.

"That's the way we do it in the Group of Six," I told him.

He blinked. "You mean Seven."

"No, no!" I said, vigorously shaking my head. "Not in *our* group!"

Due South swept the next Gemini Awards, with statuettes for Best Dramatic Series, Best Writing, Best Music, Best Sound – it was an RCMP love-in – and Paul and I both took home Geminis as well.

I had another idea for the series, which I loved, but which we didn't do, although I wish we had – that no matter what the season was, whenever I appeared I would always have to brush just a little bit of snow off my uniform. Because my character's last moments on earth were spent in deep snow, getting shot down in Skagway.

Still, at least I got to wear that sawed-off Mountie hat. Paul wrote a "hat trick" for Leslie Nielsen too, for his guest spots on the series. In the story the top of his hat got chopped off going through a tunnel, so his hair was standing straight up, sticking out of it. Leslie, whose father actually was an RCMP officer, played a character called Sergeant Buck Frobisher, and he and my Fraser Sr. got along very well, so a bit of humour came out of that, too. I enjoyed it, but I'm much better playing comedy now than I was then.

I had a good time doing *Due South*. Although we didn't have any scenes together, my son Barry Kennedy popped up in the series too, after the two Pauls hired him to play a character named Sergeant Eddie Polito in a two-episode story called "The Ladies Man." There were also *Due South* conventions in Toronto every year, and we'd sit there answering the same old questions, but I was astounded at all the paraphernalia fans had from the series. It was very strange. We were asked to sign pictures of ourselves that we had never seen before. And people were coming away with little bits and pieces. One section of the convention was devoted to playing a game in which people stood up and shouted their favourite lines of dialogue. At one convention one person came up behind me and said, "Would you sign this for me please?" and handed me the *Roots* album I had recorded for Arc records thirty years earlier! Another time I received a package from Germany, saying *Happy Birthday, Gordon*, with a whole lot of verses, signed by one thousand *Due South* fans.

Barbara Ham was enjoying a nostalgic return to the Royal Alex in Toronto. She had made her auspicious debut there in 1943 in a production of *Arsenic and Old Lace*, which, she loved to point out, was a brand-new show when she did it. "The original production was still playing on Broadway when we did it at the Alex!" she would remind us. Now she was back on the same stage, lovingly and lavishly refurbished by "Honest Ed" Mirvish, doing eight shows a week of a "new" George and Ira Gershwin musical called *Crazy for You*, and loving every minute of it. By the time she was diagnosed with breast cancer, the cancer had already spread throughout her body. It seemed like only yesterday that we had worked together, clowning around on the set of *Road to Avonlea*, playing to each other's strengths onstage in *Anne of Green Gables* and *Brass Rubbings*. Suddenly she was in a hospice, in palliative care, preparing for her final journey. We took turns visiting her. At the end we all held hands and she passed. Like Kate, she died in the winter, in February, three years after Kate. She was sixty-nine.

A staunch supporter of all my Creative endeavours, Barbara always professed to like my paintings and years earlier had asked me to do a painting, just for her, of clowns.

"Are you sure you're not mixing me up with Red Skelton?" I teased her. Skelton was celebrated for both playing and painting portraits of clowns.

"When I want a painting by Red Skelton," she snorted, "I'll ask *him!*"

A few weeks later I presented the indomitable Barbara Ham with a small watercolour of more than a dozen clown faces. She loved it on sight, and deliberated where she should hang it. "Y'know," she said, furrowing her brow, "there's something so familiar about these clowns –"

She stopped mid-sentence. "Oh my God!" she gasped. "They're all *YOU!*"

True. I had posed for myself, and all the clowns were me, in different clown makeup. She thought it was hilarious, displayed it prominently in her living room, and couldn't wait to show it off when friends came to call.

Hollywood was born for stories like Barbara's. Barbara was successfully courted by Wayne Lonergan, who had been convicted of murdering his wife and was released from prison after twenty-two years. "You kill me, Wayne!" Barbara would say. She'd introduce him to total strangers at the drop of a hat. "Have you met my new boyfriend? He's a real lady killer!" Oh she had a million of 'em! And Wayne would just sit back and grin.

I have his hat, his summer straw fedora. Barbara gave it to me after he died. I still wear it, every summer.

After Barbara left us, all three Pinsents were mercifully distracted by employment. Charm took on Mary Pickford's persona, as well as her Hollywood history, on an outstanding episode of Patrick Watson's *Witness to Yesterday*, and then joined an impressive ensemble cast (including Sandra Oh, Geneviève Bujold and *Due South* alumnus Callum Keith Rennie) in Don McKellar's debut as a feature film director, *Last Night*. Leah landed a great role, playing a Diane Sawyer wannabe in Ken Finkleman's stunning media-mashing mini-series *More Tears*, and then landed an even better role as the brainy corporate executive in Rick Mercer's sly send-up of Canuck show business, *Made in Canada* – her first significant series and one which would keep her in front of the cameras for the next five years. I myself was juggling two weekly series, *Wind at My Back* and *Power Play*, while trying to figure out what else I could fit in. What I had to fit in was another Wave Goodbye Gordon trophy – the Earle Grey Award, the Lifetime Achievement Award of the Canadian Academy of Film & Television, presented at the 1997 Gemini Awards. Barbara Ham had won one a few years earlier. So had Ernie Coombs, TV's legendary Mr. Dressup, who was no longer dressing up every morning for his audience of preschoolers. So had The Kids in the Hall. And Bruno Gerussi, just the year before, except his had been presented posthumously.

I checked my pulse.

As usual, I wanted more. I was writing again, a new idea for a movie about a man who returns home to his family after being on the run for twenty years for a murder he didn't commit.

Also, Global Television was doing a series of one-man shows, based on notable short stories, called *Spoken Art*. The idea was that you would memorize the whole short story and then deliver it to camera. You had two monitors, so you could turn your head a little. My story was called *The Clumsy One*, written by Ernest Buckler from Nova Scotia, and Charm thought it was the best thing I ever did. It was certainly her favourite. I fell for it because it reminded me of my brother and my family in Grand Falls. But what an interesting piece of work! It's about a brother who returns home after some time away – he's now a doctor or a teacher or something like that – and he tells a story about his older brother. The background is that when the time had come to decide who was going to go out in the world, only one of them could go; the other had to stay, to keep the farm going. So the older man has been in the fields, and the younger brother has come back. The whole thing is about the man's memory of how he had made his brother feel cheap, feel low, feel uneducated, feel ignorant – somehow inferior, somehow unworthy – because on a past visit he had brought two friends home from school with him, and he took part in making fun of the honest labour that his older brother did. And how he has had to live with this all these years, about how badly he made his brother feel.

I loved doing it. It was such a haunting piece. And I was touched when my peers seemed to share my enthusiasm for it, because they nominated me for two Gemini Awards that year, one for *Due South* and one for *The Clumsy One*. Meanwhile, I was still writing, and still juggling key recurring roles in two series. *Wind at My Back* was one of those splendid period pieces that producers Kevin Sullivan and Trudy Grant did so well. They had made a name for themselves with the *Anne of Green Gables* franchise and subsequently produced *Road to Avonlea*, which was a great success both in Canada and the United States *Wind at My Back* was set in the Depression with a stellar cast headed by Shirley Douglas and Kathryn Greenwood. What was not so stellar, in my opinion, were the scripts, which proved to be just a bit too windy for me. I played Leo McGinty, the owner of the town pawnshop, a former suitor of May

Bailey (Shirley) and her late husband John's prospecting partner. Which all in all sounded very promising. But I couldn't
find the same promise in the scripts.

"They're better if you read them all the way through," said
series' creator Kevin Sullivan, who was writing most of them.

Really? Was reading them all the way through going to
make my part any better? Or even any bigger? It never had in
the past. Just reading my part was a habit I'd gotten into, and
I was quite comfortable with it, thank you very much. Until
one episode we were shooting called for a group of miners to
sit down at a table with Shirley Douglas, to talk about saving
the mine. The director was blocking out the scene for camera
moves as we rehearsed, and suggested I join Shirley and the
miners at the table.

"No, that doesn't feel right," I said. "I'm a shopkeeper, not a
miner. I think I should just stand back here, behind them, leaning against this wall. That way I can convey my concern for them
without imposing on them – you know, invading their space."

The director nodded sagely. "All right," he said, "but what are
you going to do with the blind man?"

I blinked.

I had absolutely no idea what he was talking about.

"No problem," I said with a shrug. "He can lean too."

"All right then," he agreed. At which point one of our best
and tallest actors, Richard Donat, joined us on set sporting
opaque black glasses and a standard-issue white cane.

The blind man cometh.

"You have to take my hand, Gordon," Richard whispered.
"I'm blind."

I took his hand, guided him gently to our starting position, and managed to keep a straight face for the entire scene.

Later, of course, I couldn't resist sharing the incident with Charm and Leah. Charm found the whole thing hysterically funny. Leah, not so much.

"Daddy," she said sternly, "you've *got* to start reading *the whole script!*"

After a few more episodes I finally asked Kevin Sullivan to put me out of my misery. Charm was in the series too, playing a schoolteacher. She called from the set to tell me that they had killed me off.

"You're dead," she said.

"How?"

"Traffic accident."

A few months later I was amused when the Academy nominated me for a Gemini for my work on the show. I'm sure Kevin and Trudy were amused too.

I was especially pleased when I got to do a guest shot in my daughter's television series. I played the alcoholic star of the series being produced by the film company run by Leah and Peter Keleghan. Playing a drunk can be funny at a certain age, when you know you can get away with it. I knew Peter, of course, from our *Red Green* days; I didn't know that he and Leah were destined to be together, but I'm pretty sure they didn't know that either. Not then. When the series ended they asked me to come back again, to play the phoney-folksy conglomerate shopper who buys the company and fires them all – Rick, Leah, Peter – in the last episode.

Made in Canada was another series, like *Due South*, where everything was in place, everybody was totally committed to what they were doing. You felt that you could go and do your thing, because you knew that you were in good hands, and you didn't have to worry or try to compensate for anybody else, because they were just as ready as you were, except maybe even more so. Rick Mercer and his partner Gerald Lunz epitomize that high calibre of professionalism. It's always great to be invited to be part of a project of that nature, and again, to work with people you know and admire and trust. Because it's not often that way. It's mostly not that way.

In *Power Play* I played an over-the-hill NHL hockey coach, and I actually got to work with Don Cherry. We had one scene together. I walked towards him and he walked towards me, and I immediately started to speak, and he immediately answered, and we finished the scene.

I said, "That was great, Don."

He said, "WHAAAAT?? . . . WAS THAT IT??"

I said, "Yes, Don – YES, DON, THAT WAS IT."

"OH," he said, "THAT WAS LIKE REAL!"

Michael Riley played the lead, a burned-out sports agent. I had never worked with him before but I was very impressed with him and the way he committed the scripts to memory. At the first read-through he would always arrive with copious notes, on different coloured pages; he would save all the different colours, all the different versions of each script as it evolved. Not a lot of people knew how much he was putting into it, how he kept trying to make it better and better. But I knew, and a few others knew. Between the role he had to play and his desire to make the most of every moment, his workload was enormous. So he was the first guy I called when CBC gave me the green light for *Win, Again.*

Win, Again was a true labour of love. It was the story of Win Morrisey, a man who has been on the run for twenty years for a murder he didn't commit. New evidence has proven him innocent, and Win is anxious to return home, but not many in town, including his wife and son, are as anxious to see him. I took on the lead role – I had created it for myself – and brought in Eric Till to direct. But I purposely made it easy on myself by casting three terrific actors – Gabrielle Rose as my wife, Leah as my daughter (not too much of a stretch), and Michael – and the end result was, if I do say so myself, funny, touching, entertaining, and uplifting. Cheered by the response of both the audience and the Nielsen ratings, CBC drama executives seemed to agree with my contention that *Win, Again* had all the right stuff for a weekly series. What none of us knew at the time was that most of those same executives would be swept out the door in a major management shuffle. New regime, new broom, new faces, new ideas, and not much regard for the recommendations of the previous brooms.

Hello, new world. Goodbye, *Win, Again.* And yes, Irving Berlin – I agree. It's like no other business I know.

I decided I would write something completely new and fresh and unexpected. And I did. And for the first time ever, the computer ate my homework. The script was almost finished when it crashed, and when that happened, I crashed too. I didn't know if I could do it anymore, jump into that particular fray again. Certain things were not as ready-made for me as they once had been. The phone wasn't ringing the way it once did. I wasn't ready to go out there like a bag lady. *Please read my wares! Please watch my work! Please accept me again!* I felt extremely vulnerable. It wasn't something I could easily explain, even to my family. I certainly couldn't explain it to other actors, most of whom had never had the kind of luck I've had. So I felt very much alone. I took it all so seriously at that time.

And then they announced the nominees for the 1999 Gemini Awards, and I thought, *Okay, maybe I can hang in a little longer.**

Meanwhile, something exciting was happening on stage at the Tarragon Theatre in Toronto. The premiere of Janet Munsil's *Emphysema (A Love Story)* opened September 29, 1998, after six preview performances. Directed by Diana Leblanc, the play was based on an actual meeting between fifty-three-year-old British writer Kenneth Tynan and the seventy-one-year-old screen actress Louise Brooks, best known for playing Lulu in the film classic *Pandora's Box*. Playing Louise Brooks was a challenge Charm found irresistible – especially since the producers wanted Leah to play the young Louise Brooks in onstage flashbacks. Leah had just won rave reviews playing the news anchor in the CBC mini-series *More Tears*, and Frank Moore, a stage veteran with a voice as powerful as Charm's, was set to co-star as Kenneth Tynan.

* Best Performance by an Actor in a Leading Role in a Dramatic Program or Mini-Series: Gordon Pinsent for *Win, Again*. Best Writing in a Dramatic Program or Mini-Series: Gordon Pinsent for *Win, Again*. Best Performance by an Actor in a Featured Supporting Role in a Dramatic Series: Gordon Pinsent for *Power Play*.

It was an extraordinary opportunity for Charm, to be working with her daughter onstage, coming and going to the theatre with her every night, not to mention being able to watch her daughter from the wings, even if they couldn't have any scenes together.

A lot of that sexy, smoky voice of Charm's was the result of years of whiskey and cigarettes. She was seriously addicted to nicotine. She knew it, of course, and had finally had to quit. And from that point on, even when she hit rough spots in her life, personally or professionally, she was still able to resist reaching for a smoke.

What she couldn't resist was a great part in a good play.

Louise Brooks had smoked like a chimney – the way Charmion King had once smoked – and no one involved with the production had any concerns about being politically correct. So Charm, as Louise, would be smoking onstage.

When rehearsals began Charm and Frank Moore started out with herbal cigarettes, but the playwright was unhappy, and so was the director. They wanted the audience to smell the real thing.

Charm hadn't had a cigarette for fifteen years. But it was a great part. So she thought about it, and thought about it, and finally said, "It's okay, it's all right, I can do this." But she couldn't, of course. She had convinced herself that she could stop again after the play was over, but she couldn't, and by the time the curtain came down on that last performance she was smoking as much as she ever had. Maybe more.

I've tried very hard to forgive them for pushing her into it. I haven't quite managed it yet. Because in the end, that's what did her in: Emphysema. The disease *and* the play.

a turn of the century

———◦◉◦———

SOMEHOW THE YEAR 2000 MANAGED TO SNEAK UP ON me. Not that we were completely oblivious to all that manufactured Y2K panic. But we were, you know, working. So when July rolled around, and I hit seventy, I was rather shocked by the whole thing.

"I wasn't expecting to make it to seventy," I told Charm.

She shrugged. "It happens."

She herself was only a week away from her seventy-fifth birthday, but she was also starring in a new play by Claudia Dey at the Factory Theatre, doing a guest stint on Don McKellar's quirky CBC series *Twitch City*, and getting ready to play Rose Kennedy to Jill Hennessy's Jackie in a TV movie called *Jackie, Ethel, Joan: The Women of Camelot*. Leah was still shooting *Made in Canada* with Rick Mercer and Peter Keleghan, and she and Peter were waiting for Ken Finkleman to finish the script for a *Newsroom* movie spin-off.

Charm and I saw the end of Leah's eleven-year marriage to Michael Capellupo, a talented actor and writer, but before they broke up Michael had written a short film called *A Promise*, a father-and-daughter drama for Leah and me, with a cameo by

Charm. One of Leah's pals from *The Bay Boy*, actor Peter Spence, wanted to produce it and persuaded a few others, including rising feature film entrepreneur Daniel Iron, to produce it with him. Once they put it together, we shot the whole thing in a couple of days, and it turned out to be the one and only time all three of us – Charm, Leah, and me – would be in the same movie together.

I had two shiny new Geminis, one for performing in *Power Play*, one for writing *Win, Again*. I hit the road once more, flying into Newfoundland to celebrate the thirtieth anniversary of *The Rowdyman* in Corner Brook. Was it possible? Had it really been three decades? Larry and I were still working actors. So was Linda Goranson, who was now doing more theatre than film. But Will Geer was long gone. So was Ben McPeek, who had composed the score for the film. And so was Peter Carter, who directed it. So there were lots of toasts to absent friends. Around the same time, my union, ACTRA, celebrated its sixtieth anniversary, and I hitched a ride on Air Canada to join festivities in Calgary. My fellow ACTRA members in Alberta gave me a lovely gift just for showing up, a beautiful ceramic bowl. When I got home Charm took one look at it and placed it in the centre of our kitchen table, so we could be sure to see it every day.

Back in Toronto I was doing guest stints in weekly series like *Blue Murder*, hoping something wonderful would happen. And it did. As far as director Lasse Hallström was concerned, the only place to film *The Shipping News* was Newfoundland, so working on it was a treat, especially for me and fellow Rock climber Bob Joy. Based on the book by Annie Proulx, the film had a wonderful cast: Kevin Spacey, Julianne Moore, Judi Dench, Cate Blanchett, Pete Postlethwaite, Scott Glenn, all chosen for the special shades and colours they could bring to the project.

Being über-professionals, of course, they wanted to sound like the Newfoundlanders they were playing. But some found the accent more difficult than others.

"It's easy for you, Gordon," Judi Dench teased me. "You've got the beard, you've got the accent, you've got the look . . . I'm the one who has to do all this work. You just did this to get a ticket home!"

All in all, I thought they did very well. Purists on the Rock thought Julianne Moore sounded a bit too Irish, but I thought she handled it fine. Also, none of them was used to dealing with Newfoundland weather. I remember shooting one scene with Kevin Spacey, where it was spring in the morning and snow in the afternoon. About four seasons hit us before it was over. But it was great to be on a big-budget film for a change. We still struggle in this country to get films made. On *Shipping News* we had sushi breaks in the afternoons, and anyone who tells you they don't enjoy having perks like that is lying. So we had a fine time, and it didn't end there for me. At the London opening CBC commentator Ann MacMillan and I were feted by the Maple Leaf Club, a wonderful Canadian-themed pub in Covent Garden. Kevin Spacey, Judi Dench, and I were all on hand for the premiere, with Harvey Weinstein and Peter O'Toole and other celebrities in attendance.

When I think of filming *The Shipping News*, I remember it as an easy shoot. But of course it was home, so it seemed easier.

Charm was doing a Noel Coward classic, *Present Laughter*, with Martha Burns and Allan Hawco, as her first play with Albert Schultz's dazzling Soulpepper rep company in Toronto. She was back onstage. She was home. A few weeks later she would be in repertory with Albert Schultz and Diego Matamoros in *Uncle Vanya*, and a few weeks after that, with Bill Hutt and Araby Lockhart in *Inherit the Wind*, playing the Rev. Jeremiah Brown. At seventy-six she was a working actor in her prime. For me it was more gaps, more random guest shots, more waiting. It was time to start writing again. At the very least, it was time to get serious about what I was writing. Along the way I took a look at writing from the other side, playing Morley Callaghan in the CBC mini-series *Hemingway vs Callaghan*. I thought the producers did a great job of capturing that particular era, that summer in Paris and beyond. Vincent Walsh played Hemingway. Michelle Nolden, who has the most gorgeous eyes, played Hadley Hemingway. Robin Dunne played the young Morley, and I think he had more fun than I did. Callaghan was not the most exciting guy to play. Reagan Pasternak was very impressive as Zelda Fitzgerald. I was pleased to see audiences discover her for themselves a few years later on the CBC TV series *Being Erica*.

Next thing we knew Charm was back in rep at Soulpepper, doing *Uncle Vanya* again with Albert and Diego and the Jean Genet play *The Maids* with Martha Burns and Nancy Palk. The years seemed to be tumbling by, and decent parts were more than ever at a premium.

Charm and I were at a fundraiser, I can't remember which one, when Sarah Polley came up to me to say hello.

"Gordon," she added, "have you read 'The Bear Came Over the Mountain'?"

"No, no, I haven't."

"Well, you should pick it up," she said. "It's very good, you know."

I had known Sarah and her family since she was a child, so of course I was intrigued. Onscreen she had graduated from being a child star and the heart and soul of *Road to Avonlea* to playing grown-up roles in serious films – far more serious than the fluff most of her contemporaries were doing. And although she made more headlines as a social activist than as an actress, she also seemed quite intent on becoming a film-maker herself and had already directed some intriguing short films.

"It's a story by Alice Munro," she added, gently but pointedly.

"I know, I know. I'll pick up a copy tomorrow," I lied.

Meanwhile, I landed a meaty role on an episode of *The Eleventh Hour*, a weekly dramatic series on CTV, and was nominated for another Gemini. ACTRA named me as its recipient of our union's 2003 Award of Excellence, and I was both pleased and chagrined.

"Some are saying I'm not getting this most coveted award for the last performance, but to cover the amount of time I've spent in the industry," I told my fellow union members that night. "And some are saying I wore diapers to my first audition . . . all the way to where I'm wearing them again. That's a lot of crap!"

The actors running ACTRA must have agreed. By that time the union had created a free resource for ACTRA Toronto members, a space where members could record auditions or rehearse on-camera and then send those tapes to producers and directors in other parts of the country. That ACTRA space was now renamed the Gordon Pinsent Studio. As if I hadn't been flattered enough.

The following year the Banff Television Festival's Board of Directors voted me their Award of Excellence. As if I wasn't paranoid enough. *Here's your trophy, don't let the door hit your ass on the way out!* But I would, as always, defer to Charm, who was wise about such matters. It was Charm who assured me, and then reassured me, that this was not a conspiracy to get me to quit show business. And at times I almost believed her.

Michael McGowan's script for *Saint Ralph* had a nice bite to it, and I wanted to give Father Fitzpatrick the same teeth. I played him with authority, probably because I had just finished playing a cardinal in a 1974 thriller with Christian Slater, Molly Parker, and Stephen Rea called *The Good Shepherd.* That one was later released on DVD as *The Confessor* to avoid confusion with the 1976 Matt Damon–Robert De Niro–Angelina Jolie thriller *The Good Shepherd.* But I still had a good time playing Father Fitzpatrick. Then I did a bit in Paul Gross' TV thriller *H2O* (our fellow *Due South* alumnus Callum Keith Rennie was more prominently featured) and amused myself, and hopefully the audience, by playing the president of the CBC in an episode of the screwball Comedy Network series *Puppets Who Kill.*

Long before she surprised television executives with her engaging, smart series *Harry's Law,* I knew Kathy Bates pretty much the same way you did, as the Academy Award–winning actress who turned James Caan into a cripple in the screen version of Stephen King's *Misery* and who won another Oscar nomination for horsing around with Jack Nicholson in *About Schmidt*. I also knew she was a big deal on Broadway, where she'd originated roles in *'night, Mother* and *Frankie and Johnny in the Clair de Lune*, the latter with my friend Kenny Welsh. She had already directed half a dozen episodes of *Six Feet Under* and a couple of TV movies when she hired me to play a horse trainer in a movie of the week shooting in Nova Scotia called *Ambulance Girl*. We got along famously, of course, because by now it was clearly apparent to everyone, including me, that I was attracted to strong, independent, and outspoken women, and Kathy qualified on all fronts.

We were dealing with a serious subject, clinical depression, but we still had a lot of fun. One morning after we finished one scene she came up to me, patted me on the shoulder, and said, "That was terrific, Gordon, just terrific."

Later that day, after she finished one of her scenes, I just couldn't resist.

"That was terrific, Kathy, just terrific!" I told her.

"Oh, fuck off, Gordon!" she snapped.

I've got to stop being so nice.

I ended up playing the Canadian poet Al Purdy almost by accident. *Yours, Al* started with a CBC radio show, *A Night at the Quinte*, in the Glenn Gould Studio – just me and a jazz combo and Al's poetry. It took me a while to get it, but when I got it, I hung onto every word that would make a difference. And it did.

Onto another show business function. Sarah Polley stops by my table. It's two years later and, frankly, Alice Munro is not top of mind. For me, that is.

"Gordon," she says, "did you ever read 'The Bear Came Over the Mountain'?"

"No, Sarah," I confess. "No, I haven't read it."

"Well, read it, Gordon. It's very good!'"

That's all she says. But that's all she needs to say. I now realize she wants to turn it into a film. So of course I am now very interested, because Sarah is one of those individuals who knows how to get things done, one way or another.

At the beginning we only had the Alice Munro short story to read. I quite liked it. And Charm liked it too, well enough. I was aware there had been a couple of other major films about Alzheimer's disease; one of them, *Iris*, with Jim Broadbent and my *Shipping News* comrade Judi Dench, had just opened. But I knew I was going to say yes anyway, because it was Sarah. And then I read her script, and Charm and I agreed that it was just too good not to do. So we would wait for Sarah's call. I didn't know the inner history of the project, of her struggle to get it done, to get it through Telefilm. Besides, I was trying to get my own film off the ground.

I have always thought of CBC as my home studio, feeling much the same way about the Mother Corp as Hollywood actors in the fifties felt about MGM and Paramount. I've never forgotten the first time I walked into the Sumach Street rehearsal studio. The place was pulsing with its own heartbeat, with singers, dancers, actors, craftsmen spilling into the halls. It was so exciting. I loved it there. Over the years I learned, frequently the hard way, that regardless of how you feel, a studio cannot love you back. But I had been through so many CBC doors, so many CBC radio and television studios, that it always felt like home to me. Logic had little to do with it.

Accordingly, when I finished my latest script, I submitted it to CBC. The network gave us the green light, and soon we were shooting *Heyday*, my celluloid memoir of those heady days in the early forties when movie stars still roamed the streets of Gander. Consequently I'm sure you won't be surprised to learn that the character of Terry Fleming, the young busboy played by Adam Butcher, was based almost entirely on the experiences and fantasies of young Porky Pinsent. Mark McKinney played Bob Hope, Frank Holden played Winston Churchill, and, in the role inspired by the real-life visit of Maria Montez, Leah looked every inch the movie queen. And of course I loved shooting it in Newfoundland.

"Is it fun directing a period piece?" one of the younger actors asked me.

"Not as much fun as being there," I told him honestly. "It wasn't a period piece when I was living it!"

Peter Keleghan had shot a new pilot for CBC for a new weekly comedy called *Walter Ego*, about a cartoonist. The pilot, an intriguing mix of sitcom and animation, was undeniably impressive, and so was his supporting cast, led by three high-octane leading ladies: Jackie Burroughs, Diane Flacks, and Charm. By now Peter was part of the family, so we were all waiting, fingers crossed, to see if the series would get a green light. It didn't.

I blinked, and suddenly I was seventy-five, and Harry called to remind me that it was also the centennial of Grand Falls. Why he was really calling was to tell me the Board of Directors wanted to change the name of the Grand Falls–Windsor Region Arts & Culture Centre to the Gordon Pinsent Centre for the Arts. Would Charm and I attend a special Grand Falls evening in my honour?

I said Yes.

As if I would ever dream of saying No.

When we arrived in Grand Falls, centennial chairperson Paul Hennessey personally escorted me to the local radio station, ostensibly to do an interview. Unbeknownst to me, the Gordon Pinsent Birthday Committee had imported two surprise guests: my best friends Larry Dane and Perry Rosemond. They got to the radio station ahead of me and were doing a bogus interview that had been set up so that I would hear it just as I was arriving. I could hear Perry saying, "Yes, yes, he's finally come to terms with his sexuality." And Larry, adding, "Of course, he was drinking then." And then I could hear Perry saying, "Yes, but that's under control now." And right then and there I knew we were in for quite a night.

It was a wonderful evening, made even more wonderful because we could share it with our three children, Barry, Beverly, and Leah, and with all the surviving Pinsents, most of whom showed up to celebrate with us. Charm looked dazzling in her ivory evening gown, and I was appropriately black-tied. And in addition to the Grand Falls speakers we expected to hear from, Perry and Larry got the evening off to a roaring start. Or, to be accurate, a roasting start. Neither Larry nor Perry could ever let an occasion like this go by without sharing a few well-chosen barbs.

Larry took the podium first.

"Gordon, old friend," he began, "I've got to tell you, from where I stand – you look terrible." He then proceeded to read a series of bogus telegrams from everyone from Shania Twain ("Gordon who?") to Heidi Fleiss ("Gordon, because it's your birthday, you can forget about the twenty grand you owe me") to Kevin Spacey ("Gordon, after working with you on *Shipping News* I've decided you have more talent in your little finger than you have in your whole body"). And then he added a few zingers of his own. My favourites: "Gordon has done as much for acting as Michelangelo did for fifteenth-century computer repair." And, "Gordon's idea of being unfaithful is turning away from the mirror. If ego ever gets to $50 a barrel, Danny Williams will want drilling rights to Gordon's head." But it was his closing remark that was the most touching.

"Gordon," he said softly, "you are the boy who built the boat. And you are the boy who sails her."

Perry, a past master of deadpan stand-up, picked up where Larry left off.

"I'm honoured to be asked to speak about Gordon Pinsent," he began. "But this hardly seems like the time and place."

A respectful pause, and then laughter bubbled up. Perry smiled.

"I've known Gordon for fifty years. There's nothing I wouldn't do for him and there's nothing he wouldn't do for me. And for fifty years we've done absolutely nothing for each other."

Perry then proceeded to recite a verbal biography of my existence. "July 12, 1930. Gordon is born. His big brother Harry is ecstatic. For the rest of his life, Harry Pinsent will seem normal!"

He also had some well-chosen words for Grand Falls, still not the easiest place to get to. "I first came to Grand Falls about forty years ago, and I got here this time the same way Gordon did – via Kingston, Moncton, Gander, Steubenville, Costa Rica, and by mule team from Deer Lake!"

The first time he visited, he said, "my reaction to Grand Falls was probably much like yours – too many damn Pinsents!" Which, as you can imagine, sent a room full of Pinsents into gales of laughter.

Barry and Leah continued the roast. Leah informed the crowd that I was a good but strict father. "I wore this cleavage for my dad," she quipped, a little dig about the rigid rules I had set for her teenage years. And Barry turned in a boffo stand-up performance. "After this is all over," he said, "there is a good chance we may break this old bugger when we give him the bumps!"

He also noted that I had received "lifetime achievement award after lifetime achievement award after lifetime achievement award. *Oh yes, and I've got a lot more to do,*" he added, mimicking me. "A man your age just can't take a hint. Do we have to pry your honours from your palsied hands??"

An unexpected highlight was an email from the Yukon sent by an old friend who couldn't make it to Grand Falls. Shelagh Rogers and I shared a special and unusual history. One fall morning in 2002 I was her guest on her CBC *Morning* show, when I saw her eyeline shift from me to a television monitor outside the studio. I turned slightly, to see if her director was telling her to wrap it up, and then I saw the smoke pouring out of the World Trade Center towers. It was September 11, and Shelagh had just seen the second plane crash into the second tower. That moment in time had given us an inexplicably unique link, and we have been fast friends ever since. So I was very touched by her electronic greeting:

Brown is the new black.
In Vancouver real estate, 500K is the new 100K.
And in terms of age, 50 is the new 40, and 75 is the new 55.

But oh, there is a man who time does not age, with the same aptitudes and appetites he had in his 30s. And there's no mistaking his face, his voice, his presence.

He has this ability to make everything he touches more beautiful.

When he enters the room the temperature goes up, the laughter grows deeper, and the stories get better.

His art is art, and he is my favorite work of art.

He has led us and all his creative outlets to a greater understanding of what it means to be human – and how wonderful that can be.

Gordon, I just got off the plane in Whitehorse, or I would be there to say thank you for 75 years of you, and for all you have given us of you. And if I was there you would certainly get a big bosomy hug from me.

Dear Gordon – with you in the room, our revels now
never end.

I love you. Happy birthday.

Shelagh

And just when we figured nothing could top that, Beverly,
who was not scheduled to speak, approached the podium and
surprised everyone, including herself, by asking if she could
sing her tribute to her father.

Charm and I both knew, from talking with Barry, that
Beverly had sung professionally, but we had never heard her
warble a single note.

"I'd like to use my voice to sing for all of you," she told the
hundreds of family, fans, and friends who had come out for
the occasion – and then delivered a throaty, flawless a cap-
pella version of "Danny Boy," with appropriate lyric changes
("*O Gordie Boy . . .*").

Her impromptu performance earned her the first sponta-
neous standing ovation of the evening. Which seemed to
surprise her. But not us.

There were more tributes, each salute more generous than
the previous one. "Are you sure I still have a pulse?" I murmured. Charm flashed her one-thousand-kilowatt Warning
smile, and we both laughed.

After I got up to thank my roasters and my admirers, I admitted I was feeling awkward about the whole thing. "I didn't
count on anything. I thought my payment was in the work I

was doing. But you haven't forgotten me. You remembered me, bringing me back into the heart of Grand Falls again.

"When I was young," I told them, "I admired the grown-ups. I admired what they had done. My interests, my fascination with the grown-ups had a touch of forefather to it. I was in a hurry to be grown-up. I was training to be like the people in this town.

"As young people we didn't think that life started with us. We knew our history was there to pick like blueberries whenever we needed it, whenever we wanted it.

"We didn't know it then but we know it now – our family was rich beyond belief. We were rich in each other. Without exception my three sisters would show up at every live theatre event I did, no matter how small."

I looked out at the crowd. Nita's family, Hazel's family, and Lil's family were all seated at tables facing me. I had known them when they were children, and I knew them now, and it was an absolute delight to see it all coming together.

"Yes, it was showing off," I continued. "That's what I did, from as early on as I can remember. I wanted to be seen. I wanted to be heard. I was so driven, so fast-track, trying to push a career as far as I could. So I had to go into what I had to do."

My teachers, I added, would be surprised if they could see me now. "*No, no, that's not him, he's wearing a necktie, for God's sake!*"

And then I finally 'fessed up.

"When I was very young I wanted a birthday party," I admitted. "Wanted some excitement. Wanted some attention. I was ten at the time. So I told my pals, 'It's my birthday, you know – pass it on. I'm having a party. In the family woodshed. Bring gifts.'

"They did. They brought gifts they'd been given for Christmas, or their birthdays. One fellow brought an ice cream maker and all the ingredients. I went into the kitchen to negotiate with my older sister Nita and my mother. 'I need plates and spoons, please. I'm having a party.'

"One of the girls had a crush on me, and she asked what was going on. One of my pals explained that it was my birthday, and I was having a party.

"She was puzzled by this information. 'It can't be Gordie's birthday,' she said, 'because Gordie's birthday is the same day as mine.' So they all left and took their gifts with them.

"And it did occur to me, fleetingly, at this seventy-fifth birthday celebration, that the 750 guests might all decide to leave and take their gifts with them. But happily that didn't happen.

"I've just had a whale of a time. And I will not be shaken from that memory."

Before we adjourned I was presented with a special award from the RCMP. The presenter was a statuesque blonde female RCMP officer. Without thinking, I thanked her and kissed her on both cheeks. She blushed.

"I've never kissed a Mountie before," I said. "But then, there's a first time for everything."

Charm and I were still blissed out by the whole event when our Air Canada flight landed us safely back in Toronto.

away from her

No matter how much of life you eat up, there's always something left over.

How else to explain my good fortune when Sarah Polley cast me, Porky Pinsent, seventy-five years young, as Grant Anderson in *Away from Her*? Sarah wanted to work with people she knew, people she liked working with. And she was so ready, so prepared. I wasn't concerned about this being her first time directing, because I knew her well enough to know that she would be ready. It's that moment, that moment of realization, that you're about to do something you really want to do, something maybe you've always wanted to do, and I think that must have been what Sarah was feeling when we started shooting. She had come over to the house a couple of times, and walked around looking at everything, especially all the photographs on the walls, and she said, "Gordon, every picture that you're in, you're laughing!"

"Yes," I said. "What's wrong with that?"

"I don't know, Gordon," she said. "But you laugh SO much. You're *always* laughing!"

So she knew me, and she had worked with Julie Christie and Olympia Dukakis before, so she didn't have to worry about us and she could concentrate on other things. She knew we had her back.

Working with Julie was great fun. Julie is terrific. I had never seen *Darling*. I have seen her in all sorts of other stuff, going all the way back to *Billy Liar*, but not the one she won the Oscar for, so many years earlier.

Olympia was fun to work with too. On our first day of shooting together I detected a lovely scent in the air.

"You smell good," I told her. "What are you wearing?"

"*EV-rything!*" she said, and cracked me right up.

We had a week of rehearsal, which was great. Just lovely. Just Sarah and Julie and Olympia and me, and we would have sandwiches. It's like going back to school together. You get there and you bring an apple for the teacher, and try to put the piece together, try to make your own contribution to it, to make it richer if you possibly can. We had all come from different places, to play in the same kindergarten together. And suddenly it felt like you were part of their game, and they were part of yours. Suddenly you were speaking the same language.

Apparently Sarah had given Julie a choice of three actors, 1, 2, and 3, and I was number 3. And Julie said, "No to number one, no to number two, and yes to Gordon Pinsent." The first time I met her we happened to be getting out of our cars at the same time, and she opened her arms and cried, "My husband!" Which was very sweet of her. One time I picked up some coffee for us, and Julie said, very grandly, "That's all I'll ask of you, Gordon! That's all you will have to do, pick up the coffee and not forget it!"

"Be guaranteed of it," I said rather formally, "I will!"

On another occasion she caught a certain glint in my eye and somehow discerned what I was thinking but not saying aloud.

"Y'know, Gordon," she said, "you strike me as someone who's sitting on a lot of one-liners!"

"Oh no," I said, "not me. Not at all." And she just grinned back at me, not buying it for a second.

Like many stars she would choose her moments to be light, but you never knew when they would happen. We were in Paris, Ontario, shooting, and she was on the other side of the street with her assistant, waiting to be called. And she saw me on this side of the street and screamed, "*Gordon Pinsent!* Oh my God, it's *Gordon Pinsent!*" And I started to bark, "*Julie Christie!* Look, it's *Julie Christie!*" And we stood there laughing and shouting at each other across the street.

Charm visited me on location whenever she could. Back in Toronto she had returned to Albert Schultz and Soulpepper to play two classics in rep: Nikolai Gogol's *The Government Inspector* and Thornton Wilder's *Our Town*. The Soulpepper production of *Our Town* was so popular, she confided, that there was already talk of mounting it again next season, and Albert had approached her about doing Chekhov's *Three Sisters* and Saroyan's *The Time of Your Life*, and she was already bubbling with enthusiasm.

Meanwhile, we were shooting our winter scenes in the Ontario snowbelt. On the first day we were getting dressed to shoot the cross-country skiing sequence, and our trainers were there with us. Julie got into her suit, and she got out onto the snow, and she was good. She was better than I was, faster than I was, catching on quicker than I was. I wasn't catching on at all. I was having a series of falls, telling Sarah that I hoped she was getting them all, because I thought they could be inspirational, and really add a level of sincerity to the film. In the film itself, of course, they cut from me struggling to my double, who is whizzing across the horizon like a pro. But Julie was good.

Julie had done a lot of preparation. I think that was the way she approached everything. Very professional. It was a large part, and in the past few years she had been doing smaller roles, so she was feeling a bit insecure. At one point she introduced us all to Lindy Davies, a director friend of hers from Australia, who sat on the set and scrutinized her performance. "I'm not sure about that move, dear," she might say. Or, "Maybe go up the stairs a little faster." Sarah was perfectly sanguine. Her expression never changed.

Lindy went to see rushes one night, to report back to Julie, and when Julie came on the set the next morning, she told me, "Lindy said you were stunning." And I thought, *Okay, I'm home free.* So it was wonderful for me, because we got along so well.

Julie also devoted a lot of time and energy to green initiatives, working to save the planet. Which of course I teased her about.

"You're going to be very proud of me, Julie," I told her one day, "because I just bought a hybrid."

"Oh my!" she said, genuinely surprised. "That's wonderful, Gordon!"

"Yes," I said, "and it's *so* quiet! It's perfect for sneaking up on baby seals."

I decided to play the husband as an observer, someone who was playing catch-up, and I did it that way because I wanted to play him as an average guy who had no reason to know very much about this particular disease. Even today most people still don't know very much about Alzheimer's. I didn't know very much about it then. So I imagined myself as a man on the street who, suddenly faced with having to deal with it as a caregiver, has to find out as much about it as he can, and discovers a whole new world. And that way I could stand back a lot, watch the procedure, and see who was involved, and feel the shock of losing her all the more. And as long as I stayed with that, I could go anywhere.

Truthfully, I had only sort-of-read the short story – skimmed it, really – before we started shooting. But it was Sarah's screenplay I wanted to shoot. Because the writing is everything. You enter into someone else. It's rather a childlike thing, once you're into a character like Grant in that movie. It's like a day away from yourself. You go away into another life. You have no idea of time passing by or anything else. It's a lovely thing. And sometimes, if you're doing it right, you can speak with silence. I had very little dialogue to learn, but I was in almost every scene of the film, so I had to make the most of all those moments, for me and for the audience.

Months later *Away from Her* was selected for a gala screening at the Toronto International Film Festival. Sitting in the centre box that night at the festival, with Julie and Sarah and the rest of the cast, watching the audience watch the movie, watching for any sign of restlessness whatsoever, hearing no sound except what was coming from the screen, because the audience was so silent, so still, and then at the end, that explosion of applause – it was one of the highlights, maybe *the* highlight, of my life as an actor. Standing there, in the front row of the box at Roy

Thomson Hall, the spotlights blazing on us, blinking at the hundreds of little flashes from cameras all over the room, and all the time, people cheering – for a minute I thought I was in another film. David Perlmutter, a producer and an old friend, was so moved that he rushed over and kissed me on the cheek, and I was so happy to be there with Charm on my arm.

After the screening we all went out to celebrate, of course. Little did we know what a memorable post-gala party it would be.

> TORONTO (CP) - Veteran actor Gordon Pinsent was rest-
> ing at home Tuesday, a day after collapsing at a party for the
> new Sarah Polley film *Away From Her*. "He's fine. He'll have to
> take it easy for a day or two," his wife, Charmaine King,* said
> in an interview. "He'd been doing too much work for the last 10
> days or so, promoting the film. But he's fine."
> Pinsent, 76, is a companion of the Order of Canada and a
> fellow of the Royal Society of Canada. He worked in theatre
> as a teenager and moved on to roles in radio drama, television
> and film. King said doctors told Pinsent he was dehydrated.
> He stayed overnight in hospital.

I'm sure some people thought it was a publicity stunt. There we were, at the traditional glamorous after-party, at which I smiled profusely, modestly accepted the extravagant praise being showered upon me, and then, without so much as a

* Not the first time Charm's name would be misspelled in the press. Not the last, either.

by-your-leave, I collapsed. Oh sure, arrive by limo, depart by ambulance. Talk about an exit!

Okay, dehydrated. I don't suppose it had anything to do with endlessly talking about myself for three consecutive days before the screening, to any newspaper, radio, or television interviewer who would have me. This was one film I was eager to help promote, but when you're running on that particular treadmill you can sometimes mistake one thing for another. Apparently I mistook drink for food. It happens.

Needless to say Charm was terribly upset with me. No one who gets billing above the title is supposed to collapse at his own party. It's simply not done. But at least I had a good excuse.

When Charm asked me what had happened, I was perfectly candid.

"I was talking to some English producers," I told her, "and I was having a bite to eat, and a drink, and people kept coming up to us, interrupting us, to tell me how great I was in the movie. And I turned, and I tripped over my ego."

Charm loved that.

I subsequently managed to get through premieres in New York and L.A. without falling down again. Sarah and Julie and I were together for the New York and L.A. Writers Guild screenings for the film. At the New York event Sidney Lumet, a director I'd always admired, sought me out after the screening to tell me how moved he was by the film and my work in it, and Robin Williams did the same thing in L.A., which, as you can imagine, didn't hurt my feelings at all. Even if they did get a bit bruised around Oscar time.

The company distributing *Away from Her* was Lionsgate Films. Lionsgate launched an Oscar campaign for the film, promoting Julie for Best Actress and Sarah for Best Director and Best Adapted Screenplay. I too thought Julie and Sarah were the most obvious Oscar candidates and agreed with Lionsgate's choices, and professionally I did not feel slighted. I knew it wasn't personal, and I assumed that Lionsgate did not have an unlimited budget for Oscar trolling.

"This is *outrageous!*" Larry protested when he learned of this. "Lionsgate should be promoting you too!" he stormed. "Don't they read their own reviews? Let's get real here! You stand a better chance of growing angel wings than winning an Academy Award. In fact you stand a better chance of growing angel wings than being *nominated* for an Academy Award. But, by God, you should absolutely be included in their *For Your Consideration* ads in the trades! After all those reviews, they don't even mention you?? That's ridiculous!"

When the 2008 Oscar nods were announced, Julie was nominated for Best Actress and Sarah was nominated for Best Adapted Screenplay. Closer to home, when the 2008 Genie nominations were announced, *Away from Her* was up for Best Picture, Best Director, Best Actor, Best Actress, Best Supporting Actress, Best Adapted Screenplay, and Best Editing.

The Oscar buzz began. "Gordon, you've got to come down here!" Julie messaged from Hollywood. "Everyone is talking about you. Everyone wants to meet you!"

She was right. I should have gone down there. It wasn't like I didn't know the town. But instead, I stayed put. I should've gone down there and hung out, or delivered papers or something, to establish once and for all a *reputation*. But that's not who I was. It's still not who I am.

After all these years I still don't play the game very well. I've always kept my mouth shut around stars. I don't know why. Maybe because of the Pinsent anxiety. Maybe because of my fascination with them when I was growing up.

Away from Her was winning global acclaim. Would my career be different today if I had been more aggressive then? Maybe. Maybe not. My agent received two offers from Hollywood after *Away from Her* opened in the U.S. One was insignificant window-dressing; my character was not even remotely essential to the story. The other was a horror film in which a bunch of elderly characters in an old folks' home get slashed and trashed by a middle-aged serial killer who didn't get along with his parents. What you really want to say is, YOU'VE GOT TEN MINUTES TO GET THIS SCRIPT OFF MY RANCH! But this is show business, so what you say is, *No Thank You I Don't Think This Particular Script Is Right for Me at This Particular Time but Thanks Very Much for Thinking of Me.*

On February 24, 2008, Julie and Sarah, both beautifully coiffed and gowned, looked stunning on camera at the 80th Academy Awards. Julie lost Best Actress to Marion Cotillard for her stunning portrayal of Edith Piaf in *La vie en rose*; Sarah lost the Writing prize to Joel and Ethan Coen for *No Country for Old Men*. The Coens also took Best Picture and Best Director, so at least she knew she'd been beaten by the best. She later reported back to me, very sweetly, that later at the Governor's Ball she was sought out by Susan Sarandon and

Best Actor winner Daniel Day-Lewis,* both asking for me.

"Please tell him for me," said Day-Lewis, "that his was one of the best performances I've ever seen."

Sarandon was equally effusive. "This is a performance all actors should see," she told Sarah.

Yes, I should have been there.

Julie sent me a postcard from a woodland retreat in California.

Dear Gordon,
I appreciated your flowers more than any others I received.
It was so thoughtful and generous, and everyone was saying,
who is that brilliant actor? And how could he not be
nominated? More and more there was a feeling that you
deserved a nomination just as much as, if not more than,
we. I'm counting on you and Sarah to retrieve our ragged
collars. Lots of love, sweetheart.

Julie

One week later the Academy of Canadian Cinema & Television voters rewarded *Away from Her* with six Genie Awards, including Writing and Directing statuettes for Sarah, Best Supporting Actress for Kristen Thompson, Best Actress and Best Actor for Julie and me, respectively, and Best Picture of the Year. And we were all very happy when Sarah also picked up the special Claude Jutra Award for first-time feature film

* Daniel Day-Lewis won his Best Actor award (his second) for *There Will Be Blood.*

directors, because we knew she really deserved it. She is such a darling. And so smart. I don't know if I could imagine her now not having the success she's had. And she's done it here. What a girl she is.

I was surprised by the response to *Away from Her*. I was happy but surprised to see it received so well globally because the subject matter, up to now at least, has not been a household word, even though we've all been touched by it, one way or another. But it was also a great love story, so it was very gratifying to see it get such a great response wherever it played. As any actor will tell you, there is a lack of great material out there. But when you find a project like *Away from Her*, you just jump at the chance to do it.

It was close to the end of the show when my friend and fellow ACTRA champion Wendy Crewson, looking every inch a star in her elegant crimson evening gown, presented me with the award for Best Actor. And when she did, all I could think of was how I got there, on that stage, because I had not made the journey alone.

I looked out into the darkness. "Charm, this is for you," I said, "as is everything I do and everything I ever will do."

She had sat by my side, as glamorous as always, at my seventy-fifth birthday celebration in Grand Falls. A year and a bit later she was at my side again, effortlessly glamorous again, at the September world premiere of *Away from Her* at the 2006 Toronto International Film Festival.

"Gordon," she'd said, "your work in this film is exceptional. I'm so proud of you."

Four months later she was gone.

The great Kate had died in March. Barbara Ham had passed in February. Winter deaths that left us chilled.

Charmion King Pinsent left us on January 6, 2007, and we were never the same again.

charm school

What do we do when the clock strikes two
And we've dried up the bars and the wells?
Where do the scribes go to imbibe
when they're drier than old cockleshells?
Where do they go in the cold, cold snow
when the heaven's and hell's bells knells?
Well, the heart of my sweet Charmion
is the place where Pinsent dwells!

CHARMION KING PINSENT WAS A GREAT ACTRESS, A great mother, and a great wife. And she was more than that. She was my soulmate and my true partner, in everything I did.

We were not perfect people. Brutally honest when she chose to be, Charm was not shy about acknowledging it. During an on-camera session for a *Life & Times* biography of me on CBC, she told her interviewer that we'd had three breakups in one five-year period alone.

"I'll tell you frankly," she added, "a lot of it was my own fault. I was drinking at the time. So I think, you know, that was hard to take."

She didn't say, *And Gordon has a well-known weakness for flirta-tions.* But she could have. I know my extramarital diversions were hard to take. That period in my life was very hurtful to Charm, and I will always regret it. It certainly put a strain on my relationship with Leah, who to this day remains my tough-est, most honest, and most loving critic. Like her mother, Leah is not shy about expressing her true feelings. And, like her mother, she is still the first to come to my defence. In an on-camera interview with filmmaker Barbara Doran for her 2011 documentary, *Gordon Pinsent: Still Rowdy After All These Years,* Leah partly attributed our breakups to my "rowdiness," adding that show business could be hard on marriages, "because if you're a relatively attractive man, or sexy, as some people seem to think, a lot of women don't stop to think, 'Oh, you're mar-ried.' They just don't care. They just love the attention on them, or vice versa. And that's very flattering."

Yes, Charm and I had some ups and downs, but the ups were so many, and so high, that the downs become more dis-tant in memory every year. I knew when I first saw her that friends of hers would be very lucky people. And I wondered how I would ever get to be a "keeper" too. Maybe she would include me at the trailing end of a smile to others, but anything more than that would not be necessarily needed. She might well show me something about myself that would drop me from contention. Oh God, I hoped not. After we met at the Crest, me the supporting player to her star turn, there were a couple of awkward months of theatre openings and dinners, during which times I didn't know what pose to assume, so I remained mostly patiently un-decorative, until it was time to leave. The fact that her old friends might not have approved of her new choice mattered not, as she was already through her "eeny-meeny-minies" and I was her "mo." Lucky, lucky mo.

We didn't like being apart. Sometimes it was unavoidable. The jobs were sometimes at opposite ends of the country. There would be the inevitable nightly calls, then opening night wires. We used to send each other telegrams. Telegraph operators were forbidden by law to transmit messages of, shall we say, an overly amorous nature, but nonetheless I'd get away with a tricky one at times: *"I'd much rather be at your opening than mine,"* one said, and somehow slipped by the regulations.

Larry Dane used to tease Charm that she was living in a ménage à trois – Charm, Gordon, and Gordon's Career. It was funny because it was true. When she was on Broadway in *Love and Libel*, she turned down a Hollywood contract to come back to Canada. She wanted to help build Canadian theatre and Canadian theatre audiences. She did twenty-one productions at the Crest, for about $100 a show. "Labour of love," she would explain with a shrug. She would have been both amused and pleased, I think, to read obituaries that referred to her as "the Grand Dame of Canadian theatre."

Her passion for theatre inevitably reduced her opportunities to shine on big and small screens. And she wasn't as lucky as I was. When we moved back from L.A. she was very hurt because she didn't get a part she wanted on *King of Kensington*. "I couldn't even get that," she said. I could hear the deep disappointment in her voice, but she never ever mentioned it again. She was all for wining, but not for whining. So she just became more Charm, more of who she was. Who she was was a wonderful teacher. She considered acting akin to university: "It opens your mind, your soul, and makes you tap into yourself." She used to say, "We need to tell kids that if your first experience as an actor is working with awful people in a situation that has a rushed and treacherous feel to it all, don't think for a second that that's the way the business is. Because there will come a time, maybe even your next time, that will have a standard that you can really look to. You don't have to look to the standard of the bad experience with the director or whomever. Because the better standard is waiting for you, and when you come across it, you'll fit like a glove, and this business will become the love of your life."

This business was never the love of my life. Charm was. She completed me – in so many ways. Sometimes I would sit in bed like a whimpering child, complaining about the business, and she would remind me about how much I had already accomplished, how much I already had on my resumé that so many others didn't, and she'd bring me right back again. Because we had history together. I can still remember the two of us standing in the kitchen of our apartment, our arms around each other, watching the tower on top of the old CBC building on Jarvis Street come down. And then we could see the shell, and it seemed as if we knew someone who had worked in every one of those rooms.

Charm had made sense of this business for everyone she touched. She was a remarkably generous actor. I would overhear her talking on the phone with a producer or director who wanted her for a part she didn't want to play "No, honestly, it's just not right for me," she would be saying, very consolingly.

The Rowdyman.

Leah, 5, taking
me for a walk.

Clockwise, from top left: Harry, Haig, me, Lil, Nita, Hazel.

In Ottawa with Nova Scotia premier Gerald Regan and Prime Minister Pierre Elliott Trudeau. (This time I brought my own tie.)

At Rideau Hall, receiving my upgrade to Companion of the Order of Canada from Governor General Roméo LeBlanc.

When it comes to leading
ladies, I've been lucky.
Angie Dickinson in
Klondike Fever; Jackie
Burroughs in *John and the
Missus*; Julie Christie in
Away From Her; and, best
of all, Miss Charmion
King, who had the
wisdom (and, even more
remarkably, the patience!)
to wait for me to grow up.

Working with guest star Leslie Nielsen and Paul Gross on *Due South*.

With Leah and Rick Mercer in *Made in Canada*. Fifteen minutes after this photo was taken I got to fire both of them.

With Mark Polley, Sarah's older brother, in *A Gift to Last*. We were a big hit at home, but in South Africa we were bigger than *Dynasty!*

On screen in 1982 as *Edwin Alonzo Boyd*. Years later, Charm invited him to tea.

On the set of *A Case of Libel* with my attorney Ed Asner.

Going on record – in this case, a new words-and-music double CD
– with Greg Keelor and Travis Good.

Going viral on YouTube thanks to *22 Minutes* and Justin Bieber.

"But you know who you should call?" And then she would give them the name of another actress – a supposed *rival*, if you will – and then tell them how to reach her. "Because the role is perfect for her, and she'll do you proud."

She could have written the book on being professional in our industry. And she never went off track once. She was just a tremendous guide and friend and partner. She was also one of life's great naturals when it came to beauty that lasts. She had never flaunted her superb gift of rejuvenation, but it had never failed her 'til closer to the end. She never stopped smoking, but after a while, when it was just too difficult for her to catch her breath, I would take her in to the hospital, at about the same time for about five years in a row, and after her usual, three-day stay, she would not be seen in public or anywhere but her inner mirror, until the sign was there showing her she was back again. I'd never seen anything like it. Leah and I knew that she would have hated to return home only to spend her days with the oxygen attachment. That wasn't Charm. Not in the slightest. She had believed so very much in the creative spirit, and had succeeded, so expertly, in her comebacks, until it was no longer possible.

In the early years of our marriage I had a lot of living to do. And a lot of growing up to do. And Charm waited till I got there. She waited for me to grow up, through all those years, all that staggering around, trying to call myself an actor, trying to call myself an artist, waiting for that special door to open. We need margins in life, guidelines, and my life had no margins. Charm was my margins.

After Charm passed I fell into a most natural state of, well, what's left? I didn't want to do anything. And for a while, I didn't. The world was not the same without her in it. I had spent all these years showing off to Charm. She treated me as a brand-new person every day. Because we were in the business of ideas.

I kept to myself after she passed. I had said just about everything I had to say to her out loud, so many times, that I guess the time had come to share it with the computer. So, along came *The Sculptor*, a word-painting of my state of mind. It was about me; about Charm; about us.

Someone once asked Charm the secret to a good marriage. Charm said, "Laughter, darling. Laughter." We had kept each other laughing for more than forty years. We always had time for it. It was like a terminal to us. Circled it on many an occasion; got shot at and shot down by things – mostly pertaining to the sea-changing of the business – but we'd get back home and you'd never guess, we were the same people. I'll take a shot at an example, here.

We were expecting company. Both sitting in the living room. I was still in my shorts, planning to dive into my slacks just before our guests arrived. We heard a noise outside our front door. "If that's our company," said Charm, with her flawless deadpan delivery, "I would tuck that back inside." Sorry. True.

I had whistled for her every night when we were doing *Madwoman of Chaillot* at the Crest. We would continue to whistle for each other for the next four decades.

I still keep whistling. And I know she still hears me.

It's not the same.

THE SCULPTOR

He had sculpted her face. She'd liked it.

Especially the right half.

"What's wrong with the left?" he'd asked.

"I don't know, but it's more like my cousin's. You remember her."

"I disagree," he said.

And though he did, he would kiss the right profile, never the left, whenever passing.

The closer he burrowed his face into the sculptured face, the truer in nature the more real her clay features became. Not really, of course, because it was less than perfection in reality. But now he was able to think he was breathing with her, and could talk to her as he had always done – close – endearing himself to her and leaving the world behind.

He would do this easily, and her smile would seem to know what he needed and she of him. And it was a pleasure.

And with her gone, he'd have words with this image. Especially after a Scotch at cocktail time.

She must truly be gone, because with the coolness of their place, she would have warmed it by now.

Each day, he found himself caring less, needing less, moving less, almost breathing less, and missing her more and more.

After all, what had he been? Who the hell was he without her? Not enough of himself left to matter anymore. Melting now. No interest in what the calendars were saying, triggering the arrivals of one season after another.

He'd become careless, his immunity so overdrawn, that anything could invade him, bend him, in ways it would never have been possible. Yet, he didn't care. Strength wasn't necessary anymore. What would he use it for? And giving himself over to the weakness in this way was not a frightening thing to him.

Job offers had vanished from his mind, and everyone with it. Truth is, he didn't care if he got the job or not. Since losing her, he truly didn't place importance on anything; and this from a man who had laughed at himself and his foibles louder than anyone. The hiccup in which he had lived was over two-thirds done anyway. How lame was it now, in its humorous staging, after he'd been broadsided with mortality.

Without her, ordinary pain would be nothing to bear. It would be fun to wish for a wicked toothache, a crashing migraine, a stinging slap in the face, a pinch, a whack from a door, or a newly acquired broken limb, all former enjoyable things as well: the tang of salsa, smell of wet spruce, pine and fir. All jokes now, worthy of applause to God. All replaced now, with the stupidity of conversation with a boring person quiet enough to block out the noise of the world, a scar left over, so quickly forgotten after the welcome, momentary intensity of the initial pain? Promised sensations paid off in fleabites, as if they'd never happened. Gone the way of all things. Strongly tasted, and gone.

Most of all, he hated to think less of himself than she did. And didn't go out a lot. Friends had seen them together; envied the match, saw the great thing they had; why would they want to see one without the other?

Her greatness, her beauty, her mind, the world of love in her eyes for him, a daily thing, was not to be worn out by side-long glances of sympathy or cheap curiosity in a theatre lobby. What he had, was his; and he still knew he could reach out and touch her at any time – privately or publicly – when his heart needed warming off hers. But he didn't owe any of them anything right now. He owed her. Even now; because he always thought that everything belonged to everyone – anyone – but himself. The things surrounding him at all times in his early life or mid-to-late life – especially her – were always far beyond what he might expect to be his.

That night – turning in at an hour that would have been unheard of for him in his life – he thought he'd read, before falling off. The following night, he did so again. The eyes had always been good, had never needed help. But now a squinting had taken place, and this found him looking for – and miraculously finding – a pair of old spectacles. He knew right where he'd find them – in the cedar closet – and went straight for them, as if they were his own, and he'd merely misplaced them. He put them on, and wore them as if they were ordered for him. Just right for the small print of the bedside bible.

Other than the eyes, everything about him seemed stronger. He saw nothing wrong with talking to himself.

At the very moment that she died, he was robbed of his proper mind. He couldn't allow himself to sleep more than a couple of hours at a time for fear of wanting to never wake again, which would be fine with him, but hateful to her in her thinking.

He had remained in their place afterwards, as he wanted to, and he was sure that she was still with him, as her scent had remained, at any time of day or night. Her voice had clung as well, and told him there was no great difference in her going, to prod him that he should keep on. They hadn't spoken of this. He was far more the child when dealing with this sort of thing, but it was different with her. "It's okay, get over yourself!" she'd say. The understanding of death was deeper and more naturally in her bones than in his. He was not ready. Not nearly ready for shit like dying. Would never be. Oh hell no. That's what doors were for, to keep things out, like death. That's what songs were for as well; about lasting love. EVER lasting love. Yes, there were deaths of friends, and their funerals, and they would attend, but he had perfected a practice not to take them in completely. He'd always look for scraps of amusement about them. These moments were not always available of course. On one occasion, they had left a funeral with another grieving friend, whose idea of dying equalled the perfection of the best movie he'd ever seen.

"We're having too many of these, my friend," the friend said. "And the one I'm not looking forward to, is yours."

After that, he couldn't drive.

Nearing her death, he was close to wishing he could go himself. He seemed made up of small, stuck-together photo fragments of many personalities, none of whom added up to a solid enough caregiver when needed. She was all he needed. To remind him how to go on. To love. And not stop living just because she had. To teach him how to breathe. He'd never recognized dying in either of them, so when it came through the door at last, he slammed the door on it.

To the end, she had worried only for him. "Get out of here now. I don't want you to see me like this."

Guiltily he did what she'd suggested, and removed himself to another vacant hospital space until at last they came to him to inform him that it was over. They expected him to go to her for a final moment with her in repose, but he sank into himself, from which he has since been afraid of completely surfacing.

How did she die? Natural causes. *Natural causes?* What the fuck are they? Natural causes. That all? Notice how some people just hurl those generals around like turds from a tall cow's arse, and leave you to break it down into details while they head off to more heightened lives. How the fuck do we know if they know what they meant? He'd just like to nail them into having to explain themselves once.

And what's he going to go from? Dic, I mean. Give him a good one. A great cramp when doing something heavy. Don't make it a natural cause. He doesn't want to drop dead without a mark on him. Got to have a wound! Must. To give them some idea of what happened to him at this age. He does not want them calling it natural causes without stopping to guess there might have been triggers to it. Lazy bastards.

He gives a quick look at the face, or what's left of it. Nobody's seen him naked, so would they get a surprise, when they stripped him for the morgue? His body would need to be better looking. He'd perform there as well. They'd have a look and there he'd be. Never seen without his clothes. By anyone. Done up to the throat, and the mystery body underneath. A perfectly formed body! Not a scar. This body wasn't old. Not matching the face at all. Younger and trimmer and unused by a good fifty years than what anyone would expect. Bloody near alien! . . . you think?

He is beginning to appear somewhat. . . unreal. He is sitting or moving about in some fictional state of life perhaps where any other person of normal understandable needs would not want to be seen.

The segue has not occurred that quickly. Nor would it, if he didn't wish it to be so. And he didn't. She would have wanted to be certain that his continuance would be a secure and safe one. God knows, she had waited 'til he grew up within their marriage, and yes, she had witnessed the maturing. The stability of this would convince her when he was fit and able to graduate to a new page in his unknown life. How he would step out of their life and into his life alone would be worth her extra time with him to see.

He's not in a hurry to change that. Nor should he be. And that's fine with her as well. She'll wait 'til he's ready, if that ever will come about. It doesn't matter. Not to her and not to him. It wouldn't be natural for either of them.

You, he's talking about you, dear. That won't change. He'll keep you as long as he can feel your breath upon him. As long as the ringing of your rich voice will brush his skin, and as long as you want to continue life with him, as you would if you were here as usual – before your "natural cause clause." And while you both – one here, one gone, one alive, one not – refuse to accept your one hideous day of dying from all of the thousands of days of sweetness in his life with you.

But now, with your help, he's got to be the man you knew. Starting with his imagination. He's got a trout in his trunks, and it won't let him sleep.

He will enter into someone else. Always a good way to spend his day.

Does she want to come along? Could he stop her? For certain, she couldn't stop him. And what harm? Was it real? Could it ever be real?

Would he lose himself, stray into fields bravely imagined? And would this field have an edge he had not registered, and end himself as well if she could not completely go without him? If he could not entirely let her go, then she might curiously assume the strangers he would meet within himself in whatever drifting worlds he allowed himself to go.

And of course she could never stop his mind, nor would she want to.

Then, a sliver of rationality.

Day will break, and mend again, and then again.

Dear Charm,

I forgot to tell you this, until now.

I was scuffing the snow outside our apartment block, waiting for a cab to arrive. This was only three days after your funeral, having learned now to dip my head so as to not be accessible to neighbours and such-like, knowing they would understand why my watery eyes would be that way. Not that this manoeuvre would work on a homeless, drifting by.

"Any change?"

"No," I said.

The homeless sniffed and trudged on. Then I recalled how you, my darling wife, had always carried change for homeless. So I called back homeless, and dug for coin.

Homeless sharply returned, twinkling elfishly. "I truly admire the way you changed your thinking there," he said, hand out.

When he received the change, he took it upon himself to sit down on a cement block, completely ignoring my perpetually water-filled eyes and purposely distanced body language.

"Is there anything better than freezing your arse off in Canada?"

I said nothing.

Then another one: "Lives here do ya?"

"Yes."

"Must be nice."

"It's okay."

"Yes, I bet. But know what I always say? I say it all evens out, y'know. What you got is probably a hundred times better than what I got, but that's yours, and what I got is mine."

Nothing.

"And what you eats no doubt tastes a whole lot better to you in your mouth than if you had a mouthful of what I eats, and likewise backwards."

No proper appreciation forthcoming.

"At the same time, I'd most likely heave up yours and you'd probably heave up mine. That's the way of the world, idden it?"

"Please," I said, and for a reason unknown to myself, shared: "I'm sorry. I've just lost my wife."

"That right? I lost t'ree of the bitches!!"

The entire city of Toronto must have heard that, and waited for my reaction. There wasn't one — at least, that you would have heard. But a whole well of crying and laughter collided inside me, and try as I might, the laughter stayed as long as it wanted to.

Missing you.

G.

charmless

———◦◉◦———

I hear her through the morning
riding waves of music's ocean
breakfasting with my emotion
mindful of the tune she plays
upon my heart, into my day
to swell my world, to cool my way
to teach love's majesty again
make distant all existing harm
I praise the miracle of Charm.

WHEN I WAS NOTIFIED BY THE FOUNDERS OF CANADA'S
Walk of Fame that they wanted to add my name to the Toronto
firmament, I automatically asked them to hold on for a minute
so I could tell Charm – until I remembered why I couldn't.
Those first few months after her death were challenging
ones, full of habits I had to break and dreams I had to erase.
So I called Leah instead, and she was very pleased to hear that
I would be celebrated in very good company. My fellow 2007
inductees were Johnny Bower, Rick Hansen, Jill Hennessy,
Catherine O'Hara, Lloyd Robertson, and the popular West

Coast rock band Nickelback, and Eugene Levy was set to host the gala evening at the Hummingbird Centre. And despite the fact that I couldn't help wishing Charm was by my side, taking it all in, it was a great night. At my request, Leah and Peter Keleghan presented my award to me, and I'd been getting so many sad looks from sympathetic audience members that I purposely decided to keep it light.

"You can't do this!" I protested meekly. "I happen to live here. This is just the kind of thing that can turn a Canadian's head. This is going to make me take side streets. Can't walk this way any more. What happens when they see you pass by your star? *'Look at him. Passing by his star! He'll be calling himself an icon soon.' 'We got the Mountie and we got the beaver! Those are the only two icons we need!'*

"Anyway," I continued, "I'll happily take it. If only to be part of this great list of fellow inductees. This has to be the best list of them all. I can see alumni reunions coming out of this one: With the brilliant Catherine O'Hara; the heroic Rick Hansen; Jill Hennessy, who for the longest time had been a second ambition of mine; Ivan Reitman, who deserves a street of stars; Lloyd, who needs no other name by now, he is known and loved that much; Johnny Bower – *those* were Leafs, Johnny! – and Nickelback!! I got all their LPs and 45s!!

"All said, this couldn't be a better day. And I'm truly honoured. To have been introduced by my wonderful daughter Leah, most talented, and truly beautiful, and her Peter Keleghan, brilliant actor," I added, wrapping it up. Then I held up the award, so everyone could see it. "And this is yours, Charm, as it is with all I have or will ever have!"

Alone again.

A kindly old friend sent a "toke" by way of a designer lady guest. I looked at it, beautifully done, as a designer would have it – with a wee filter even – but where would my mind go that it had not been? Could be that our Spanish cleaning girl could find a few grounds in our place in a couple of days and report it. That would be worth a mug shot next day, maybe. And maybe no one would recognize me now, if Charm wasn't with me. We were forever one.

I could also – perhaps thanks to the toke – forget all that had been said by the charming ladies down the long hall outside our place.

"Whenever I saw you two together I said, That's how it's supposed to be."

"What you two had is what everyone wants."

"What memories you must have, though. How does married love last that long?"

I didn't just smoke what the lady guest brought and rolled. I ate the mother.

The advice had been to have a couple of puffs, a sip of single malt, and fall down. That's what someone, somewhere, unremembered, offered up. The designer lady guest had kindly brought this gift from someone in the building, and it was a sweet thing to do; a favour, not politely paid back by a stagger, puke, and crash about our place in search of anywhere horizontal to sit, or fall, die-like. On nails would be good.

Upon waking somewhere between bedroom and bathroom, I hadn't recalled a whole lot about the designer lady guest, except her kindness in leaving a note reminding me to lock the door as soon as I somewhat resembled myself again. The place looked all right when I'd recovered sufficiently, and not a speck of the spooky smoke stuff for the Spanish cleaning girl to discover.

On June 2 the Royal Ontario Museum in Toronto opened its controversial Michael Lee-Chin Crystal addition and I honoured my commitment to an evening gala, *World of Possibilities*, set on three outdoor stages. Paul Gross was the ringmaster, with Jann Arden, Isabel Bayrakdarian, the Canadian Tenors, Deborah Cox, Seán Cullen, David Foster, K'naan, Leahy, Natalie MacMaster, and David Suzuki among the notable crowd-pleasers on hand. Director Rob Iscove choreographed the cameras to capture the event for producers Mark Shekter and Bernie Rothman, and the whole shebang was broadcast on Global Television. So I was glad to take part, but I didn't go out very much after that. And when I did I often wondered why. At what used to be Charm's favourite restaurant, Richard the waiter said: "I meant what I said. You look fifty-five, not a day more." But it was clear, by the way he'd fled without eye contact, that he'd not been entirely truthful. Chris the chef waved from above the day's special. And got a wave back. As did the waiters Nadine, Rosita, Heidi, Michael, and David. Plus a kiss from Susan, and a hug from Fernando, our lifelong friendly managers. Well-meaning smiles from all, in the worst acting ever.

Back to hiding out.

Leah came up with new and frequently enticing ideas to keep me preoccupied, and she and Peter were a godsend – an island of stability in a suddenly shaky existence. It took me a couple of years to pull myself together, to retrieve my old self, to want to go back to work.

Receiving an ACTRA award for Best Actor for *Away from Her* helped stir the embers, but it was a totally unexpected tribute from the Company Theatre that got me fired up again. In Toronto the young Company Theatre was still very much the new kid on the block. It had been founded in 2004 by two ambitious and talented young actors, Allan Hawco and Philip Riccio, who wanted to build a stage showcase for some of our most engaging actors – Nick Campbell, Rosemary Dunsmore, Eric Peterson, Gary Reineke, Sonja Smits, Maria Vacratsis, and Joe Ziegler, to name only a few. And Hawco and Riccio too, of course; I think that's why it works, Company Theatre shows are all about the talent on stage – Hawco and Riccio are committed to presenting "the best actors at their best," and so far their track record has been stellar. Their 2005 production of *Whistle in the Dark* and their 2008 production of *Festen* both made it onto the annual best-of-theatre lists of both national newspapers, and both earned critical notices that read more like love letters than reviews.

Consequently, when I received a call from Hawco and Riccio, I was flattered to think they might invite me to appear with their already illustrious ensemble. But instead they were calling me to tell me that they wanted to create a new award of excellence for artists whose careers were marked by creative risk-taking; that they hoped I would agree to be the first recipient, and that they wanted to call it the Gordon Pinsent Award of Excellence. I don't remember exactly what I said, although I think it was mostly "Pardon?" with a dash of "Sorry, say that again?", a pinch of "Are you sure you have the right number?" and the all-but-inevitable "Is this a crank call?" At the end of the day I was elegantly feted at a black-tie dinner at the Windsor Arms Hotel. Allan Hawco and *Canada A.M.* commentator Seamus O'Regan, a member of the Company Theatre's board of directors, co-hosted the evening, which was easily one of the highlights of my professional life. In addition to me, Hawco, and his buddy O'Regan, there were several other Newfoundlanders in attendance, and they made a bee-line for me as soon as I arrived.

"I'm sure they didn't mean to swarm you like that," said Hawco apologetically.

"Are you kidding?" I said. "I loved it! Who are they?"

"My family from St. John's," he confessed with a sheepish grin.

The idea of not being on stage or screen for even a year had always been unthinkable to me in the past, but now it happened, and I tried to cushion the fall by easing myself into the market again as painlessly as possible. Mostly I did voice work, a couple of shorts, a bit on Brent Butt's hit series *Corner Gas* on CTV. An offer to co-star in a pilot for a smart and funny new dramatic series was very flattering, and when I read the script I was sure it would get a green light, but the thought of doing a weekly series again, so soon after the upset of Charm's untimely exit, was frankly overwhelming. So I reluctantly took a pass. But I did agree to do a guest spot on Christina Jennings' ambitious dramatic series *The Listener* for CTV and NBC and by the time I got the call from Ridley Scott – yes, that Ridley Scott – I had my sea legs back.

Ridley Scott and his brother Tony were two of the fourteen producers behind a mammoth international co-production of Ken Follett's best-selling novel *Pillars of the Earth*, and the producers were looking to Donald Sutherland and me to represent the Canadian investment onscreen. Ian McShane, who had become something of a cult anti-hero in America after starring in *Deadwood* on HBO, was top billed, and I shot my last scene on location with him. We were in the makeup trailer when I looked at myself in the mirror and grimaced.

"Jesus!" I exclaimed. "I look so rough today they'll have to shoot me through Doris Day!"

McShane shrieked with laughter. It was one of the oldest gag lines in show business, but he had never heard it before. Clearly, I was on a roll.

"You know, Ian," I added, in a hushed, confidential tone, "My wife Charm never swore 'til she saw you in *Deadwood!*" And he doubled up with laughter again.

Ken Follett himself was working on the script with seasoned screenwriter John Pielmeier, and the production had budgeted for Donald and me to each do four episodes. They offered me the role of the King, but I didn't want that, because he dies right away, in Budapest, and I didnt want to go all the way to Budapest for such a small part. So I said no, and then they offered me the Archbishop of Canterbury, and I said yes, because I wanted to go to Vienna, and I wanted to bring Leah and Peter with me, for moral support. Besides, I'd played padres, priests, ministers, cardinals, everything but the Pope – but this would be my first Archbishop.

The cathedral they built was just magnificent. Big budget

shoots are great for that. Everything looks so much more real, more finished. There's something about a cast and crew all pulling together, all trying to give their very best work to a director they love working with, which brings you back up to the peak, to that joy and pleasure that reminds you why you got into this business in the first place. There were more than 250 people just on the crew. And then they started throwing big robes on me, and the cap, and I thought, *This is me!* I felt completely at home in all those extravagant trappings.

Chris Plummer and I had chatted before I left for Austria. "Make sure you wear a mitre!" he insisted. "Only a mitre!" Which I never would've known if I hadn't spoken with him.

Given the nature of the project, and my specific role in it, I couldn't keep the wardrobe. I had to leave my mitre there. And my velvet robes, which were pretty muddy by then. But I did walk away with one pair of shoes, and I kept the Archbishop's ring.

Pillars of the Earth fits a certain category – the epics, the sagas – in which there's so much melodrama that everybody gets his sooner or later. So you watch it thinking, *I don't want to miss this, because I think so-and-so's number might very well be up tonight!* And I'm sure they were cheering in homes all over the world when I got killed in Part 7. With stories as monumental as *Pillars* you never know quite what to expect.

Returning from Vienna I found myself welcomed back home in St. John's, doing a guest spot as a small-time crime boss in a new hit CBC series called *Republic of Doyle*. I've done three *Doyle* episodes now, and I have the highest admiration for the way it comes together on the first day of shooting, the way everybody on this team is at the top of their game. The series is fun to watch, but it's also fun to do. I have been part of a good many shows over the years that just started to get off the ground, just a little bit, only to find there wasn't enough money or support to really enlarge the idea – so that you were stepping into the middle of it but you were surrounded with the finished possibility. That's what made me feel so good about this one. It was finished. It has a finished look to it. It shows. Everything has that finish, from craft services to the guy who maintains the trailers. And I have nothing but admiration for Allan Hawco. Hawco was sure that he was going to stay in this business, do this business, do it well, and enjoy the hell out of his life while he was doing it. And after all he had done, it had to happen sometime for him. He's a young leading man, a strong actor, a strong writer, a strong producer – he's the whole package, which is very important, because in our industry it's very important for him to be seen as that.

A fair amount of growth had to happen in Newfoundland for a show like *Doyle* to succeed. It didn't happen very quickly. But it happened. And for it to happen now underlines all the possibilities. It's all good. And very, very good for Newfoundland and Labrador tourism, as well as for the Newfoundland film industry. And for me, and for so many other ex-islanders like Robert Joy, because we get to go to work on the Rock where we were born. Whenever I'm writing, Newfoundland has always been a rich source for me to draw on, because the place is so wonderful and yet so tragic – so full of loss. The cod moratorium put about thirty thousand people out of work – the single largest mass layoff in Canadian history. Hundreds of coastal communities virtually died overnight. Yes, many fishermen realized the cod stocks were in trouble, but most had worked in the fishery since high school, and some had invested their life savings in fishing vessels and fishing gear, and they had nowhere else to turn for employment.

I sometimes wondered, when I was a kid, what life would be like if the sights and sounds of my hometown were no longer there. What would happen if it all went? Just shut down and closed up? And of course later on it became a certainty, not for my hometown so much, but for so many others. That's the question, of course, at the heart of *John and the Missus*. Because, finally, it's all about home.

And yet, despite everything, the Rock's still such a vibrant place. When you're surrounded by water, you tend to serve yourself first. You take special pride in what you do. We had many terrific musical groups, in every town, even before Newfoundland became a province. They never left the place. They created beautiful music, but they were doing it for them-selves, in a way. Whenever I'm back in Newfoundland I'm torn between the two worlds, between "knowing my place" – another Pinsent family hang-up – and crossing the street where I shouldn't be. And suddenly it's *Hey Gordon! How are ya, buddy?* And getting that recognition, so friendly and familiar, feels like a lovely kind of bath. You just sit there and it cushions you like velvet. And there's always someone by my side to make sure it doesn't go to my head, because adulation of any kind is consid-ered bad manners by most Pinsent clan members. As far as they're concerned I'm still Porky Pinsent from Fourth Avenue, and they would consider it a personal disservice to me if they ever let me forget it.

My brother Harry called me one day to tell me that they were going to rename a street for me in Grand Falls.

"Really!" I said. I was quite touched by the gesture. "Which street are they going to name after me?"

Said Harry, without missing a beat: "The one they used to call Dump Road."

Honours do not sit comfortably on Pinsent shoulders. Sadly, neither do feelings of self-worth. Charm would get quite agitated when she heard me say that I had married "above my station," but I can assure you that no one on Fourth Avenue disagreed. I married someone from Forest Hill, "out of" Bishop Strachan School. Which could hardly compare with my terrible little school days in Grand Falls. When I was her age, I wouldn't have been allowed to cross the road at St. Clair and Forest Hill, looking the way I did. I was brought up to keep my head down. As a schoolboy, when I needed to go to the bathroom, I was the last one to put up my hand. I didn't want to make any waves. God no, never wanted to do that!

Leah thinks my anxiety attacks come from being the youngest of a family of six, always wanting to please, never wanting to be left out. She thinks I still have that little kid in me – that I want to be loved and accepted, and that I don't want to disappoint. She may be right. Harry has it too. When friends or neighbours passed away in Grand Falls, some people would pay their respects by going to the funeral service, or bringing homemade cakes or casseroles to the home of the deceased. But Stephen and Flossie taught us to let the bereaved get on with their mourning in privacy. We were not to intrude.

A couple of years ago I had to reapply for my green card, so I could work in the United States, and for some reason I managed to work myself into a frenzy of self-doubt and worry, to the point where I couldn't sleep the night before I was scheduled to go to the consulate. The next morning I staggered in and was greeted with *Oh, Mr. Pinsent, so nice to see you* and *Oh, Mr. Pinsent, I love your work* and *Oh, Mr. Pinsent, can we bring you a coffee or tea or water or anything?* And of course I had had no legitimate reason to get so upset, but once that Pinsent anxiety takes over, no one can drive me around the bend faster than I can, with or without appropriate psychological transportation.

Consequently, when you come from a family with a peculiarly Newfoundland mindset, you find it somewhat mind-boggling, and more than a bit hilarious, when people start referring to you as an *icon*.

Part of this, you realize, is due to the longevity of your career and the length of your teeth. And part of it is now Newfoundland folklore.

For example, there's the time Tina Turner was performing in St. John's and we were both staying at the Hotel Newfoundland, and there were a lot of young people waiting for her at the main entrance with cameras and autograph books. We just happened to be leaving the hotel at the same time, and when the young people saw *OMG. GORDON. PINSENT.* standing there – smaller than he is in the movies but much bigger than he is on TV – they swerved over to me instead, leaving poor Tina and her entourage all by their lonesome in the lobby. I was later told that she subsequently inquired, *"Who the fuck is that??"* – and who could blame her?

Similarly, Newfoundland poet and writer Des Walsh, the man who wrote that stunning *Random Passage* mini-series, loves to tell the story about the time Kevin Spacey and I shared a cab on the way to our *Shipping News* set. The driver had picked us up without even making eye contact, and it wasn't until we were well on our way that he actually looked in his rearview mirror and discovered who his passengers were.

"Omigod!" he cried. "It's really you! I can't believe it! If I wasn't seeing this with my own eyes, I would not believe it!"

The modest two-time Oscar winner smiled graciously. "Really?" he said shyly.

"Really and truly, b'y," our driver responded enthusiastically. "Geez, Gordon, wait 'til my missus hears you were in my cab today!"

Part of it comes from remarks that have been made by people who other people listen to. For example, the time John Crosbie, the present lieutenant governor of Newfoundland and Labrador, insisted that *I* was the real lieutenant governor. Or the time when Paul Gross told a captive audience at the National Arts Centre, "As loved as Gordon may be in the rest of the country, he is a living god in Newfoundland." That's the sort of thing that could turn a boy's head, providing the boy wasn't Porky Pinsent.

My nephew Ron Smith, Lil's son, once praised me publicly for coming home to visit "not as an actor, not as someone famous, but simply as our Uncle Gord." False modesty aside, I never knew there was any other choice. Still, you can only receive so many Lifetime Achievement awards without wanting to take your own pulse, and even though you're secretly hoping that internet surfers fail to see the *Huffington Post* reference describing you as "the elder statesman of Canadian theater," you instinctively know better. So when your fellow Rock natives Mark Critch and Cathy Jones invite you to come on their long-running comedy series *This Hour Has 22 Minutes* to send yourself up – way, *way* up – you do what you've always done. You say Yes.

Like most good ideas, this one was exceptionally simple. Stratford, Ontario *wunderkind* Justin Bieber had just published his first autobiography – well, I assume it's his first, since he was only sixteen at the time – and *22 Minutes* asked me to do a dramatic reading of some of the more pertinent passages, giving them a faux *gravitas* which we hoped viewers would find affectionately amusing.

Best of all, I got to introduce the piece on camera by saying, "Hello. I am Canadian icon Gordon Pinsent," delivered quite solemnly, as if I actually believed it. I was all decked out in a rather formal pearl-grey suit with a smart black bowtie, and sitting in front of a roaring fire. The roaring fire was courtesy of The Keg, who let us use one of their waiting areas as our set. "And," I continued, "I would like to share with you some selections from the memoirs of another famous Canadian, sixteen-year-old Justin Bieber." I then read some sweetly inane statements from the Bieber book – "*Singers aren't supposed to have dairy before a show. But we all know I'm a rule breaker . . . pizza is just so good.*" As I finished my literary homage to Bieber – "*I'm just a regular 16-year-old kid. I make good grilled cheese sandwiches and I like girls*" – I stared longingly at the cover of his overnight bestseller.

"Ah, the girls . . . the grilled cheese," I murmured with a wistful sigh. "I wish I was you."

The piece was very well shot and produced and was wonderfully well-received when it was played back to the audience at that week's 22 *Minutes* taping in Halifax. The producers of the show then posted it on YouTube, where it suddenly became a viral phenomenon. People were calling me on the phone, full of compliments, still laughing. And I'm told that young master Bieber took it very well.

Charm, honey,

I'm losin' control here! Our things refuse to obey me! How about
that? They did as you would have them do, but not for me. Nothing
works! Since you, the sofa bulges, the toilets gag, the kitchen knives
rebel, spooning the forks, and whispering all together in their drawers;
the door handles snag; a bottle of ink that hasn't been seen since
moving in found time to tip itself onto the unpaid bills; and an English
muffin smeared itself with some un-branded fucking jam, which has
started wearing its lid Capone style. After you – I haven't had the
brains of Lillian the lounge chair.

Yes, I've given names to our household items, they're family
members now; or at the very least, company. Trouble is, they've
become so superior, thinking they're Rhodes Scholars in charge of
my befalling. The Lowboy has turned into a Lowgirl, ordering me
around. All kinds of things are screwed or stuck to other things, not
to move for evermore. Having smoked a touch, I sat on the lamest
of your Chippendaley chairs, who's been humming innocently while
waiting for my weight to fracture it.

All in all, everything we owned together has been firmly intent
on doing me damage. But I fouled up their planning by getting to

myself first. And believe me, the interest has piled up. On the third night, following you, I put the brush to my unsuspecting maverick teeth, who now had also turned on me, voting for an ache-fest, and were not mine anymore, in their old-boy's club, thinking they were too goddamn good to bleed! Well, said I, "Fuck that! Gums still bleed by God! Is it blood you're after? Then, here it is. That enough? I got more! See it swirling down the basin!" Then, I left the teeth to their smirks and smiling, mid-sentence, and since, have had no more in common with any of them than pigs in frigging panty hose.

Still, I'm not afraid of much now. Almost not afraid of anything that's not able to move. Things. Even the crystal we used to have. Even crystal. Crystal is what it wanted to be, and it became that. Surely to God it should be somewhat responsible for what it is, like us. Like me. What would it do if I knocked one over? Slap the snot out of me? I don't think so. It'd have to be pretty damn school-smart crystal for that. And tough. Which it ain't. Last time I looked I had a fair amount of strength. Strength I started out with. Could've handled crystal. Any old time.

In the kitchen now, and a quick wish that if I were to purposely neglect to keep the place clean and intact, I might hear you lovingly admonish my feeble efforts.

I'm having a chicken leg this evening. Nothing fancy. God knows. Just a leg. Have not done the complete body yet. Scared the rest of it would jump the table and be on its own through the country. While I was at it, I thought I'd throw in the other one. Leg. They were small, and as long as I didn't have to worry about the critics, I could carry that off. No spices, maybe, but still.

I don't even use the oven timer anymore. Touch of pride there. Is that an accomplishment? Feels like it.

Your layout in the spice drawer is a thing of beauty. I used the Garlic Salt. Once only. Stopped when I reminded myself that I am now in charge of using salt or not. So I don't. Kind of proud of that as well. Must remember to add this to my list of accomplishments. Mind you, I probably wouldn't think of these things myself. That's okay. Your voice is still mine. Our wiring, one. I'm more than pleased to assure myself that it's you who taps into my fuse-box when caution is needed for my well-being.

Being watched. Being watched. That's okay. Heat was heat. Boiling. Bubbly. Get it out onto the plate. Done. Dinner. Brussels sprouts won't hurt. Touch of home. Hunk of cabbage, of all things. One carrot only. For colour. Okay, Honey? Couple of colours on the plate. Sprig of parsley. Parsley was among the list of growing vegetables. Good for future humans to know.

Beans are okay. They can be handsome unless on the prettiness of a placemat. Don't know if you ever think about it, sweetheart, but the bean is still having a bad time, socially. He's still cursed with the same socio-economic status of his grandfather in the dirty thirties. Still gets inhibited when there are better things on the plate. Beans are even snubbed by Brussels sprouts these days! But if you've got the decency not to put anything else on the plate with them, then – watch out! They puff up like royalty! They know that by themselves on the plate, beans are the very least of what they are. Now that's not vital, I know, but that's the way it is, for the bean.

In our kitchen – and yes, into the streets – I'll work around you, satisfied with your shadow, in astonishing tune with me, even as I would practice changing step, not knowing what new story in my life I would struggle to know, regardless of its fictional hold on me.

When I circle the condo, I half expect to hear your steps in unison with my own.

Alone is not the kindest word.

Missing you.
G.

away with words

Of course it's a cliché now. For one thing, no one seems to remember exactly who said it for the very first time. Maybe it was one of those now near-mythical "angels" who used to invest in Broadway shows just for the fun of it. My guess is it was an actor, struggling to make a script work against seriously impossible odds. I'm sure you know the next-to-ancient theatre axiom I'm referring to, because it's just as true now, maybe even truer, then it ever was: If it ain't on the page, it ain't on the stage. And as any actor will tell you, you can have way too much of nothing.

I did most of my writing after we came back from L.A. I think those things just come to you when they are supposed to come to you, the same way they come to a songwriter or anyone else. The bank is there, that saintly deposit is there. It just depends on when and how you decide to draw on it, so that when you go to it, you will find it. It's just that you don't go to it, for years, because you're out there simply loaning yourself out to the world, instead of sitting there and looking inside yourself for the answers. You just don't report to yourself that much, because you're so busy reporting to everyone else.

If I'd had to retreat into my own resources, I wouldn't have had enough faith in them. And I say I wouldn't have had enough faith in them because I was not scholarly. I was not an academic in any sense. There were so many others who were, and who made their impressions that way, and I never made my impressions that way. So it didn't make sense that I would come out that way. I really would have a difficult time deciphering the life that might have happened if I had never left the Rock. I knew that I wanted a certain kind of life, but I did not know how to acquire it, so I certainly did not expect it. And I certainly could not put a scholastic wrap around it. So I went for the fanciful, the imaginary.

I never took a writing course, but I should have. Maybe I will someday. A three-week writing course would've told me the plot was important. I wrote for ten years without a plot. So that might have been helpful.

I started writing in L.A. when I was forced to make my own career opportunities. I would have been much happier to have someone else do it. But in fact I had always been writing. I wrote a play called *I Only Play George* when I went to Boston to do *The Thomas Crown Affair* for Norman Jewison. Over the years I have written twenty-four, maybe twenty-five scripts. I used to throw them out. I keep them now. I threw out a couple of them just to recycle my brain. I like them all, but some I like better than others. With some it's the idea that grabs me, more than the actual script. After *Easy Rider* came out there was a sudden appetite for small films, so I wrote a movie for Charm called *Gloria Unglued*. It was about a woman who moves into a seedy

L.A. hotel after her husband leaves her. This hotel is only a few laps away from a huge park, very dark, where bad things happen, and the whole film was about her gathering her courage to cross the park. I liked that script a lot at that time. But, it didn't happen.

As a writer I like to take my work to a certain point and then leave some breathing space. I don't finish it, but I don't finish it on purpose. The whole idea is to leave room for creative input, to see how you can adjust to the needs or specific requirements of the producer or the director or the actors or the network or, sometimes, all of them. But sometimes they're not up to it, and you have to finish it for them.

Charm was a genuine fan of my writing. Yes, she was a doting wife, but she was also bright, educated, and well read. When someone asked her what she thought of my skills as a playwright and screenwriter she said that, for her at least, I captured the Canadian conscience.

"I think he creates men of humour, men of dignity, men of strength and men of compassion," she said. "He doesn't play arrogance. He doesn't play stupidity. I think Canadians are like who he portrays. And even if they're not," she added with a shrug, "they see it and they want to be!"

My son Barry, an accomplished writer himself, asked me if I had developed a specific philosophy or methodology over the years. "Because," he said, "so many people seem to recognize themselves in your stories."

"If you want to write anything from the heart," I told him, "take some major decision you made in your life, and reverse it, and tell the story from that angle."

Meanwhile, the world around us keeps changing. Another new game, another new set of rules to learn. Today when you send scripts to producers and directors, and they turn you down, it's not about personal taste, or because you sent them a drama and they are really longing to do a musical. It's about What's Going, what's sellable, what's pitchable to the studios and the broadcasters. And what's going usually has more than a little to do with what's going across the border with our big neighbour next door. They give us very good seats to watch what they're doing, but we will not be heavily involved.

Only four of my scripts have been produced so far. But I'm to blame for that. One of my genuine regrets is that I've never been proactive. I've never been one to put myself out there. I like writing. I like doing it. And I know I'm a good story person. But I just can't be any more proactive than that. I just don't like the idea of bag-ladying around the country with my wares.

Besides, I'd rather be writing. Or directing, for that matter. The two directors who had the greatest influence on my performances and, in some ways, my life, were John Hirsch and George McCowan. In 2008, as part of the fiftieth anniversary celebrations for the Manitoba Theatre Centre, the Mainstage at the MTC was re-dedicated as the John Hirsch Theatre. Last year saw the arrival of a new biography by Fraidie Martz and Andrew Wilson, *A Fiery Soul: The Life and Theatrical Times of John Hirsch*. And this past summer's theatrical events at the 2012 Stratford Shakespeare Festival included Alon Nashman's high-octane one-man show about John, *Hirsch*.

I still find it hard to believe that John is gone. When I met him in Winnipeg for the first time it was clear to me, even then, that he knew where he was going. And we all just wanted to be part of that journey. His introductions of plays to his actors, the preambles he would give us before we started learning and rehearsing, were absolutely brilliant. You could have filmed them. And here he was, Hungarian, speaking to us in English, which was not even his native tongue. It took a young man from Hungary to create theatre excitement in Winnipeg. John always looked like a flamingo on his way to or from his own creative urges. But his knowledge, his instincts, during that time, were astonishing.

He was also unpredictable and frequently surprised me with his bursts of bizarre behaviour. After we opened *Glass Menagerie* at the MTC, we had a cast party, of course, and I remember sitting there with a drink in my hand, cocky young leading man, surrounded by three very pretty girls, at which point John ambled by, wagged his finger at me, and said, "Gordon! Be sensitive!" (*Whaaaa?*)

On another occasion he and his manager Catherine McCartney were driving north along Church Street in Toronto when he spied me approaching in the southbound lane. He immediately rolled down the window, stuck out one flailing arm and effectively stopped traffic so he could talk to me, driver window to driver window.

"Gordon!" he cried somewhat indignantly. "Why aren't you home writing!"

"I – I – I'm on my way home now!" I protested, stammering. "That's where I'm going now!"

"Well, stop wasting time then!" he snapped. "Go home and write!" After which he rolled up the window and sped off.

George McCowan had many of the same uncanny instincts as John. Except he would never tell you. Oh, he knew. He had a photographic memory, just to start with. He stepped in two days before Toby Robins opened in *Two for the Seesaw* at the Crest after the leading man dropped out. And as you know that's a two-character show! So not only did he direct it, he stepped in and did the whole goddamn show!

You could see it. He was like an arrow going through plays and TV shows. And even with that arrow-like precision he didn't have to solve anything. He just *knew*.

An actress in one play I did for him, years ago, got very anxious because she felt she was running out of time.

"We open tomorrow night," she said nervously, "and George still hasn't given me any direction!"

"Yes, dear," I told her, "that's why he hired you."

He didn't have to give her any direction. And he knew he didn't have to. I remember one time when we were about to shoot a scene in which I had to interrogate ten people at once, and what I remember most is how well George handled it. I showed up bright and eager on the set, and George knew that I was ready. By then I had memorized it ten ways to Sunday. So we took our places, and he called "Action," and we shot the scene. It was that kind of thinking. And that did more for me than almost any other thing. Also, George seemed to learn the technical side almost overnight. Not by studying, not by observing, but by common sense. He had a very visual sense. He knew where he was going, technically, with a film. He knew how to get things done – things that might have been difficult for other people. When I showed up for something and George said, "Here comes Gordon," he was treating me like I was the most experienced actor in the world. And he knew, he just knew, that I would work myself into the ground before I would let him down.

I used a lot of the lessons I learned from John and George when I started directing. I remember it being particularly useful on one project, *Exile*, a hot-topic drama about wartime Japanese internment camps in B.C. The lead actor was Robert Ito, a respected principal dancer from the National Ballet of Canada who was doing his level best to create a new career for himself as an actor. I was very sympathetic to the baggage he was carrying, and his concerns about stereotyping and casting limitations. He was already planning to move to L.A. permanently, and went on to play opposite Jack Klugman for seven years on Klugman's series *Quincy*. At the end of the day I like to think *Exile* served as an effective showcase for him, and I hope he was as pleased with the end result as I was.

I must confess, however, that in later years John Hirsch had a dark side. Although I never experienced it firsthand, I heard enough about it that I was prompted to confront him.

"John," I said, "I hear you're being quite mean to some of the actors."

"Well, Gordon," he replied, without a moment's hesitation, "I'm not running an old folks home." And that was the end of that.

At this point in my life I am more focused on acting than directing, but I take every opportunity I can to work with young or new directors. The Canadian Film Centre, the demanding high-standard film school started by Norman Jewison when he came back to Canada, has honed and fine-tuned some very talented people. So far I've worked with Clément Virgo on *The Listener*, Vincenzo Natali on his quirky film *Nothing*, and, of course, with Sarah Polley on *Away from Her*. And in time I hope to work with all of them.

I hold fast to the virtue of imagination. When things are bad, imagine that they're going to get better.

That's what your bank manager does, when he imagines that next year will be better than this year. Norman Vincent Peale called it the power of positive thinking. Some people call it visualization. Call it whatever you want, we all imagine our lives as we would like them to be. Even as I write this, I imagine I hear the telephone ringing, and when I answer it, I'm informed that a courier is on his way to me with a wonderful, innovative, bold, and daring new script.

I was offered two movies this week. I was very pleased to be offered two movies. I don't think I'll do either one of them. Same old story. "But did you read the whole script?" I don't have to read the whole script to see how my character impacts the story. There's a little bit here, then there is a twenty-page gap, and then there's a little bit there, and then there's another twenty-page gap. Is my character development the thrust of the story? I don't think so. And if the story is not dependent on my character, why do I need to read the whole script?

Then again, I've just been offered two short films, with some really good people. And I'm going to do them both.

These days it seems to me that I spend half my time working and the other half defending it, that I'm still working.

"You're still doing it, Gordon? Jesus!" I get that everywhere. "Yes, and I made four dollars this week." Because the big properties are few and far between.

I am often asked: "Why are you doing so many different things?" It has struck me, at this late date, that I was entertaining enough as a kid, but that I was beginning then to believe everyone who had said I was "useless" – which most assuredly meant everyone I had passed on the street where I lived. And, I was. Useless, I do believe it now, in the deepest part of my foolish self. Not a part of me was real. You can try on every cowboy hat in the store, but that still won't make you a cowboy.

I've always looked ahead. What's next? What's next? As if it was the very first thing I was going to do. And people say, "My God, Gordon, you've done a lot of work." People look at me with that fishy expression and say, "Wow, you're still at it!" Which is another way of saying, hey, Gordon, maybe it's time for you to leave, to sign off. *You're still at it for God's sake! You gotta be 200!*

Honestly, sometimes you forget you were even part of certain things. My brother Harry calls every so often and gently tries to nudge me to give it all up. He's waiting for me to come home to Newfoundland and sit on a bench with him and watch the world go by. But I'm not ready for that. Sometimes the work is slow, and then you get a movie like *Away from Her* and, bang, you're right back in it and doing your best work.

Maybe it's peculiar to my particular generation. Look at Chris Plummer. Chris is doing so great now at this late stage in his career. *The Girl with the Dragon Tattoo* with Daniel Craig,

Beginners with Ewan McGregor, *The Last Station* with Helen Mirren, *The Tempest*, *Barrymore* . . . when you're in your eighties, you can still have your best idea tomorrow. Which is one of the reasons why retirement is never an issue. Retire from what? Use the word "retiring" in front of Donald Sutherland and he'll assume you're using a synonym for "shy." Retire? Just because you've hit a certain age, a certain number, that our culture has defined as Quitting Time?

Don made his first movie with Tallulah Bankhead – yes, *Tallulah Bankhead*, for God's sake! He's been directed by Altman, Bertolucci, Fellini, Mazursky, Redford, Roeg, Schlesinger, even Dalton Trumbo. He's done more than 150 shows, on big and little screens, from *Ordinary People* to *Bethune* to *Buffy the Vampire Slayer*, and even tackled Edward Albee's *Lolita* on Broadway. So far he's picked up a Genie, an Emmy, two Golden Globes, a star on Canada's Walk of Fame and another one on Hollywood Boulevard. This year his film *The Hunger Games* set new box office records, and he has five more in the works, and he's not even eighty yet! Just a simple lad from New Brunswick with a dream.

We had fun working together on *Pillars of the Earth* in Vienna, some grand lunches and dinners. His wife Francine Racette is still movie-star stunning (remember her great work with Jeanne Moreau in *Lumière?*) and his best down-to-earth counterpart. She keeps him grounded in reality. Francine is his margins. And Don is very diligent about maintaining his privacy. He has built his "castle" as he had meant to; its moat, solid enough to cross for those he wants to spend time with. It's a safe bet that The Sutherland has many bright things on his horizon, and it's an even safer bet retirement isn't one of them.

Look at Bill Shatner. In fact, just try *not* to look at him! How many TV series is he doing this year, on how many networks? *Star Trek* proved to be such a strange phenomenon that I think most actors' careers would have been dwarfed by it. Leonard Nimoy had to struggle to break out of its boundaries. But Bill keeps reinventing himself, constantly surprising us. There are younger audiences out there who only know him as Denny Crane, the eccentric lawyer sparring with James Spader and Candice Bergen on *Boston Legal*. They have no idea he starred on Broadway. He did *The World of Suzie Wong* on Broadway. He did *A Shot in the Dark*, too. When he appeared for three seasons at Stratford, Charm said his handling of the material was excellent, that his voice was the only one that she could hear at the back. He really knew what it was all about. He just seemed to be the wisest kid in class. Before he got those breaks, people thought he was just another actor pounding on desks in Toronto, wanting to be heard. They have no trouble hearing him now.

Both Bill and Chris have always had a sly sense of humour about themselves. They realize it's important to have some fun with the business you're in, and Bill especially has done it remarkably well.

I always loved doing the stand and deliver, but now I'm becoming even more partial to the Ulysses speech from *Troilus and Cressida*. You know the one. Because the more I do it the more I realize that it's about people like me, who *have* to keep going.

For time is a fashionable host
That slightly shakes his parting guest by the hand,
And with his arms outstretch'd, as he would fly,
Grasps in the comer: welcome ever smiles,
And farewell goes out sighing….

(Act III, Scene 3)

You hear about *ageism*, or whatever they call it, and you don't think that much about it, and then one day your hair turns white and they think, yes, we better make this deal now, so he can go out and walk the dogs. You get to a certain age and they label you and they treat you like you should be standing in line to play Santa Claus at Eaton's.

And what's to be done about it? Nothing that I know of. Except, of course, landing a really great role, even greater than the good ones you may be lucky enough to be working on now. Top billing may not be the best revenge, but it will have to do until something better comes along.

My friend R. H. Thomson, an accomplished actor and director himself, has been conducting a series of interviews for Theatre Museum Canada, capturing an oral history of our theatrical accomplishments before they fade into oblivion. We spoke of many things when he interviewed me, but I thought he was especially prescient when he asked me if I was just making up my whole career as I went along. Because yes, that's what I did, and that's what I'm still doing. As for my so-called mercurial drive, I told him, it comes from a fear of failure, a fear of losing. I was no good in school. Failed everything. But I loved the friendships. Loved life in general. I was a happy kid. I said to my teacher, "The trouble is, I'm sitting so far at the back that I can't hear you." But I never got moved up to the front.

I still have that fear of failure, and the Pinsent Anxiety, a family trait I share with my brother Harry. I said to Charm, "I'm getting to the point where I don't know if I can go into a crowded room." And she said, "You're a performer. Perform." So I did. I acted my way into those crowded rooms. And after I circled a bit, I had a wonderful time.

I've just finished rewriting one of my plays, a piece originally called *Corner Green*. This time I've done it as a screenplay, and it's all about anxiety. Not the Pinsent family anxiety so much as that terrifying black-hole anxiety that haunted people like Nijinsky, Lord Byron, Churchill, and Hitler. Years ago I even wrote about it in verse:

> *It's a desperate thing without a name*
> *It's not a dream. And it ain't no game*
> *could be bad, could be good*
> *it can't be seen, but it's understood*
> *a desperate thing has taken flight*
> *don't come out of your house tonight*
>
> *one thing certain and it's a fact*
> *if you kiss it, it'll kiss you back**

Is it a poem? A song? It feels fresh and new again, but like the Pinsent Anxiety, it's been with me, weighing heavy on me, for

* From "It's a Desperate Thing," by Gordon Pinsent.

some time now. Probably because all these things are tied up together, and you have to be careful when you pull the string, so you won't unravel more than you can handle.

I've probably kept some of it under The Ledge. The Ledge is what I call it; you may have a different name for it. Hidden resources are stored under The Ledge, and when I go there I'm eighteen again, or twenty-five, or whatever fragment of my past I need to be, or see, or revisit, or re-examine, to help find what I'm looking for. Because the best answers often come from a place you kept only for yourself. Granted, the journey back inside can be a bit intimidating, maybe even a little frightening at times. But it's a journey well worth taking, always, especially if it helps you find your voice. Your own voice is the first voice you heard when you said *I'm going to be a writer, I'm going to be an actor, I'm going to be a dancer with the Winnipeg Ballet.* And when you start getting in your own way, and we all do, you need to go back to that voice, and listen to it again, so you can move forward, so you can move on. Don't give it away. Take it with you wherever you go. Because if you lose that voice, it's over. And as my old friend R. H. Thomson says, that's one cliff no one wants to go over.

Some in our field are continually faced with threats to their potential that seem impossible to overcome and, because of it, they will quit their dreams, leaving them on someone else's doorstep. They walk away, reluctantly falling in step with the going throng, content to walk in ruts that have been created by others, instead of remembering that the most important voice they heard was their own, and to know not to stop listening to themselves, and to never return their natural gifts for giving to someone else's store. Never being a tenant of their own talent, but owning it; being the landlord of it. And lifting it high for all to see and to hear in a voice distinctly their own.

Am I the only one concerned, at times even distressed, by the fact that there does not seem to be any thread between young talent today and the actors, writers, and directors who built the highway they drive on? Years from now, others will be in the same spots as we are now. They won't be related to us; they may in fact bear no resemblance to us. And if they see no sign left by us in the best work we do, they could conceivably have the notion that they are the first ones here. But not if our footprints are deep enough, and our example clearly drawn!

When I was doing publicity for *Away from Her*, my stops included a visit to an Alzheimer's home for seniors in St. John's. While I was there I noticed a local politician who had been running for an upcoming election, in search of votes perhaps, bending down to a wheelchair, to speak to an elderly patient.

"Hello, my dear," he said. "Do you know who I am?"

"No, I don't," the dear woman replied, "but if you go to the desk, I'm sure they'll tell you!"

To leave those footprints, we need to know who we are. To leave those footprints, to set that example, we have to acknowledge what we already know to be true. If that truth is hiding under The Ledge, we need to extricate it, and the sooner the better. Because it's a profound but simple truth: It *is* better to be happy. It *is* better to walk with your head held high, and not with a victim's walk. Because I still think that the Creative individual is the most glorious individual in our society.

making them wait

You'll work and play and scratch and bite
You'll learn to kill with sheer delight
You'll only come alive at night,
when you're in a show
Welcome to the theater!
*You fool . . . you'll love it so.**

OVER THE YEARS I'VE BEEN FORTUNATE ENOUGH TO get a lot of stage work. And despite my giggling debut in Winnipeg as Sebastian in *Twelfth Night* I've been lucky enough to do a lot of Shakespeare, too. And loved doing it – loved being onstage. There's something about that peak – when you're up there – because it's the true reason why you got into the business. And when you get up there it comes and slaps you in the face, but it's quite a lovely feeling. So when you see some strange new wonderful character waiting to be played, something odd happens. It sort of takes you over. And it gives

* From "Applause," with lyrics by Lee Adams, music by Charles Strouse, from the Broadway musical *Applause* (1970).

you a sense of how it might be, to inhabit someone else's personality, someone else's character, in the human comedy. A rare and unique opportunity to enter into someone else. And you go with it.

Doing an experimental play, or a play that's has never been done before, can give you a sense of comfort. Because it's never been done before, there's no precedent. You are originating the role. No one is comparing the way you play the role to the way Brian Bedford played the role. Maybe the buck stops here, but it also starts here, which can make for very exciting theatre.

At one point in my career I was so focused on doing film and television that one day I realized I'd given up a lot of stuff I adored. Musicals, for example. I had gone to the Royal Conservatory in Toronto for singing lessons so I could play leads in musicals. I did *Guys and Dolls* in Winnipeg, *Anne of Green Gables* in Toronto, *The Music Man* in St. John's. *Music Man* went very well, I think, and yet, not one telegram of *Bravissimo!* from Robert Preston, so I'm not positively sure. It was one of those deals where your understudy does it in the main body of the rehearsals, until you arrive, fur top coat and white fedora, with your pair of Prussian wolfhounds on a leash, shouting, "I'M HERE!" And then you do not do as well as your understudy, who has now become a hero to the other kids. And then, before you leave town, you have the nerve to suggest you wouldn't mind doing *Man of La Mancha* next. As in, *as if*. And with all of it you are reminded once again how gorgeous it is, how great it can be to arrive on rehearsal day and really enjoy the stuff you're doing. And that the other stuff, the TV, is getting in the way of that pleasure. But invariably you come back to earth and do another series, so you can afford to play hooky every once in a while and run away to do a musical. Or even just a well-conceived play.

After all these years my memories of being onstage at the Manitoba Theatre Centre and Theatre Calgary and the Vancouver Playhouse remain surprisingly vivid. I can still hear the audience murmurings when we premiered Bernie Slade's play *A Very Close Family* in Winnipeg. And I still remember working with Ted Atherton in Calgary in a play by the Aussie writer David Stevens called *The Sum of Us*. It was a four-hander, just four actors, and Ted played my gay son. Every night he had to push me onstage in a wheelchair, because by the third act I've had a stroke, and he had to deliver a speech to his father, me, and every night I would silently respond to his speech, right on cue, with tears streaming down my face. And one night after we'd taken our final bows he turned to me, his eyes shining, and said, "Gordon, how do you *do* that?" Which, of course, was music to my ears, and very generous of him to say.*

It's not all love letters and roses, of course. When I went back to Winnipeg to do one play I got a bad review, and I was feeling pretty down about it, until a woman sent a note to me backstage which read, *High station in life is earned by the gallantry by which appalling experiences are survived with grace.* So that saved me for a long, long time. Did my performance in the play get any better? Probably not. But I felt a lot better about it. When the play finished its run, I took the woman's note back to

* Aussie actors Jack Thompson and Russell Crowe played father and son in the 1994 screen version.

Toronto and stuck it on the fridge. I was in love with it for a while, and in time it had company – another note from another sympathetic theatregoer, after I received a decidedly unsympathetic review from a Toronto critic. The review in question all but demanded a strong reply, but the sympathetic Toronto theatregoer urged me not to take the bait. "*Never wrestle with pigs*," he advised me. "*You both get dirty, and the pigs love it.*"

Words to live by.

In my salad days my family turned out to see me onstage whenever they could. My brothers refused to make a fuss over me. *Don't tell him too much.* But my sisters were always there. All three of them. If I was in a play, they were there. And in their souls they were built for this. The whole family was. They had a great taste for better times, if they could only get to taste more of them.

One of the many rewards of being chosen by Miss Charmion King to be her consort were the many privileged insights she would share with me over time. Over the years we did four plays together, two of which I wrote just so I could be onstage with her. About twenty-five years after *The Madwoman Of Chaillot* – we didn't want to rush into anything – we did my play, *Easy Down Easy*, at the Gryphon Theatre at Georgian College in Barrie, Ontario. Two years later we did my next play, *Brass Rubbings*, at the Factory Theatre in Toronto and at the MTC in Winnipeg. I specifically wrote *Brass Rubbings* as a vehicle for Barbara Ham, and the three of us had a lot of fun being onstage together. Jackie Maxwell directed the show, and having the legendary Eric House in our merry little band didn't hurt the audience's feelings *or* ours.

The last show Charm and I did together left us with some wonderful memories, especially since the two of us were the only people onstage. We performed A. R. Durney's wonderful two-hander *Love Letters* in Ontario and B.C. and loved every minute of it. Years later Leah and Peter got the idea of adapting it for television as a sixty-minute special by using well-known couples to read excerpts from it, and using me as host to link all four couples. In addition to Leah and Peter, the celebrity couples who added their own lustre to the project were Debra McGrath and Colin Mochrie, Samantha Bee and Jason Jones, Carlo Rota and Nazneen Contractor, and Sheila McCarthy and Peter Donaldson. Peter had been diagnosed with lung cancer two years earlier, and he and Sheila both knew his days were numbered. So Sheila was especially happy to have this permanent record of them performing together as a loving couple.

It was also around that time that I decided to revisit *Easy Down Easy*. Berni Stapleton, a Newfoundland actress I greatly admired, had become the artistic director of the Grand Bank Regional Theatre Festival in Newfoundland, and Berni wanted to present the play in her July Festival. As if that wasn't flattering enough, Mary Walsh wanted to direct and possibly revamp it. We all knew the play needed work, and we all seemed to feel the same way about the work it needed. Before its premiere in Toronto two decades earlier I had written one of the roles specifically for Charm, as a way of getting to work with her again. Charm had done the play with me somewhat reluctantly, as she realized that her role, regardless of the stylish trappings in which I had dressed it, was superfluous. Cutting that role was at the top of Mary Walsh's creative hit list, and I couldn't really argue with that.

"Gordon, I want to go for the jugular on this," Mary told me. "I want it to be like a fast train. I want it to *move!*"

I wished them well. Over the next few months we conferred mainly by telephone and occasional emails, and when July rolled around I flew to Newfoundland to attend the July 9 premiere in Grand Bank. The play was inspired by my hikes with Wally Cox in the Hollywood Hills, and Lewis, the central character, was loosely based on Wally. So it was fascinating for me to see what Mary had done with it. She had wanted it *to move*, and boy, did it ever! It was at least an hour shorter than it had been.

After the performance Mary cornered me.

"Well, Gordon," she said, "what do you think?"

"Well, Mary," I said, "it moves like a train – but there's no dining car on it!"

After more tinkering *Easy Down Easy* was selected for the official grand re-opening of the famed and newly renovated LSPU Hall in St. John's. The play ran eleven nights in October and in my opinion was exceptionally well received. Berni Stapleton got wonderful notices for her performance as Lewis' enigmatic wife, Mary was praised for her "crisp" direction and I received the now-familiar "Canadian Icon" accolades. What's not to like?

Was it hard for me to watch another actor play a role I wrote specifically for myself? Yes, and no. Because most of them don't do it the way I did it. Charm used to watch me and say, "You're making them wait, aren't you," and I woud say "No, no, I'm not." But I was, of course. At times. I would take a breath, and take in the moment. And the audience would take a breath too. Or maybe hold their breath, if I took too long a moment. I had adopted the dumbest rule ever: *Don't let yourself get to three.* And, *Jump – the net will be there.* (I'd borrowed that last bit from Julia Cameron.)* Okay – maybe not so dumb. Because we're conditioned to threes. So instead of waiting for a full count, I would plunge in at two, which would sometimes startle the other actors and would always startle me. Because if you let yourself go before you get to three, you get a chill. You get a chill at the same time. And that was the point of it, of course. To keep me out of my comfort zone, so I couldn't do it by rote. It becomes a natural moment if you don't allow yourself to get to three. Because you purposely jumped in before you're ready. You purposely played a trick on yourself. To prevent myself from getting into the habit, every night I broke the habit. And counted on my belief that the net would be there. That's what all actors learn in time. Take the leap, and the net will be there. It just takes some of us longer to leap than others.

I'm not doing many plays now because so many are co-productions. You do a play in Winnipeg and they expect you to do it again in Ottawa six months later. I like the fast ones. Get in and get out. With the wardrobe. Especially if you like the clothes your character wears, and look good in them; always get the wardrobe. But do the play in one city, in one theatre, and get out.

There's another reason, too. A couple of years ago I finally went public and admitted that I suffer – and that's the right

* See Julia B. Cameron, *The Artist's Way: A Spiritual Path to Higher Creativity*, 1992.

verb for it – from trigeminal neuralgia. Before they came up with medication to treat it, they used to call it the suicide disease, because the pain literally drove people to kill themselves. I've had it for at least twelve years. It's very debilitating. It causes these excruciating stabbing, electric shock-like pains in your eyes. The pain is very intense. It feels like being bitten by a tiger, or what I imagine that feels like. Sometimes I have to take time off work because of it. And that's why I've had to take time away from the theatre, because I worry that the pain will return while I'm in the middle of a scene or, worse still, a great Shakespearean soliloquy, and I will be unable to continue. But I'm getting used to it, and I'm getting better at handling it. It used to send me to the floor, and now it doesn't.

I've had several offers to do *Lear*, and an awful lot of people still tell me I should do *Lear*. The jewel in the crown, and all that. But when I think about it I always end up with the same question: *Why?* Why put myself through that? For the slim possibility of coming up with something a little different, discovering something in the character that nobody else before me has discovered? I guess it would be a great exercise. God knows, *Lear* is a wonderful piece.

I love the thought of sitting with an audience, watching Chris Plummer do it, or Bill Hutt. Since Bill shuffled off this mortal coil we have been left without another of our voices. His was not a voice which will fade easily in our memory, made up of so many rich and glorious character portrayals on the many stages of this country. Now his voice will be heard in the memories of what he has left us: his Prospero, his Lear, his Tyrone, his Lady Bracknell, his Valpone. With his passing the theatre has lost one of its most faithful friends, and so has the oldest and the youngest of us, and the scenery is not quite as bright as once it was.

But no, no *Lear* for me. Not at the moment. On the other hand, if a great new stage role comes along tomorrow, something glorious, something that makes me believe that my life will be unfulfilled and incomplete if I don't do it, I will do what I always do. I will say Yes. And it will continue this way, until the only thing left for me to play will be a revival of *On Borrowed Time* with the Homeless Repertory Company of Allan Gardens. Because at the very end, I'll be dragged offstage. And they won't know if it's me or the play that stinks. I'll just go right off the stage and right into the holes. Because I won't be stopping voluntarily. It's just too great a love.

> *Our revels now are ended. These our actors,*
> *as I foretold you, were all spirits and*
> *are melted into air, into thin air:*
> *And, like the baseless fabric of this vision,*
> *the cloud-capp'd towers, the gorgeous palaces,*
> *the solemn temples, the great globe itself,*
> *Yea, all which it inherit, shall dissolve*
> *and, like this insubstantial pageant faded,*
> *leave not a rack behind. We are such stuff*
> *as dreams are made on, and our little life*
> *is rounded with a sleep.**

* From *The Tempest* (1611), by William Shakespeare.

chromosome 11

———◆———

AS AN ACTOR YOU'RE SIMPLY AT THE MERCY OF OTHER people's perception of you. It can be a terrifying feeling. The rewards can be great, but there is no steady happiness in this business. There are peaks of joy and valleys of gloom. As you get older, you forget that it was an adventure at one time, that you were able to take the falls. You think, "I know I'm good. I've had it proven. Then why is it not working now?" You feel you can't take the falls. You say to yourself, "Gee, I need this. This is all I can do in life." And you need it so desperately that just the thought that it could disappear is enough to scare you.

Does that make me a member of an endangered species? Not today, no. Better to be an actor in the twenty-first century. It's no secret that it has taken centuries for us to erase the ancient opinion that the actor belongs in one of two places in our society, on the stage or in the stockade. In the echelons of higher society, the actor would have been seated below the salt, and checked for silverware before leaving. In iron curtain times, in Prague, for example, many of the artistic calling were considered to be "non-persons." And as far back as the Roman era, it was proclaimed, regarding the rites of marriage, that "if a daughter, grand-daughter or great grand-daughter should marry a freed man or a man who practices the profession of an actor or whose father or mother did so, that marriage will be void."

I think it's safe to say that these archaic notions have been vanquished from the more modern and sophisticated social behaviour. Nothing would support that more clearly than my being invited, over the years, to so many lovely places. But with that kind of history, is it any wonder actors sometimes huddle together against the slings and arrows of outrageous agents?

I never took an acting class, or a dance lesson. I didn't have the money to go to RADA or any of those famous schools. I just had to pick it up as I went along. But I'm a big fan of theatre schools, because I think they can help you find out if you're any good, and what you're good at, much faster than you can find out on your own. You'll still have to go through all the other stuff, digging ditches, waiting on tables, driving a truck, whatever it takes to keep you going while you look for your big break. And en route to your big break in this profession you have chosen – yes, I know, you believe *it* has chosen *you* – you learn to become intimate with rejection. I used to get the feeling that if rejection was a cereal, my picture would be on the box. Which is the way most actors feel most of the time. And which is probably why, no matter where we're born or raised, we speak the same Creative language.

I remember one time, in Beijing, when Charm and I were at a rooftop dinner hosted by the Canadian Consul, and among the invited guests were a number of Asian actors who were quite sullen and withdrawn. When we invited them to join our table they just ignored us – until their translator told them that

Charm and I were actors too. And suddenly they brightened up, and opened up, and couldn't have been more wonderful. And we knew exactly how they were feeling. *At last, there is someone in the room with the same understanding, the same sensibility as me.*

Chalk it up to Chromosome 11. Someone once said that actors and writers and artists have a different chromosome. These are the people with attention deficit in school, the kids who are sure they are more suited to something else. Even if it's not true, it means we should be forgiven. Because clearly we can't help it.

I'm very doubtful about whether I can analyze my technique as an actor. People are always saying, How do you approach a role? How do you do this? How do you do that? In my Winnipeg theatre days Tom Hendry regarded me as a naturalist actor, the kind of actor who uses a lot of sense memory from his past to build the character he's playing. The thing is, I've always been conceited enough to say of myself that I'm an actor. It's as simple as that. I can act. And all these days later – years later – I'm an actor. I scratched and clawed to find other fossils in me which might have suggested that, down through the ages. there would have been others. At least one. A *Pinsent, Pinson, Pincon.*

I did find that we had all hailed from a German bird, by the name of Finch-sen and – how's this? – that according to an elderly retired Doctor Pinsent in London, we had flowered, remarkably, from no less than the captain of the *Pinta*, an ancestor by the name of Martin Alonzo Pinzon.

The Captain, no less! This had me hoping like hell that the good old doctor was just that, and not an inmate. I might not even have to be that good an actor, with that on the CV. And apparently there have not been a whole lot of dissenters to that connection. Not that I've looked for one. Plus the fact that my brother Haig had been blessed and stamped with the middle name of, get this, *Alonzo*. (Come on now, you surely don't think you can talk me out of that one?) But I would have been pleased as punch to locate one who had called himself Legitimate where theatre was concerned. A messenger for one of the Henrys, say, or a servant to Burbage in anything. I'd even settle for a relative down through the ages who might have taken tickets.

I always resented the rule in Canada that, yes, you could try your hand at this, but you better learn to do something else as well. But I still thought that was the richest part, to be able to do all these things. I thought, *Well, I'm not going to sit here like algae on a pond*. So I was a painter before I was an actor, and I was an actor before I was a writer, so I knew I could dabble in all three. That made sense to me. Acting was what I really wanted to do, and when you're an actor, you get a lot of spare time. So I would paint, but even when I was painting I would have to stop and go back to Waiting. Because I was a Waiting actor – waiting for the phone to ring. Acting is a truly wonderful profession, but it is not an easy one. Whenever it looks easy you can be sure that we are working very hard to create that particular illusion.

One of the great showbiz stories – and don't stop me if you've heard it – is sometimes attributed to the celebrated Shakespearean actor Edmund Kean but most commonly attributed to the film actor Edmund Gwenn, who popped up regularly on the silver screen at the Nickel when I was a boy. According to Hollywood folklore, the ailing thespian, then eighty-two, was about to take his last breaths on earth, surrounded by his family at his bedside. Distressed by the sight of the old man's discomfort, one of Gwenn's young grandsons leaned forward and rested his hand gently on the actor's arm.

"Grandpa," said the young man, "is dying hard?"

The old actor slowly shook his head.

"Dying is easy," he replied softly. "*Comedy* is hard."

How many different ways have I died onstage? Onscreen? Not that often, actually, unless you count those deaths I might've deserved through performance. I didn't mind being killed, but "lying" dead while the play went on was far more difficult than I had expected, due to my incurable giggling.

The first and most memorable time: Rainbow Stage, the fifties, melodrama, *The Pitfalls of Pauline*. The hero Allan Allworthy leaves the villain (that would be me) as he intones the historic line, "I shall remain to see that he expiates his diabolical depravity." All the while my supposedly inactive corpse is bubbling and choking with laughter, for my own amusement. The giggling, by the way, was a joyous one, brought on mainly, as I lay there, by counting my blessings for having been accepted and nurtured by my marvellous discovery, theatre.

I died a few film deaths, and maybe a couple more on TV, but never after I became established enough to play the good guy. My absolute favourite death scenes on film all belonged to James Cagney. If you look at his films, there were three beauties – *Public Enemy*, *Tomorrow Never Dies*, and *White Heat* – and in all three, when he hits the floor, his feet lift off the ground, for a last bow. In those days stars really knew how to die.

Why do we do what we do? Yes, the applause is sweet, but that's only part of it. We are gamblers playing the ego lottery, and we know the odds are against us. Still, somebody's got to win. And maybe this time we'll get that series. Granted, the thrill of landing a series is frequently greater than the thrill of doing a series, playing that same character over and over again. But offer us a guarantee of twenty-six weeks and we'll jump at it. Because now we don't have to keep wondering if we'll ever work again, because now we know we will, if we don't screw it up, for at least another twenty-six weeks. And if the series should run five or six or seventeen years, we'll complain about it, and moan about having to play the same character again and again, and send our kids through college, and love every minute of it, and on our good days, on our very good days, be just as grateful as we should be. And then we'll suddenly find ourselves "on hiatus." And then we will have to wait and wait and frequently wait some more before we can actually find out if we're just "on hiatus" or just out of work.

The regular working man has a nine-to-five existence; he quite rightly assumes that he will be working from 9 a.m. to 5 p.m. for pretty much the rest of his life. As actors we don't have that. We have these gaps. Down time. Hiatus. And meanwhile, you just keep working on the dream.

choose me

⎯⎯◉⎯⎯

No minor musical statesman, the brilliant American lyricist Stephen Sondheim said it with music:

Even when you get some recognition
Everything you do you still audition . . .[*]

I'm almost getting used to tuning into a new series and not recognizing anybody on it. Or going to an audition with a lot of new faces – well, new to me, anyway – with Kenny Welsh sitting in the corner.

We've all been there. Prepping the resumé. Shining up the ol' curriculum vitae. Putting our best face forward. Doing our damnedest to get the job.

Some corporations hire you on a trial basis – a three-month let's-see-how-we-get-along period, ostensibly. But of course what it is really is a three-month test drive, so they can see if you can do the job and you can prove that you were

---

* "Putting It Together," music and lyrics by Stephen Sondheim, from the Broadway musical *Sunday in the Park with George* (1984).

only fibbing about half the accomplishments on your CV.

People in my business don't get a three-month trial period. Sometimes, if we're lucky, we might get three weeks. We call it "rehearsal." And by then of course we've already got the job.

Actors audition. We read for a part. We get the part or we don't get the part. A terrifying process, really. Ask anyone – except me. From the very beginning, overall I had the same feeling going in for auditions whether they were good or not, and I had the same feeling about them whether I got them or not. I was not afraid of them. Certainly there were a number of things generally agreed-on about auditions, that they were terrible and demeaning and everything else. But I've never felt that way. For some reason I always felt that if I didn't give them exactly what they wanted, I wouldn't get it, thank you. Because their idea of what it is wouldn't necessarily be mine. But no, it didn't bother me, the possibility of failing at an audition. And no, I don't know where that confidence came from. I think it came from stirring up, at the last minute, just enough stuff of my own, to make the thing work for me, even if it didn't work for them. It was a very odd thing. In a strange way it was like painting with me. And I'd had the experience of painting before that. And I could layer it. I could do my layers and get in there and say, *Well, that was interesting*, even if I came out and didn't get the part. Because I was always happy to find out a little something more.

I've always been excited by life around me. Even when I was a little kid I admired adults who had lived a certain life, I remembered the businesses they were in, the drama of the workaday world around me. And I was happy to take part in it. I didn't want to have to be the leader of anything. That didn't bother me at all. So not to get something, to feel like it was going to be the end of the world if I didn't get it, wasn't really an issue. I knew that they had an idea of what they wanted, and that maybe I could give it to them. Or maybe I could if I went back a second time. I didn't always get that chance. But I was part of something that I was glad to be part of – this business, this work, this stuff. Fitting in and getting things done and feeling good about it and having somebody say that you're right for the part, that you're good for the business. In times when nothing was happening I felt like I was still part of the club.

I've always wanted to be part of the club. I've always wanted to be part of a going thing with a lot of fine people to talk to. All of that would make a great deal of sense. I wasn't thinking of any kind of stardom. Tony Curtis said, "Fame is an industry unto itself." And a different world. But the working world, the world you're part of until fame happens, well, you're either going to have great fun in it, or say, *What a waste of time!*

And you learn things, because there are lessons to be learned. You need to learn how to say Yes. Barry Morse told me that he always said yes to everything. You can always say no later, he said. This also made sense. So I learned to say Yes, as if I knew what they were talking about. And people thought they could depend on me. Maybe they thought I had something really important to say. What I had to say was, *nothing*. But I guess they thought I did.

All these characters – who do you see yourself playing? All of them, I said. Because I was just so anxious to get into that wonderful place called the rehearsal studio. Wouldn't it be fun? Bring in coffee, have a cigarette. It's all about that. Beats working for a living, absolutely.

When I auditioned for a role in *Last of the Mohicans*, a TV series that was shooting in Toronto, the casting director asked me if I knew how to ride a horse.

"English or Western?" I replied somewhat grandly.

I didn't know how to ride a horse.

I got the part.

I think this boldness came from situating myself in the life around me, whatever was going on. And seeing the value in it. And watching it, and appreciating it. And everything was new, so I was seeing it for the first time. For the longest time, everything was new.

A lot of people had learned far more than I had in the same amount of time. But I was not dismayed because I didn't know how to swim or ride a bike, because there was plenty of time to learn.

I never did learn some things. I'm still not a great swimmer. And I still can't ride a bike.

Some of the parts you audition for, you get. Some you don't get. Sometimes you're not right for the part. Sometimes you're not who they have in mind. They are secretly looking for someone taller/shorter/fatter/thinner/older/younger than you. Sometimes it's so secret that they don't even know it themselves. And then, every once in a while, you just do yourself in. When *The Godfather* was announced, I had a meeting with one of the producers, Al Ruddy. I wanted to play Thomas Hagen, Brando's *consigliere*, a role that eventually went to

Robert Duvall. But when I read for Ruddy I was just too confident. Overconfident. Which of course is a clear indication of low self-esteem, a condition that has plagued me all my life.

You can also be overprepared.

In the early nineties Robert Redford, who had already won an Oscar as a director, was putting a film together called *A River Runs Through It*, about a minister and his two sons. Redford had a keen eye for fresh talent. He had cast Brenda Blethyn as the mother, Craig Sheffer as one of the sons, and as the other son, a young up-and-comer named Brad Pitt.

So far, so good.

Redford saw a demo of mine from *A Gift to Last* and asked me to read for him. And Larry Dane was also going to read for him, for another part. So he and I were both preparing to go to New York for this meeting with Redford, and Larry said, "What are you going to do?"

"Well," I said, "I will read whatever he gives me to read, and we'll see where it goes from there."

"No, no!" said Larry, "no, you've got to prepare for this!" And Larry is *always* right. "Okay, Gordon, here's what we're gonna do. Go over to CBC wardrobe and borrow a priest's cassock – get the collar, get the whole thing. Then get a haircut." As if I was four years old. "And then we're going to set you up, in a nice little corner of the house here, and we're going to shoot some video of you in the role. And I'll direct it."

So I did. And he did.

"That's right, turn in your chair. No, a little more to the right. No, not that much. Okay, now say what you have to say.

Okay, that should do it. Because you know, the better you're prepared . . ."

So that's what we did. We prepared. And I prepared myself right out of the movie. Oh yes.

Down I go to New York City, a clean white shirt tucked into my carry-on. I was staying at the Paramount, I think, and I went into one building, and I was way early, and waited for ages, and it was the wrong building.

"No, you want the Times building," they said, and then added reassuringly: "It's okay – it's not that far."

But it *was* that far, and by the time I got there I was a total wreck, sweating like a pig, and meeting Robert Redford for the first time. And I could see that he was very busy, but he saw me waiting and came over and said, "Hello Gordon, thanks for coming, I'll be with you as soon as I can." Which was very nice of him, very professional.

And then I got to read for him. And I don't remember if Redford has dark brown eyes, but after we started they turned pale, and I think he was catching up on a little bit of sleep while I was reading for him. And after we finished I said, "Would you like me to do it again?" And Redford said, "No thanks, Gordon, that was enough."

Tom Skerritt, who I worked with on *The Silence of the North*, got to play the minister. And I never did that kind of preparation again. Because it's great to be prepared, but it's always a good idea to leave a little room for the director!

Actors audition. It's what we do. When we're not auditioning, we're thinking about auditioning.

Or, in my case, writing about auditioning.

THE AUDITION

"Perform!" she'd said. "You're an actor. Use it, where you are overwhelmed! If your well-known anxiety stops you at the door – any door – where the unknown threatens to swallow you up, then perform. You've still got the merest black Irish twinkle left. Use it. Use it on strangers, who will like you if you don't reveal your entire litany of ailments, and on your friends, who think they know you. Perform. I don't have a whole lot of time for this, being as dying has cost me patience when it comes to such things as nerves. But this I know, and want you to know. You have a lot more death ahead of you than life. So get the fuck on with it!"

I showed myself to a mirror in a thick large sweater half pulled over my frame, as if I'd been halted in dressing completely for the day. From inside the sweater, I thought: I like this. I see only fragments of noon through the weave; and the day – and those few old friends of ours who lived to see this far – could see nothing of me, except hair sprouts through the neck of the turtle, and lower body.

Another glance of casual interest. Yes, there's something about him that might suggest strength, but try and look beyond that.

I was sure that my steel-blue eyes and steady countenance were intimidating my fellow auditioners, which suited me fine as it could throw them off; and I could use that. They would not take long, their voices, high and shaky next to my *profundo*, able to peel the walls of the corridor. By now, I could safely race through the amount of French I would need for the audition. Fine too was the fact that I would be the last to go in. For now, be bold, for God's sake; and try and act as though you know that you must have learned something in your long career compared to these youngsters, first time out.

Only one, a smartly turned-out sexpot, had it right. She'd cut her session with the producers short, making it easy for everyone, with this character-revealing intro: "I play whores!" she said. No one worked more, apparently. Sixteen hours a day. Two hours in front of the camera, and fourteen in the backs of limos.

The others entered one at a time; in and out, living up to their milk-faced appearance and body language, and leaving me bullet-eyed and experience-laden by God. As they came out of the office one by one, I wanted to thank them for failing, but it might have them heading for open window exits.

My turn. Entering – thinking much taller than I actually was, and dipping my head to avoid the door size – I made the most of each step from door to desk, imagining my shoes were size elevens and planting them in front of the producer types. I had planned to laser my eyes along them – American Producer, Co-producer, Director, an especially pretty lady Writer, and Casting couple – with the hope of mesmerizing them long enough to have them cast me in their partially interesting film. Instead, I was quickly asked how I was.

"Good." I said. (Recalling not to overdo my replies, having made that mistake on too many other occasions.)

"Did you have a chance to read the script?" said the Director.

"Read it? I ate it," I answered, quite sure that my classically trained projection would cause the lady Writer to caress herself.

"I'm sorry," said she. "Didn't quite hear."

(What? This to Caesar, for Christ's sake! This to a voice that I would usually have to pull back in a three-thousand-seat theatre, stuffy little shit, with – on second thought – thick legs?)

"Oh, yes!" I said. "Loved it! Exciting! Fell right into it! Amazing material! Totally unusual! Never read anything like it." (Couldn't stop by now.) "You wait a long time for this kind of thing! Felt we were all on a great journey together. By the time I finished, I was them and they were me. Knew them and could play them. Any one of them. All of them! Loved them! Backwards."

(Too much. Said too much. Too loud as well. They had to hold down their fluttering sheets. But so what? I needed that much to make it sound truthful.)

The male Co-Producer spoke next. He was short. All of them were. Short. Good. Kept thinking that as I continued to over-power. Now, I was even taller. Really, really tall. What if I fell over from this height?

"How tall are you?" said a Bela Lugosi.

Couldn't believe my ears.

"How tall d'ya want me to be? I can be any height. An actor can do that."

"Yeah," said a cigar, "But the camera can only do so much!'"

"No," I offered. "It's called IMAGINATION."

Whoa, Nellie. Producer-types must not be made to seem asshole-ish on such short notice.

What look will I give them now? A stare, a double stare. A take, a double take, a freeze take and a fade-away squint. Oh

God, I love this business. Look at what you can do with a fade-away squint: It can say "Come on" or "I'll be in the bar at five." Thick Legs should be so lucky.

Not important now. Focus now.

Pushing my fingers through my thick mane, I rolled it back, sort of, taking myself to the fifties or sixties when the story was set.

"Do you have a rug?" asked the little shit next to him.

"A RUG? I can ACT hair!"

Too loud? Who cares? I didn't take this trip across town after a terrible night's sleep and a go at self-hypnosis to be treated like fucking Oliver Twist.

After a series of mumbled goodbyes and one thank-you, I stayed just long enough to ask them where the can was, and got out of there, capping the meeting with a fart. Not silent and odourless, but memorable, colourful, warlike in its audacity. And Canadian, buddy! One that, when closing the door behind me, would cause them to head for the plane.

All in a day's work.

working on the dream

———◦◦◦———

WHEN YOU GET OLDER YOU CAN'T ALWAYS SEE AS WELL, especially the distances. But you get to see deeper.

Now I realize what a good family I was born into. None of us, neither my brothers nor my sisters nor I, were ever really great family people, even though we had a terrific family, as it turns out. Our lives didn't allow for a love of playtime. And certainly we were not demonstrative. We certainly didn't stop to say, *Don't we have a great family*. And now I'm truly able to look back on those days, and those times, and think those things.

My three sisters were wonderful. Hearing them laugh when they got together, when they were all in the same room, was sheer delight. And as they grew up and started to make lives for themselves, they had a chance to laugh more, and enjoy life more. I remember one time standing in our kitchen in the house we grew up in, when my oldest sister, Nita, was visiting my younger sister Lilith – Lilith Leah – and they were all crowded into the living room, with Lilith's children, watching an old movie with Shirley Temple, on this little black-and-white television. They were transfixed by it, and Nita looked over at me, as I was standing in the kitchen watching them, and mouthed the words, *Shirley. Temple! Isn't. That. Wonderful?* Because Shirley Temple was in our living room in Grand Falls.

I have fond memories of my brother Harry from those bygone days. Harry's wife was a divorcee with three children – a wonderful girl, Dot, just the best – and after they married she got pregnant with twins, and so within one year he gained five children! And this for a man who never wanted to get married. "Harry," I told him, "you're never going to be able to close your eyes again!" Little did I know they would have nine more children. But Harry has developed a fascinating relationship with all fourteen of them. One of his grown children will come in and say, "Dad, the fence in the back is practically falling down. You really should do something about that." And Harry will say, "No, no, there's nothing wrong with that fence, it's just fine the way it is, and I don't want to hear any more about it." And the next thing you know it's fixed.

He tells me he has four computers now. *Four.* How did he acquire four computers? Simple. He kept telling his kids, "No, no, I don't want to get into all that Internet stuff." How ingenious is that!

One day a parade was passing by his house, and there he was, out on the sidewalk, nodding his head ever so slightly in time with the marching bands. I think the neighbours were surprised to see him, because Harry is not a flag-waving, parade-viewing kind of guy. What they failed to notice at first was that Harry was standing there with a shovel behind his back, and when the last cluster of horses finally paraded past him, Harry got to work with his shovel and added a few wagonloads of fresh, still-warm horse manure to his garden mulch.

Harry has an exceptionally dry sense of humour. He's very much a man's man – pulls a moose out of the woods every year, that sort of thing. Says to Dot one day, after he's been tramping through the woods, "I really need to soak my feet." So she gets him a big pan of boiling water, and he soaks his feet 'til they're ready to come out, and she goes to hand him the towel, and he says, "Dot, Mom always wiped my feet on her hair." Of course, she caught on to him over the years, the longer they were together. But you really had to watch yourself around him. Because he could say the most outrageous things and make them sound absolutely normal.

"Do you know Raymond Burr?" he asked me one day.

"No, I don't," I said.

"Oh, too bad," he said. "Dot's watching reruns of *Perry Mason* and she just loves the guy. If I could get a picture of Raymond Burr signed to Dot . . ."

"Well, let me make a few calls," I said. I called a friend in L.A. and asked him to go to Raymond Burr's office on the Universal lot and see if he could make it happen. And he did. And he sent it to me. And I put it in another envelope and passed it on to Harry.

"Gordon, thank you so much for that picture of Raymond Burr!" said Dot. "You must've gone to a lot of trouble!"

I was about to say "no trouble at all," but then of course I remembered she lived with Harry.

"Well, the *Raymond* was easy," I said, "but the *Burr* was a bit difficult." And Dot slapped me and said, "You bugger! You two buggers!" And I thought Harry was going to fall off his chair laughing.

By the time I left home Harry had already taken over the family reins, and my sisters were already married. All three had gotten married in the last two years of the war. And Haig was, well, Haig. He was just two years older than me, and he worked in the paper mill until he was old enough to leave. I left just after Haig left. He got married, started a family, then joined the Air Force, then came back home. One day he said to me: "You think you're the dreamer! I've always been a dreamer." I regret not having tried harder to create and spend a closer time together; and perhaps shifted life around a bit more to make that happen. I miss him greatly now in later years, and have, as it turns out, not enough memories to make the rounds with.

In his day Haig was a clever boy, and a clever man. Perry Rosemond described my brothers and sisters as "equalizers" who kept my feet on the ground. Haig embraced the assignment of keeping me humble with unabashed gusto, and over time it became something of a hobby for him. When CBC did that *Life & Times* profile on me a dozen years or so ago, Haig was more than happy to lay it on the line. "We've always said, you never really know yourself 'til you come home," he told the CBC interviewer. "We would never let him get above himself. We'd cut him off and say *Who the hell who d'ya think you are!* ... this type of thing. So when he came home, he knew it. He got put in his place."

I had left the Rock because I was looking to live a thousand different lives. When I look back now I can't help but wonder – did my brothers and sisters ever have time to consider other lives as an option for themselves? I don't know if the older members of my family ever had a chance to stop and look around and think about it. Somehow, I doubt it. And yet, somehow, all three of my children carved out successful careers in the arts, no special thanks to me. I can't begin to describe the emotional wellspring I experienced on my seventy-fifth birthday, sharing a head table in Grand Falls with Charm, Leah, Beverly, and Barry. What a remarkable family. So much greater than I ever could have hoped for. So much greater than I ever deserved.

Barry and Beverly's mother, Irene Reid, left us in 2010. I look back at our courtship and our wedding and our marriage, and wonder, *What were we thinking?* But then I remember how young we were, and how we weren't thinking of anything much at the beginning, besides being in love. It was such a different time.

The hospice is one of life's great gifts to us, and the caregivers who work there are just as sweet and kind as we need them to be. Irene was in a hospice at the end. She had been ill for a year and a half, and I called her to say goodbye. I knew she would never call me. She was the last of her family – she was one of nine children – just as Harry and I are the last of ours. And after she passed I was able to talk to Beverly, and bring her some comfort, I hope, giving her my best advice about how to deal with your feelings after you lose someone you love. Before I spoke to Beverly that day I had often wished that I didn't know quite as much about that subject as I do. But suddenly none of that seemed to matter, and we consoled each other and had a good talk.

Like her sister and brother, Leah continues to grow intellectually and spiritually. Leah has everything her mother had, and more. I cannot tell you the degree to which she improved our lives simply by being part of them. She's a strong, independent woman with a mind of her own. When I was directing her for a movie we were doing, I said, "How about saying the line this way?" To which she replied, "Maybe I will, maybe I won't." But Ken Finkleman and Rick Mercer and some of this country's top directors seem to like what she gives them. Which is probably why, for her television work alone, she's already earned six nominations and three Geminis.

As an actor herself she fully understands the vanity that necessarily comes with the job, and how easily that vanity can spiral out of control. She is also blessed with her mother's wicked, take-no-prisoners sense of humour, which I'm reminded of at least once a week. She started one recent phone conversation by saying, "Hello, Daddy, this call is not about you." To which I responded, in the most hurt, wounded, and disappointed voice I could muster: "It's *got to be!*"

Very early on I advised Leah not to bring her work home with her, so she could maintain a real life as well as the make-believe ones. "Perspective, Leah, perspective," I would tell her. That, she tells me, has become an invaluable mantra for her. She also tells me that keeping perspective is one of the things I have had the most trouble achieving (or even remembering) in my own life. And I think that's probably true too. *Do what I say, not what I do.*

On the other hand, despite seeing Leah shine in dozens of films and television and stage stints, I'm still overprotective. I'm not nearly as obsessed with her safety as I once was, because now she has Peter – her husband, Peter Keleghan – who says all the things I used to say, much to her chagrin. If we're together and she has to go to a meeting, she may casually mention that she plans to get to her meeting by taxi.

"I'll call one for you," I will say.

"No, I'll go out on the street, I'll get one for you," Peter will say.

And she will just look at the two of us and groan. "*Please!* . . . I can hail a cab all by myself!"

Peter and I are tied for Gemini wins at the moment. Not that I'd ever dream of competing with a son-in-law. As you can imagine, that's just not me. No, not at all. Just thought I'd mention it in passing.

In any case, there are three of us again, waiting for the phone to ring. Not just waiting, however. All three of us understand the need to keep things in order, before your life looks like a loose clothesline. Some twenty years ago, in an autobiography called *By the Way*, I wrote: "Watching your child take some of those same roads and turns as you did years before, and possibly gathering identical scars to yours, can make you hold your breath in a business where less than 2% make a living wage. But even that's not important these days. Until we square the economy again, we won't know where anyone stands."

Pardon my French, but *plus ça change, plus c'est la même chose.*

At the same time, I believe that you can change some things, in an instant. You can say, *I'm in charge of me, and I can do this.* Lynn Redgrave was diagnosed with cancer, went through the treatment, and had supposedly beaten it. When she found out she had a second cancer, she was in the midst of doing a play on Broadway, and she said something then that has stuck with me to this day. She said, "Why should I stand in my own way? Other people are going to be standing in my way. Why should I?" And that made sense to me. Why should I, of all people, keep standing in my own way? I've done it too. We all do it.

A few months ago I woke up in the middle of the night laughing to myself about the absurdity of the Gordon Pinsent Award of Excellence. Now don't get me wrong – I was genuinely touched when Allan Hawco and Philip Riccio first proposed it. And at time of writing I've personally presented it twice now, to two richly deserving honourees, Eric Peterson and Jayne Eastwood, and I look forward to presenting it again. But honours don't rest easy on Pinsent shoulders. I was raised with values that have stayed with me like a parade. The possibility of being honoured for what you chose to do was simply not on the table. That's probably why I resisted Lifetime Achievement awards for so long. Lucky for me that no one ever pays any attention to my feeble protests.

Over the years I have collected a lot of trophies and statuettes. And yes, I've had more years to collect them than most working actors. But in hindsight, where 20/20 vision is more often than not the norm, there are two or three special moments that still stand out for me above the rest. Why? Because they meant the most to Charm. And they weren't show business awards. The first moment was when I received my Order of Canada in 1980 from Governor General Edward Schreyer; the second was when I was upgraded to Companion of the Order of Canada in 1998 by Governor General Roméo LeBlanc; and the third came when a group of ACTRA members, including Charm and myself, made our annual trek to Ottawa to lobby our elected masters to increase arts funding. While we were there, some of us paused to watch the proceedings in the House of Commons. When we got up to leave, the Speaker of the House interrupted the proceedings and said, "I want to acknowledge Gordon Pinsent," and the members stood up spontaneously to cheer. I was stunned, but mostly I was thrilled, because Charm was by my side, shining in the moment. Charm had given so much to me in so many ways during our "actors' marriage." She had, with hardly any notice, curtailed her own career, for mine. Yes, to become a mother, but afterwards as well, giving so much encouragement – and, when needed, silence – throughout our lives together, while riding this sometimes terrible and unforgiving horse called "Acting." She gave me time to climb over and through my own anxieties regarding winning or losing, in this divisive, difficult, hysterical, soul-satisfying, lovely busyness of mad activity, or in a field of dead silence. At the time, I certainly would have hated to face being the one to make that sort of decision; yet there she was, extracting time from her own work, to allow me that same time to spend on mine, without complaint. And she was there with me in the gallery in Ottawa, with a look on her face of utter pride and happiness; yes, for me, but also for the validation of an actor's acclaim, given in such a bold and satisfyingly public way – and the actor now happily, completely, unmistakably Legitimate.

Awards are funny things. I love them, but I am totally aware of the fact that they cannot love me back. I think that's why some people find them confusing. So often they seem to say more about the people who give them than about the people who get them.

A couple of years ago Chris Plummer was nominated for an Oscar, for Best Supporting Actor, for his breathtaking portrayal of Tolstoy in *The Last Station*. Until he was nominated, however, no one seemed to have noticed that he had never been nominated before. Sensing real or imagined previous snubs, reporters asked Chris if he was surprised to be nominated, considering that his performances had been overlooked by Academy members so many times before. Chris told them he was very pleased to be nominated, but that he was now past the age where he could be surprised by such apparent discrepancies. "It happens all the time," he added with a shrug. "Gordon Pinsent should have been nominated for Best Actor for his work in *Away from Her*, but he wasn't. We all have our times."

Yes, we do. One night we were at the same function and when Chris, who is always full of mischief, got up to speak, he said, "Gordon Pinsent is here. He does *everything*. He makes me sick!" Having Chris Plummer in my life, as a friend for more than half a century, has made my times just that much sweeter. And when he was nominated for an Oscar again this year, and then went on to win his first Academy Award, I suspect I was more excited than he was. Yes, we all have our times, and this is Chris' time.

Each experience in this business is a little lifetime. And when you realize that acting is what you want to do for the rest of your life, that discovery is wonderful. What a splendid, splendid way it can be to live a life. The thing that can make a difference is that you have even less time to think about yourself. And the less you think about yourself, the more open you remain. So when happy surprises come along, they don't have to scour the nation or even the neighbourhood to find you.

One happy surprise was my 2010 Gemini Award, for voicing King Babar in Nelvana's animated series. Again, imagine getting a prize for doing something you love! Irving Berlin was right; there really is no other business like it. At the ceremony I thanked the producers at Nelvana for watering me down and cleaning up after me, but I know they knew I was quite delighted by the recognition. After voicing sixty-five episodes of Babar I assumed I would not be doing any more of them, because I was pretty sure that the episodes that we had just completed would last longer than I would. Wrong again. Fast forward a couple of decades, et voilà – a delightful new animated series called *Babar and the Adventures of Badou*. Who is Badou? My eight-year-old grandson! Well, King Babar's grandson, technically. The new version cleverly plays into the way things are in the world today. And the new show has the smoothest, most beautiful look to the animation. It's really quite something.

Another happy surprise was the audience response to a Sunday night CBC special, *Sunshine Sketches of a Little Town*. Never had so easy a job: I played the brilliant Good Humour man, Stephen Leacock, in a Leacock show, with only a few lines on camera and a small ton of voice-over, with the rest of the show being so beautifully done by the large, great cast – Jill Hennessy, Seán Cullen, Ron James, Debra McGrath, Patrick McKenna, Colin Mochrie, Eric Peterson, Caroline Rhea, Rick Roberts, Michael Therriault, and more. Peter had a key role, Leah did a beautiful cameo, and the young man who played Leacock as a boy, Owen Best, is a terrific young actor. I haven't been on such a happy set for many moons. Strange, isn't it? With so many styles and noises coming from the Chase to Be the Most Prominent, the plain old Sunday "roast beef shows" still hold a special place in our hearts. Plus, it was a great gig. I got to walk on, say next to nothing, and get star billing. Which is not quite fair. But, what the hell – I'll take it!

After I finished my scenes for *Sunshine Sketches*, I flew home to St. John's to shoot a new episode of *Republic of Doyle* with Allan Hawco and his tireless team of show-makers, then returned to Toronto to read the Bible. Yes, you read that right. One of several outstanding features of the Word Festival at the Young Centre for the Performing Arts in Toronto was a live-streamed reading of the King James Bible. I read the first chapter of Genesis like I'd written it. I was followed (as if anyone could really follow that!) by more than one hundred readers, including Cynthia Dale, Peter Mansbridge, and Albert Schultz, who read it all, chapter and verse, homily and benediction, for a total of seventy-six hours.

At this writing, despite the doomsday predictions of the Mayan calendar, 2012 has been a very good year for me. In early February I had a wonderful time shooting a short film for Stephen Dunn, a young Newfoundland filmmaker with an extremely promising future. Look up "go-getter" in your family dictionary and don't be surprised if you find his picture there. It was Rick Mercer who introduced us. (It's true, we islanders are thick as thieves.) Rick's rise to fame has been somewhat meteoric, and when he won a Governor General's Performing Arts award a few years back I felt the need to write a limerick in his honour.

A radical Mercer named Rick
left his home to try every trick
Did he take his aplomb?
"I don't know," said his mom,
"but he went up the ladder some quick!"

In any case, it was The Mercer who acquainted me with the young master Dunn's credentials: how he attended the Cannes Film Festival with his first short film and wound up on Roger Ebert's new-filmmakers-to-watch list; how his short films had screened at the Toronto, Miami, Atlantic, and St. John's international film festivals; how he was the youngest person ever selected for the Toronto International Film Festival Talent Lab, where he won two awards in TIFF's RBC Emerging Filmmaker Competition.

The idea for his new short film was intriguing. A dark comedy called *Life Doesn't Frighten Me*, it was about a twelve-year-old girl, on the eve of becoming a teenager, who gets her first period and thinks she's dying. Would I consider playing her grandfather? I would. And, he didn't even ask me to audition.

"Is it all right to tell people you're going to be in my film?" he asked politely. He was now a fourth-year film student at Ryerson University. "Can I use your name?"

"Sure," I said. "Can I use yours?"

"When I told my mother I was going to work with you," he added, grinning like a Cheshire cat, "she said she shit her pants."

Accordingly, I responded in verse, which was reprinted verbatim in the press release young master Dunn issued the following day. Which led off with the headline "Help Gordon Pinsent and Stephen Dunn Make a Movie," and followed up with the news that Dunn, now in his final year of film school, "has been given the gift of working with Canadian Legend, fellow Newfoundlander and long time hero, Gordon Pinsent, on his final thesis film. Gordon enthusiastically accepted the role in Dunn's film through a poem."

"Stephen Dunn, are you there my son?
"T'is Gordon P who's callin' ye.
"to tell you if he gets the chance
"to work for ye for f*ckin' free,
"t'is he who'll shit his pants!"

Which was then followed by the pitch:

Filmmaking is no easy feat, especially for a group of broke film students. The film's budget is over $9,000 and Dunn and Pinsent are inviting the public to help materialize this dream. In exchange for donations they are offering an array of exciting prizes, including signed posters, DVDs and a prestigious Executive Producer credit on the film.

Not since the Holy Mother Church started selling indulgences had I seen such naked ingenuity. It positively smelled Spielberg. "Good luck with that," I told the boy with the solid-gold brainpan; but privately, I hoped he wouldn't be too disappointed by the response.

He wasn't. In the first twenty-four hours he managed to raise more than $2,500, which was about 28 per cent of his budget. By the time all the would-be executive producers had sent in their cheques, young master Dunn had raised $14,000. And then attorney-turned-agent Michael Levine stepped in with Bravo!FACT funding, and suddenly *Life Doesn't Frighten Me* was in the black – Dunn like dinner! – before he'd even shot a foot of film (not that filmmakers use film anymore).

I had a wonderful time with cast and crew and especially with young master Dunn. Best part of the whole shoot for me was when Linda Dunn, Stephen's mother, flew up from St. John's to personally make me some bakeapple tarts. Oh yes, there are still some things that money can't buy, and bakeapple tarts remain high on my list. So all in all I think I can honestly say I will never work for Stephen Dunn again. Unless he asks me.

By mid-February 2012 I was in Mexico shooting *The Flight of the Butterflies* for the British director Mike Slee. Slee specializes in making those IMAX 3-D epics, and he had called me two years ago to pitch me on this one, before it was even financed. I must confess that I was quite taken with his passion, his commitment, and his persistence. In reality, this sprawling docudrama was still only an idea, because he was still searching for the money, but after we spoke I could tell that he had already started making the movie in his head. Some eighteen months later he called to say he'd put it together.

In *Flight of the Butterflies* I play an Ontario man named Fred Urquhart who spent his life trying to track the nesting place of monarch butterflies. It's a fascinating detective story. Urquhart's painstaking research first led him to Texas, until he finally discovered that the monarchs actually nest in the Sierra Madre Mountains in Mexico, and fly to Canada from Mexico every spring. Mind-boggling.

Making the film in Mexico was an exhilarating experience. After shooting in Mexico City for about ten days, we were transported to a small hotel halfway up the volcanic mountains of the Sierra Madre Occidental mountain range, and remained there for two days so our bodies (and, especially, our brains) could adjust to the altitude. On the third day we climbed into a series of vans and were taken to a considerably higher point. Then we set off on horseback for our still-higher location. Two or three dozen crew members had gone ahead of us with heavy IMAX cameras, setting up the scenes for the best 3-D visuals possible. They'd already been shooting bits and pieces when I donned a crumpled hat and traced Humphrey Bogart's steps, ten thousand feet up, popping my blood pressure pills. I could already envision myself descending, wrapped around a donkey, having gone up as Tim Holt but coming down as Walter Huston. Which was not quite the swan song I had in mind.

As we approached I could see a group of tall trees whose trunks and branches were dripping with what appeared to be Christmas lights, in big yellow cascades. The young Mexican lad leading my horse was wearing a bright red shirt, as vibrant as the yellow of the Christmas lights, but as we got closer we could suddenly hear the strange, unique sound of millions of fluttering wings, and could see that the Christmas lights were actually hundreds of thousands of monarch butterflies. On the ground ahead of me were thousands of their dead, covering the ground like an ethereal, pale yellow blanket. My young Mexican minder stopped at the edge of this sight, and I made my way around the rim on foot, to the set.

We repeated the climb, and the careful skirting of the butter-flies, every day, until Mike Slee was satisfied with the day's takes.

We came back down, returning to reality. Looking up at the Sierra Madre made us wonder if we'd really been up there, or if we'd simply dreamed the whole thing. I had had the strange sense, while being with the monarchs, that we were only as much a part of their world as they had allowed us to be; the monarchs had been given to Mexico as a gift, and now, would be seen by the world. At any rate, we were allowed to be there for only so long. But at least we had photographs. I had sent Leah a snapshot of myself astride the small horse they had provided for me to ride to and from the set every day. "Oh, Daddy," she emailed back, "that horse has even shorter legs than you do!"

When Newfoundland producer Barbara Doran was shooting her biography on me in 2010, she asked me to recite some of my poetry on camera. Unbeknownst to me, her cinematographer Michael Boland liked what he was hearing and called his friend Travis Good, of the Sadies. Travis liked what he heard too, and called his friend Greg Keelor, of Blue Rodeo. And that's how our musical adventure (and resulting CD) began.

> Boy of fiction, future wise
> I cannot see tomorrow in your eyes
> Got no more rights, got no more say
> So maybe you should think of movin' on today.

The CD's title track, "Down and Out in Upalong," came out of the memory of a slighter, poorer, flat-footed chapter of myself, working the highways out of North Sydney, Nova Scotia; taking aim at the dream-belt of Toronto; praying nicely, past the steadily barking night-time farm dogs, for each morning light; with half-baked confidence, half-decent foot-wear, and a too-far farmhouse, and not enough breadcrumbs to get back home to a crying girlfriend. Upalong was what we Newfoundlanders called the mainland, Canada; if you look at a map you'll see why.

> *Down and out in Upalong*
> *Got no story, Got no song*
> *Down and out in Upalong*
> *Comin' back to you where I can do no wrong**

I had written and would strum these songs to Charm in the kitchen as she was making dinner. I'm pretty sure that, in her mind, that took care of me, and kept me out of her way, but these were good, warm moments. I never considered col-laborating with someone else. I'm a child of Lightfoot's time, where the poet comes out in the writing. So my words meeting up with Greg and Travis's music was a bit like finding relatives I never knew I had. I gave them the material, performed some of it for them, and they came back with eleven songs. They grabbed their guitars and came over to my place, and started to play what they'd written, and I was thrilled.

Some of the songs had come from my roots, and some had stuck to my boots crossing the country over time. As for the roots, Newfoundland does that. You're surrounded by water, and all of these little gems are sitting there, waiting for you to dig them out of your own past and make something happen with

* From "Down and Out in Upalong," by Gordon Pinsent.

them. What you don't know is how other people will hear them. Greg was particularly taken with "Let Go" – "Let go, music, so I can sleep." He's done some damage to his hearing over the years, and as a musician the idea of not being able to play music terrifies him. So "Let Go" holds a whole different meaning for him. I wrote another song, "Shadows in the Sun," about a vibrant community becoming a ghost town after the local industry shuts down – every Newfoundlander's fear. But Greg and Travis heard it as a mournful salute to our fallen soldiers. So apparently it works on that level too, which the poet in me finds fascinating.

In the months that followed I went on stage with Travis and Greg, test-driving the tunes in Peterborough, Ontario, and kicking the musical tires in Toronto, and I won't be too modest about it   some of my lyrics sound pretty bloody good! (When we played Peterborough, I told the audience that I hadn't performed in that city in twenty-five years. "But here I am," I added, "back by popular demand!")

The original idea was to do an acoustic album, just guitars and voice, but of course it grew and grew. I was going to recite a couple of poems on one track, and the next thing I knew, it was a two-disc album, with their songs on one disc and my spoken words on the other. Greg still insists he likes my disc better. "Gord's metre is so impeccable!" he told the *Globe and Mail*'s Brad Wheeler. (Did you get that? *Impeccable.*) And Travis told one interviewer that when I perform on stage with them, "He's like the Young of Crosby, Stills, Nash & Young." Hey, you've got to live a lot of years to get a review like that.

Much to our delight, when the CD "dropped" (yes, that's what we say in the music business), it was warmly received by critics and fans. So far it's been a wonderfully unexpected adventure, which happened because I let it happen. I didn't stand in my own way. I let it happen, just in case it could ever get this far and I could end up sitting next to Anne Murray at the Juno Awards!

In any case, it was genuinely satisfying to be back on radio. I wish I could be back on radio, working for producer Mary Lynk. Her CBC Radio series *The Late Show* was a compelling, beautifully crafted series about people who have made a difference – unsung heroes whose "songs" were being heard for the first time. It really was what it claimed to be – an unconventional take on the art of the obituary – and the key word here is "art." In 2010 Mary asked me to host ten of these stirring stories, and then ten more, and then ten more, and three seasons later I was hoping she'd ask me to do ten more. But her *Late Show* was another casualty of still more government cuts to our notoriously underfunded public broadcaster's dwindling budget. In my opinion, *The Late Show* gave Canadians an exciting, important, and richly rewarding radio experience, and as long as she kept asking, I would have kept saying Yes.

This past April brought another unusual opportunity my way, when I was invited to participate in memorial ceremonies for the one-hundredth anniversary of the sinking of the *Titanic*.

When I was a young fella in Grand Falls, every second house had an etching of the *Titanic* going down. A reminder that the Atlantic, shiny and beautiful and blue as it was, was also bloody dangerous. Living on the coast, we had a close relationship with the sea, with all its vicissitudes, its perils, and the way it could swallow you up. Thinking about the *Titanic* still shakes me, that it could happen so quickly. I have seen the story in its many versions on screen, as most have, and each time, I swear off watching them. Someday, maybe.

Some 150 of those 1,500 who perished are buried in Halifax, and Halifax has not forgotten them. On the Saturday evening, April 14, 2012, a funeral carriage pulled by horses led a procession through the city's downtown streets to the wail of bagpipes, and hundreds of people, some carrying candles and wearing period costumes, followed the hearse. The procession made its way to the Grand Parade, the public square in front of city hall, where we were waiting for them. They tucked me into stage right, seated, with tea and suchlike, where I belted out the evening's material to the mostly blanketed and loyally attentive audience. Reminded them, that "people marvelled, not just on hearing of the *Titanic*'s sheer size, but on learning of her grand opulence. She was a sight to behold – massive and majestic, shiny and sleek. Everyone wanted to be part of her maiden voyage to America." And after she sank, swallowed by the frigid waters of the North Atlantic, south of the Grand Banks, "Halifax was a city in mourning, a City of Sorrow."

That night's performance outside on the square ran almost four hours, with a devoted audience who defied the blustery cold wind chilling us on the open stage. The only major hitch came after midnight, when a moment of silence was scheduled for 12:27 a.m., the same time when the last wireless messages from the *Titanic* were heard at Cape Race, Newfoundland. But our moment of silence was delayed by about forty minutes after the performances ran longer than planned due to some technical challenges.

The next morning we stood united under blessedly warm sunshine at the Fairview Lawn Cemetery for another emotionally charged ceremony, heightened by an RCMP bagpiper playing "Nearer, My God, to Thee," the hymn, legend has it, that *Titanic*'s band bravely played on the open deck as passengers scrambled into lifeboats.

"The Atlantic is both generous in sharing her bounty, and greedy in claiming her victims," I told the assembly. "We are gathered here today to commemorate the 1,500 people she indiscriminately stole from us. Tragedy, not chance, brought some of them to these shores to be buried here, far from their families, far from their homelands, far from forgotten."

In closing I recited lines from "The Sinking of the Titanic" by the American poet Clarence Victor Stahl.

> Yet let us weep not for her treasured hulk
> That sank leagues deep into the sea,
> But for the toll of ill-starred voyagers
> Who rode her to eternity.

A night, and a day, to remember.

It's almost July as I write this, and going over my kitchen calendar for 2012, so many of the white spaces have already filled up. *Peter and the Wolf* with the Newfoundland Symphony Orchestra in St. John's; a little Prokofiev for the soul. A performance at Massey Hall with Greg and Travis to honour new Glenn

Gould Prize–winner Leonard Cohen. Another gig with the boys in June, this time at the Glenn Gould Studio itself, at home, at CBC. (I probably should mention, too, that *Life Doesn't Frighten Me* premiered at the TIFF Student Film Showcase in May 2012 – and took the top prize! Oh he's one to watch, that Stephen Dunn.) Still to come: Narrating *The Carnival of the Animals*, with Camille Saint-Saëns's music and Ogden Nash's poetry, at the Ottawa Chamberfest (my Chamberfest debut). Then, with James Parker at the piano, performing Strauss's musical treatment of Tennyson's "Enoch Arden." I'm told the first guys to do it, the ones who made the LP, were Claude Rains and Glenn Gould. May have to bone up a bit for that one. And more offers to consider. An offer to do a guest spot in a new NBC dramatic series. The character they want me to play needs a lot of work, and I'm not sure they know it; don't think I'll do that one. An offer to play a Cardinal in a current miniseries shooting in Europe. Maybe. An offer to join the ensemble cast for a film Don McKellar's directing. Yes. I'll start growing a scruffy beard for that one. Another call from Allan Hawco, always a pleasure, to do another episode or two of *Republic of Doyle*. All in the future, of course. But by the time you read this the future will be the past, and I'll be looking to see what's next, looking at new white spaces on my calendar, and hopefully some of them will be filling up too.

Why do I keep saying Yes? Because I love working. And because I'm still restless. Charm used to tell people that I was always restless because I was not easily satisfied. "It's the lack of satisfaction that drives him on to the next thing," she would explain. "And he always wants there to be a next thing. Another opening, another show."

Even now, as I'm reading new scripts, or writing new scripts, or both, people still ask me why I'm still doing what I'm still doing. It's not all that complicated, really. I want more.

I love people. And I love stories. And I love something new to be happening all the time. And I love being part of it. Rejection, bad reviews, whatever – nothing is going to stop me from my part of this glorious life. And when I start to lose my nerve, I'll just do what I always do.

I'll say Yes.

And then I'll start counting to three.

acknowledgements

———◦◉◦———

UNLESS YOU STARTED READING THIS BOOK FROM THE back, by now you know it contains more than a few "thank you" moments.

This is another one.

On behalf of my collaborator, George Anthony, and myself, I want to thank all the interviewers, past and present, with whom I've enjoyed chatting over the years. Some of your words served as excellent memory joggers – and I had a lot of personal history to remember.

George and I must also acknowledge the creators of Google and, especially, YouTube, which not only provided us with magical flashes from the past but also revealed how it is quickly becoming the Original Cast soundtrack album of our lives.

Televised biographies were also a huge help, reflecting not only how I felt at the time but, perhaps even more significantly, who I was becoming at those particular times. Especially useful were the *Life & Times* biography produced by Laszlo Barna for CBC Television; Barbara Doran's lively film essay, *Gordon Pinsent: Still Rowdy After All These Years*, for Bravo! Canada; and

R.H. Thomson's inspiring and engaging oral-history interview for Theatre Museum Canada.

Thanks, too, to my steadfast chums, stout-hearted pals Perry Rosemond and Larry Dane, for sharing their stories and insights and to my agent Penny Noble – ours is one of the longest-running partnerships in show business history.

George Anthony says that he is seriously indebted, once again, to Jack Bond, Kevin Shortt, and Kim and Roberto Chiotti for the use of their glorious straw bale house on the hill, which he describes as "the best writer's hideaway any steno-to-the-stars could imagine." He is also deeply grateful to another old friend, June Chalmers, for providing him with ten idyllic days at her idyllic cottage on an idyllic bay off Lake Muskoka. Without the kindness of these friends, he insists, he would still be struggling with the first draft and be many months away from writing notes of gratitude.

And although this book is technically a Michael A. Levine-Douglas Pepper production, almost all the heavy lifting was done by our editor, Jenny Bradshaw, who managed to make sense of what we were trying to accomplish, even when we couldn't, and George Anthony's not-so-secret secret weapon, McClelland & Stewart publicity manager Ruta Liormonas, commander-in-chief of Team Gordon, whose enthusiasm for this project from the very first mention was spectacularly and consistently unflagging.

In closing, I confess that I have decided that I will never work with George Anthony again. Unless, of course, he asks me.

Gordon Pinsent, October 2012

photographic credits

Page numbers refer to photographic inserts.

SECTION I:

p. i: courtesy of the author

p. ii: courtesy of the author

p. iii: courtesy of the author

p. iv, top: courtesy of the author; bottom: Manitoba Theatre Centre

p. v, top left: CBC Winnipeg; bottom left and right: Manitoba Theatre Centre

p. vi, top: Crest Theatre; bottom: Straw Hat Players

p. vii, top: CBC Still Photo Collection; bottom: Roy Martin/ CBC Still Photo Collection

p. viii: courtesy of the author

SECTION II:

p. i: *The Rowdyman*, courtesy Lawrence Z. Dane

p. ii: courtesy of the author

p. iii: courtesy of the author

p. iv, top: *Klondike Fever* (CFI Investments); bottom: *John and the Missus* (Big Island Motion Pictures)

p. v, top: *Away From Her* (Lionsgate Films); bottom: Charm and Gordon by Tom Sandler

p. vi, top: *Due South* (Alliance Atlantis); bottom: *Made in Canada* (Salter Street Films & Island Edge) (photo: Alan Chan)

p. vii, top: *A Gift to Last* (CBC Still Photo Collection); middle: *Edwin Alonzo Boyd* (CTV); bottom: *A Case of Libel* (Showtime/PBS)

p. viii, top: Warner Music; bottom: Halifax Film

selected performance history

———◦◉◦———

(bf = stage/theatre)

Years Ago (Winnipeg Little Theatre) (1954)
Just Married (Winnipeg Little Theatre) (1954)
Angel Street/Gaslight (Winnipeg Repertory Theatre) (1955)
Twelfth Night (Winnipeg Repertory Theatre) (1955)
Coriolanus (reading)(Winnipeg Little Theatre) (1955)
Romeo and Juliet (reading)(Winnipeg Little Theatre) (1955)
Peer Gynt (reading)(Winnipeg Little Theatre) (1955)
The Little Hut (Winnipeg Little Theatre, Shoestring
   Theatre) (1955)
The Moon Is Blue (Shoestring Theatre) (1955)
An Italian Straw Hat (Theatre 77) (1955)
The Voices of the Dead (CBC) (1955)
Ray Bradbury's The Martian Chronicles (Winnipeg radio)
   (1955)
Arsenic and Old Lace (Theatre 77) (1956)
Death of a Salesman (Theatre 77) (1956)
Alice in Wonderland (Theatre 77) (1956)
Dear Charles (W.L.T. Shoestring Theatre) (1956)

The Ladies in Love with Learning (Winnipeg Little
  Theatre) (1956)
Pitfalls of Pauline, or Passion, Pride and Peril (Rainbow
  Stage) (1957)
Twelfth Night (Winnipeg Little Theatre) (1957)
Man in a Window (CBC) (1957)
A Bird in a Gilded Cage (CBC) (1958)
A Hatful of Rain (Manitoba Theatre Centre) (1958)
Of Mice and Men (Manitoba Theatre Centre) (1958)
The Glass Menagerie (Manitoba Theatre Centre) (1959)
Music for a Quarter (CBC) (1959)
Noah (New Play Society) (1960)
Machinal (New Play Society) (1960)
Legend of Lovers (New Play Society) (1960)
Fifteen Miles of Broken Glass (CBC) (1960)
Rehearsal for Invasion (CBC) (1960)
Substitute Soldier (CBC) (1960)
The 21st Floor (CBC) (1960)
The Madwoman of Chaillot (Crest Theatre) (1961)
Roots (Crest Theatre) (1961)
Two for the Seesaw (PACE, Beacon Theatre) (1961)
Mr. Roberts (Manitoba Theatre Centre) (1961)
  (one performance only, as 'Ernie')
Wedding Breakfast (Straw Hat Players) (1961)
State of the Union (Straw Hat Players) (1961)
Lullaby (Straw Hat Players) (1961)
Scarlett Hill (CBC) (1962)
A Very Close Family (Manitoba Theatre Centre) (1962)
Stratford Shakespearean Festival (1962 season)

Cyrano de Bergerac (Hallmark Hall of Fame) (NBC) (1962)
Ten Little Indians (Straw Hat Players) (1963)
Subway in the Sky (Straw Hat Players) (1963)
The Long, the Short and the Tall (Straw Hat Players) (1963)
A Very Close Family (CBC) (1963)
Lydia (Libra Films) (1964)
Twelfth Night (CBC) (1964)
The Spirit of the Deed (CBC) (1964)
Angels in Love (Actors Equity Showcase) (1964)
Arms and the Man (Crest Theatre) (1964)
Caesar and Cleopatra (Crest)
Three Approaches to Leadership (National Film Board of
    Canada) (1965)
The Forest Rangers (CBC) (1966)
Seaway (CBC)(1966)
Don't Forget to Wipe the Blood Off (CBC/ITC)(1966)
Show of the Week: A Germ of Doubt (CBC) (1966)
Quentin Durgens, M.P. (CBC) (1966)
Telescope (CBC) (1967)
Hatch's Mill (CBC) (1967)
Dominion Drama Festival Awards (St. John's) (1967)
The Thomas Crown Affair (United Artists)(1968)
Adventures in Rainbow County (CBC)(1969)
Bits and Pieces: Gordon Pinsent (CBC)(1969)
It Takes a Thief (ABC) (1969)
Traveller Without Luggage (CBC)(1969)
Quarantined/The House on the Hill (ABC) (1970)
Colossus: The Forbin Project (Universal) (1970)
The Young Lawyers (ABC) (1970)

Dan August (ABC) (1970)
Hogan's Heroes (CBS) (1970)
Sarge (NBC) (1971)
Chandler (Metro-Goldwyn-Mayer) (1971)
Invitation to a March (Hollywood Television Theater/PBS)
    (1972)
The Rowdyman (Crawley Films) (1972)
Blacula (American-International)(1972)
Banacek (NBC) (1972)
Guys and Dolls (Manitoba Theatre Centre) (1972)
Marcus Welby, M.D. (ABC) (1973)
Cannon (CBS) (1973)
Incident on a Dark Street (NBC) (1973)
ACTRA Awards (1974)
Only God Knows (CBC) (1974)
Newman's Law (Universal) (1974)
Ocean Heritage (NFB) (1974)
The Heatwave Lasted Four Days (NFB) (1974)
The Play's the Thing (CBC) (1974)
The Collaborators (CBC) (1974)
Horse Latitudes (CBS) (1975)
Trumpets and Drums (Stratford Shakespearean Festival)
    (1975)
The Rowdyman: The Musical (Charlottetown Festival)
    (1975)
The Great Canadian Culture Hunt (CBC) (1976)
The World Is Round (1976)
A Gift to Last (CBC) (1976)
John and the Missus (Neptune Theatre) (1976)

Who Has Seen the Wind (Janus Films) (1977)
Canadian Film Awards (1977)
Blackwood (NFB) (1976)
A Gift to Last (CBC) (1978)
Drága kisfiam (International Cinemedia Centre) (1978)
The Beachcombers (CBC) (1979)
People Talking Back (CBC) (1979)
The Suicide's Wife/A New Life (CBS) (1979)
Up at Ours (CBC) (1979)
Famous People Players: Carnival of the Animals (CBC) (1979)
ACTRA Awards (1979)
Klondike Fever (World Entertainment Corp.)(1980)
Once (CBC) (1980)
A Far Cry from Home (CBC) (1981)
The Devil at Your Heels (NFB) (1981)
Silence of the North (Universal) (1981)
Escape from Iran: The Canadian Caper (CBC) (1981)
The Tempest (Vancouver Playhouse) (1981)
John and the Missus (National Arts Centre) (1981)
The Life and Times of Edwin Alonzo Boyd (CTV) (1982)
A Gift to Last (Vancouver Playhouse) (1982)
Ready for Slaughter (CBC) (1983)
High Schools (1983)
A Case of Libel (PBS/Showtime) (1983)
Sam Hughes's War (CBC) (1984)
And Miles to Go (CBC) (1984)
Seeing Things (CBC) (1984)
Cyrano de Bergerac (Stephenville Theatre Festival) (1984)
Cyrano de Bergerac (Neptune Theatre) (1984)

Uncle T. (Atlantis Films/NFB) (1985)
John and the Missus (Big Island Motion Pictures) (1987)
Easy Down Easy (Gryphon Theatre) (1987)
Two Men (CBC) (1988)
Danger Bay (CBC) (1988)
9th Annual Genie Awards (CBC) (1988)
Friday the 13th: The Series (CBS) (1989)
Babar: The Movie (New Line Cinema)(1989)
Brass Rubbings (Factory Theatre) (1989)
The Half of It (Canadian Stage) (1989)
Blood Clan (Monarch) (1990)
The Red Green Show (Global) (1990)
Gemini Awards (CBC) (1990)
The Hidden Room (Lifetime) (1991)
Babar (CBC/HBO)(1991)
The Red Green Show (CHCH-TV) (1991)
Anne of Green Gables (Elgin Theatre) (1991)
The Sum of Us (Theatre Calgary) (1991)
Ray Bradbury Theater (USA Network) (1992)
A Passage from Burnt Islands (NFB) (1992)
Counterstrike (CTV/USA Network) (1992)
Beyond Reality (USA Network) (1992)
In the Eyes of a Stranger (CBS) (1992)
The Ray Bradbury Theater (1992)
Bonds of Love (CBS) (1993)
E.N.G. (CTV) (1993)
Secret Service (NBC) (1993)
The New Red Green Show (Global) (1993)
The Music Man (Grand Falls Arts and Culture Centre) (1993)

Kung Fu: The Legend Continues (1994)
Road to Avonlea (CBC) (1994)
Lonesome Dove: The Series (CBS) (1994)
Street Legal (CBC) (1994)
A Vow to Kill (USA Network) (1995)
The Red Green Show (CBC/PBS) (1995)
A Gift to Last (Theatre New Brunswick) (1995)
A Holiday For Love/Christmas in My Hometown (CBC)
    (1996)
Due South (CTV) (1996)
Les amants de rivière rouge (France) (1996)
The 1996 Gemini Awards (CTV)(1996)
The Red Green Show (1996)
Magic Time (NFB) (1997)
Spoken Art: The Clumsy One (Global) (1997)
Pale Saints (Norstar Entertainment) (1997)
Pippi Longstocking (Legacy Releasing Corp.) (1997)
The Outer Limits (Showtime) (1997)
The Red Green Show (1997)
**Corner Green (Newfoundland Amateur Drama Festival,
    St. John's) (1997)**
Made in Canada (CBC) (1998)
The New Red Green Show (CBC/PBS) (1998)
Relic Hunter (CityTV/Space) (1999)
The Old Man and the Sea (IMAX) (1999)
Due South (CTV) (1999)
Win, Again! (CTV) (1999)
The Red Green Show (CBC/PBS) (1999)
Jewel on the Hill (CBC) (2000)

We Stand on Guard (Family Channel) (2001)

The Shipping News (Miramax) (2001)

Mentors (Family Channel) (2001)

Blind Terror (Hearst Entertainment/TVA) (2001)

Blue Murder (Global) (2001)

Wind at My Back (CBC) (2001)

Power Play (CTV) (2001)

Corner Green (Blyth Festival) (2001)

The New Beachcombers (CBC) (2002)

Life & Times of Moe Norman: The King of Swing (CBC)
(2002)

Stranded Yanks: A Diary Between Friends (PBS) (2002)

A Promise (Atticus Films) (2002)

Fallen Angel (Hallmark Hall of Fame/NBC) (2003)

Snow on the Skeleton Key (Dickray Films) (2003)

Nothing (Senator International) (2003)

Just Cause (W Network) (2003)

Hemingway vs. Callaghan (CBC) (2003)

Inventing Grace, Touching Glory (2003)

Shattered City: The Halifax Explosion (CBC) (2003)

Comedic Genius: The Work of Bernard Slade (Bravo!/
Canal D) (2003)

The Seán Cullen Show (CBC) (2003)

Made in Canada (CBC) (2003)

**Acting In Canada: Our Northern Stars (National Screen
Institute, Winnipeg)** (2003)

**A Conversation with Gordon Pinsent (National Screen
Institute, Winnipeg)** (2003)

The 2004 Gemini Awards (CBC)(2004)

amazinGross: Life & Times of Paul Gross (CBC) (2004)

Fairy Folio: A Field Guide to the Faerie (2004)

Saint Ralph (Alliance-Atlantis)(2004)

H2o (CBC) (2004)

The Good Shepherd/The Confessor (Peace Arch
　　Entertainment Group)(2004)

The Eleventh Hour (CTV) (2004)

Nothing (Odeon Films) (2004)

Legends and Lore of the North Atlantic (Global)(2005)

Ambulance Girl (Lifetime) (2005)

Puppets Who Kill (Comedy Network)(2005)

Ride Forever (CTV) (2006)

Angela's Eyes (Lifetime) (2006)

The Sparky Book (2006)

Away From Her (Film Farm/Lionsgate Films) (2006)

Heyday! (CBC) (2006)

Yours, Al (CBC) (2006)

Miss DownHome Pageant (St. John's)(2006)

A World of Possibilities (2007)

The 28th Annual Genie Awards (E! Network) (2008)

The Red Green Story: We're All In This Together (PBS) (2008)

Vancouver Vagabond (2009)

Playing the Machines (CBC) (2009)

At Home By Myself . . . with You (Pocket Change Films)
　　(2009)

The Ron James Show (CBC) (2009)

How Eunice Got Her Baby (Canadian Film Centre) (2009)

The Spine (NFB) (2009)

The Listener (NBC/CTV) (2009)

Corner Gas (CTV)(2009)

The 10th Annual Canadian Comedy Awards (Comedy
    Network) (2009)

The 11th Annual Canadian Comedy Awards (Comedy
    Network) (2010)

Making a Scene (CBC) (2010)

Love Letters (CBC) (2010)

Babar and the Adventures of Badou (YTV) (2010)

Republic of Doyle (CBC) (2010)

The Late Show (CBC Radio) (2010)

The Pillars of the Earth (Channel 4/Starz/The Movie
    Network) (2010)

Easy Down Easy (LSPU Hall) (2010)

Sex Scandals in Religion (Vision TV) (2011)

The 31st Annual Genie Awards (CBC) (2011)

Republic of Doyle (CBC) (2011)

22 Minutes (CBC) (2011)

An Unlikely Obsession: Churchill and the Jews (Vision TV)
    (2011)

Sunshine Sketches of a Little Town (CBC) (2011)

Republic of Doyle (CBC) (2012)

22 Minutes (CBC) (2012)

**King James Bible – Live Reading (Young Centre for the
    Performing Arts) (2012)**

Titanic Centennial Tribute (Halifax) (2012)

**Peter and the Wolf (Newfoundland Symphony Orchestra)
    (2012)**

**Governor General's Performing Arts Awards (National
    Arts Centre) (2012)**

Glenn Gould Prize Gala Concert in Honour of Leonard Cohen (Massey Hall) (2012)

Life Doesn't Frighten Me (LDFM Films) (2012)

Typesetter Blues (2012)

The Carnival of the Animals (Ottawa Chamberfest) (2012)

Flight of the Butterflies (SK Films) (2012)

++ The Grand Seduction (Max Films) (2013)

++ The Borgias (Showtime/Bravo!) (2013)

(++ = Deal pending)

index

Welch, Raquel, 106
Welsh, Jonathan, 157
Welsh, Kenneth, 94, 217, 305
Westgate, Murray, 88
West, Mae, 106
Westmore brothers, 98
Weyman, Ron, 65-66, 127
Wheeler, Brad, 331
Whistle in the Dark (play), 258
Whitehead, O.Z., 62
Whittaker, Herbert, 68
Who Has Seen the Wind (film), 159-60
Wildeblood, Peter, 158, 159n, 163
Wilder, Thornton, 229
Williams, Billy Dee, 146n
Williams, Robin, 233
Williams, Tennessee, 88
Willis, Austin, 88
Wilson, Andrew, 276
Win, Again (film), 209n
Wind at My Back (television program/ series), 203, 204-6

Winnipeg, theatre audience, 49-50
Winters, Shelley, 105
Wisden, Robert, 191
Wise, Robert, 143
Witness to Yesterday (television program/series), 202
Wood, John, 175
Wood, Natalie, 88
Word Festival, Young Centre for Performing Arts, 324

Years Ago (play), 44-45
Young Centre for the Performing Arts, Toronto, 324
Young Lawyers, The (television program/series), 109
Young, Robert, 151
Young, Stephen, 80, 88
Yours, Al (film), 217

Ziegler, Joe, 258
Zolf, Larry, 61